Carpentry and Joinery
for Building Craft Students
2

by the same author
Carpentry and Joinery for Building Craft Students 1
Carpentry and Joinery for Advanced Craft Students: Purpose-made Joinery
Carpentry and Joinery for Advanced Craft Students: Site Practice
Multiple Choice Questions in Carpentry and Joinery for Building Craft Students
Industrial Studies: a workbook for building craft students

Carpentry and Joinery for Building Craft Students 2

Peter Brett

Hammersmith and West London College

Stanley Thornes (Publishers) Ltd

Originally published in 1981 by Hutchinson Education

Reprinted in 1990 by:
Stanley Thornes (Publishers) Ltd
Ellenborough House
Wellington Street
CHELTENHAM GL50 1YW

98 99 00 / 10 9 8 7

British Library Cataloguing in Publication Data

Brett, Peter
    Carpentry and joinery for building craft students:
    2
    1. Carpentry
    2. Joinery
    I. Title
    694   TH5604

    ISBN 0 7487 0301 2

Set in Times

Printed and bound in Great Britain by
Redwood Books, Trowbridge, Wiltshire

Contents

Preface

Carpentry and Joinery for Building Craft Students 2 is the second of two volumes designed to cover the CGLI 585 syllabus to craft certificate level.

The presentation of the books is one which will greatly aid today's building craft student. The text has been written in a clear, concise and factual style, fully integrated with numerous illustrations and photographs. Each chapter begins with a list of learning objectives and ends with a series of self-assessment questions, to which the answers are given at the back of the book. This will enable students to evaluate their understanding of the relevant chapter and to check their progress through the course. The books also have a comprehensive index for easy reference.

In addition to being ideal course textbooks for CGLI 585 students, this two-volume work will provide useful background reading for a wide range of building construction courses with a carpentry and joinery element.

Acknowledgements

The author wishes to thank Hilti (Great Britain) Ltd, Dominion Machinery Co. Ltd, Multico Company Ltd, SGB Group Ltd and Wolf Electric Tools Ltd, for supplying information on their products, and Her Majesty's Stationery Office, for permission to reproduce The Abrasive Wheels Regulations 1970.

chapter 1

Woodworking machines and powered hand tools

After reading this chapter the student should be able to:

1 Name in sequence the machines used to produce a typical item of joinery.

2 State the probable causes of and remedies for a number of machining faults.

3 State the machining operations that require special guards to be fitted to sawing and planing machines.

4 Recognize each of the following portable powered hand tools and state their uses and safe working procedures:
circular saw
jig saw
planer
router
drill stand
cartridge-operated fixing tool (ballistic tool)
bench grinder

5 List the general safety precautions to be observed while using portable powered hand tools.

6 List a number of the requirements of The Abrasive Wheels Regulations 1970.

7 Describe the principles of the various types of cartridge-operated fixing tools, their safety devices and fixings.

Woodworking machine shop layout and work flow

The layout of a woodworking machine shop is most important to its efficient running. A shop must be planned to keep the timber moving, as far as possible, in a continuous flow with the minimum of back tracking, from the timber store right through all the machine operations to the finishing, assembly, painting and dispatch areas.

Small to medium joinery shops will normally contain the majority if not all of the following machines:

cross-cut saw
rip saw
dimension saw
band saw

surface planer ⎫ or a combined machine
panel planer ⎭
mortiser
tenoner
spindle moulder

Note: The first seven machines are covered in *Carpentry and Joinery for Building Craft Students 1*. The last two are more advanced machines and are not within the scope of this chapter or your course at this stage. For information and recognition, the tenoner shown in Figure 1 is for cutting tenons and scribing, while the spindle moulder shown in Figure 2 is used for machining rebates, grooves and mouldings.

Figure 3 illustrates a typical layout and work flow for a woodworking machine shop.

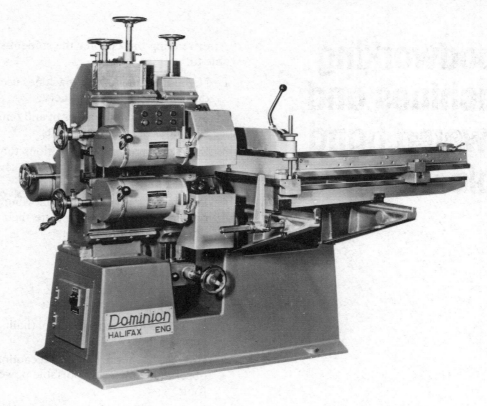

Figure 1   *Single-ended tenoning machine*

Figure 2   *Spindle moulder machine*

Note: The movement of component parts from one machine or area to another is normally done with the help of trolleys. Component parts are taken off one trolley, passed through the machine, stacked on another trolley and then moved on to the next stage.

The work flow or stages for producing a typical item of joinery would be as follows:

Cross-cut all timber to the required or manageable length in the timber store.

Note: This does away with the need to bring long lengths of timber into the shop.

Rip saw all the timber to the approximate section.

Machine face side and edge on surface planer.

Plane to the required width and thickness on the panel planer (thicknesser).

Mark out the timber for joints and mouldings, etc., on the marking out bench.

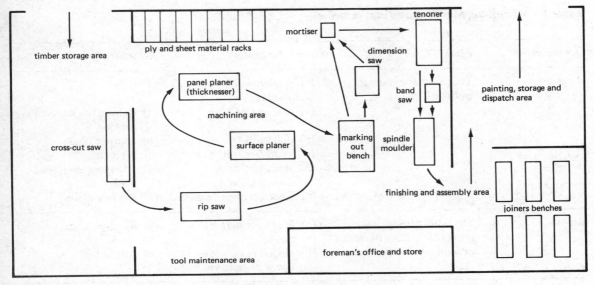

Figure 3   *Typical woodworking machine shop layout and work flow*

Cut plywood, blockboard, etc., and follow by fine dimensioning to length, if required, on the dimension saw.

Cut joints on the mortiser and the tenoning machine.

Note: Mortises before tenons, as chisels are set sizes.

Cut any curved work to the required shape on the bandsaw.

Run the required rebates, grooves and mouldings, etc., on the spindle moulder.

Pass all components to the finishing and assembly shop for joiners to finish, assemble and clean up the joinery items.

Note: In larger shops more than one of each machine may be found, particularly the mortiser and the spindle moulder. Also more specialist advanced machines such as four cutters and high speed routers may also be installed.

Machining faults: causes and remedies

The chart shown in Table 1 lists some of the more common faults that can occur when machining timber, along with their probable causes and remedies.

Special guards for sawing and planing machines

Although the standard guards on sawing and planing machines are suitable for all normal straightforward machining operations, special guards must be fitted when carrying out certain operations. Some of these are as follows.

Saws: Grooving, trenching and moulding, cutting sheet material (desirable).

Planes: Rebating, moulding, bevel edging.

Note: All of these operations, with the exception of the cutting of sheet material, can be carried out on the spindle moulder, where available.

These guards normally take the form of shaw or tunnel guards which, as well as applying pressure to the workpiece and keeping it in place, also protect the cutters in order to prevent the operator's hands from coming into contact with them.

Figure 6 shows the guards suitable when timber is being grooved out using a circular saw. Figure 7 shows the guards suitable when timber is being moulded using a moulding block in a circular saw. Figure 8 shows the guards suitable when sheet material is being cut on a circular saw.

Table 1 **Machining faults: causes and remedies**

Operations	Fault	Probable causes	Remedies
Ripping	The saw blade starts to wobble	Blade overheating because of: (a) too tight packing (b) dull teeth (c) insufficient set (d) abrasive timber (e) incorrect blade tension	 (a) Reduce thickness of packing (b) Sharpen blade (c) Set teeth (d) Use tungsten-tipped blade (e) Replace blade
Ripping	The timber being sawn moves away from the fence or binds against the fence	(a) Fence not parallel to blade (b) Arc on fence not set in line with gullets of teeth	(a) Re-align fence (b) Adjust fence
Ripping	Rough sawn finish	Uneven setting or sharpening of teeth	Resharpen and reset correctly.
Ripping	The blade binds in the saw kerf	(a) Dull teeth (b) Insufficient set (c) Case hardening or twisted timber	(a) Sharpen blade (b) Set teeth (c) Avoid if possible. If not, use tungsten-tipped blade and feed slowly forward, easing back when binding occurs
Surface planing and edging	Tail end of board drops at end of surfacing or edging operation, leaving a dip in the end of the timber	Out-feed table set too low	Raise out-feed table
Surface planing and edging	Timber will not feed onto out-feed table	Out-feed table set too high	Lower out-feed table
Edging	Edge of timber is not planed square	Fence is not square to table	Adjust fence
Surface planing, edging and thicknessing	Large number of cutter marks visible	(a) Timber fed too fast (b) Unequal projection of cutters, therefore only one cutting	(a) Feed more slowly (b) Set cutters. This may be done using the cutter-setting attachment as shown in Figure 4
Surface planing, edging and thicknessing	Poor irregular finish (grain picked up)	Timber fed against direction of grain	Reverse timber and plane with the grain

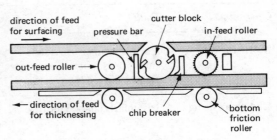

Figure 4   *Planer cutters being set using a cutter setting-attachment*

Figure 5   *Section through a combined planer*

Operations	Fault	Probable causes	Remedies
Thicknessing	Timber will not feed, or has difficulty in feeding	(a) Too much timber being planed off in one go (b) Resin build-up on rollers (c) Incorrectly adjusted feed or bottom rollers	(a) Reduce amount to be planed off (b) Clean off with solvent (c) Adjust rollers
Thicknessing	Bruise marks or scores on the face of the timber	(a) Resin build-up on rollers (b) Knots or splinters of wood wedged in gap between table and rollers	(a) Clean off with solvent (b) Remove knot or splinter
Thicknessing	Chatter marks or ripples appear at the end of the board being thicknessed	(a) Incorrectly adjusted rollers or pressure bar (b) Long board not being supported as it nears the end of its cut	(a) Adjust. A section through a combined planer is shown in Figure 5 (b) Support the end of the board
Mortising	Chisel overheats	(a) Not enough clearance between chisel and auger (b) Too much clearance between chisel and auger (c) Dull chisel and auger (d) Resinous timber clogging chisel and auger (e) Bent auger	(a) Reset clearance (1–2 mm) (b) Reset clearance (c) Sharpen chisel and auger (d) Clean with solvent (e) Replace auger
Mortising	Mortise has zigzag edges	Chisel not set square to fence	Square chisel to fence
Mortising	Stopped mortises and haunches have uneven bottoms	Too much clearance between chisel and auger	Reset clearance

Operations	Fault	Probable causes	Remedies
Mortising	Chisel or auger will not fit into mortiser or will not tighten correctly	Incorrect size collets being used	Select correct size collets for chisel and auger
Chain mortising	Irregularly shaped mortise	(a) Chain too slack (b) Worn guide bar and rollers	(a) Adjust chain (b) Replace
Chain mortising	One edge of mortise breaks out	Incorrectly set chip breaker	Reset chip breaker
Chisel or chain mortising	Mortise not vertical	(a) Timber not seating correctly up against fence (b) Badly sharpened chisel with uneven points, causing it to pull to one side (c) Worn guide bar and rollers	(a) Ensure timber is correctly seated (b) Square up points and resharpen correctly (c) Replace
Band sawing	Rough sawn finish	(a) Uneven setting or sharpening of teeth (b) Timber being fed too slowly causing teeth to become dull	(a) Resharpen or reset correctly (b) Sharpen blade and feed timber faster
Band sawing	Blade twists and wanders from vertical	(a) Incorrectly aligned or adjusted guides (b) Incorrect blade tension	(a) Reposition guides correctly (b) Adjust tension
Band sawing	Band saw breaks	(a) A too wide or narrow blade being used for work in hand (b) Offcuts wedged in mouthpiece (c) Incorrectly aligned or adjusted guides and thrust wheels (d) Cracked or badly jointed blade	(a) Use correct blade, wide for heavy work, narrow for small radius work (b) Renew mouthpiece (c) Reposition guides and thrust wheels correctly (d) Blade requires rejointing

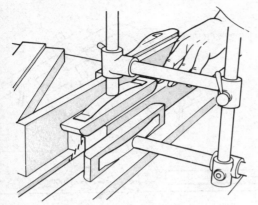

Figure 6 *Grooving on a saw*

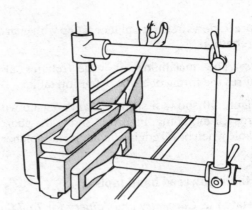

Figure 7 *Moulding on a saw*

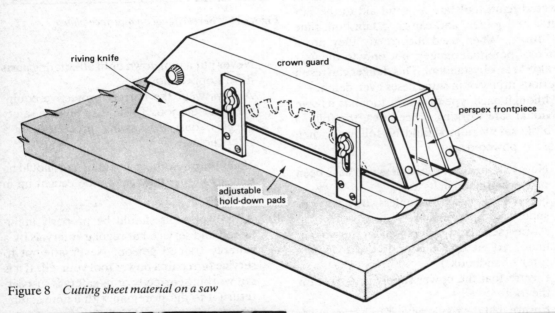

riving knife

crown guard

perspex frontpiece

adjustable
hold-down pads

Figure 8 *Cutting sheet material on a saw*

Figure 9 *Guards set up for rebating on a surface planer*

Figure 10 *Guards set up for moulding on a surface planer*

Figure 9 shows a surface planer set up with guards for rebating.

Note: The machining of wide rebates also requires the fitting of a side extension table.

Figure 10 shows a surface planer set up with guards for moulding. Figure 11 shows the guards suitable when bevel edging on the surface planer.

Portable powered hand tools

As stated in *Carpentry and Joinery for Building Craft Students 1,* when used correctly, portable powered hand tools are a useful aid to the carpenter and joiner, and can save him both time and effort. When used incorrectly they are a source of potential danger, not only to the user but also to any bystanders. This danger can result in serious injury or in some cases even death.

Although each type of power tool has its own individual safe working procedures, the following basic safety rules should be followed when using any powered tool.

1 Never use a power tool unless you have been properly trained in its use.
2 Never use a power tool unless you have your supervisor's permission.
3 Always select the correct tool for the work in hand. (If in doubt consult the manufacturer's handbook.)
4 Ensure that the power supply is correct for the tool.
5 Ensure that the tool's cable is free from knots and damage; firmly secured by the cord grips at both the plug and tool ends; and unable to come into contact with the cutting edge or become fouled during operation.

Note: This can be done by draping the cable over one shoulder during the tools operation.

6 Before making *any* adjustments always remove the plug from the socket. Also ensure that the tool is switched off before replacing the plug in the socket.
7 Always use the tool's safety guards correctly and never remove or tie them back.

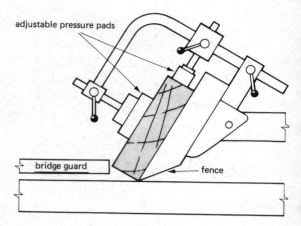

adjustable pressure pads

bridge guard

fence

Figure 11　*Bevel edging on a surface planer*

8 Never put a tool down until all rotating parts have stopped moving.
9 Always wear the correct protective equipment for the job. These may include safety goggles, dust masks, ear protectors or a safety helmet.

Note: Loose clothing and long hair should be tied up so that they cannot be caught up in the tool.

10 All power tools should be properly maintained and serviced at regular intervals by a suitably trained person. Never attempt to service or repair a power tool yourself. If it is not working correctly or its safety is suspect, return it to the storeman with a note stating why it has been returned. In any case it should be returned to the stores for inspection at least once every seven days.
11 Ensure that the material or workpiece is firmly clamped or fixed in position so that it will not move during the tool's operation.
12 Never start or stop a tool under load. Always let it obtain its maximum speed before applying it to the job and remove it from the job before switching off.
13 Never use an electric tool where combustible liquids or gases are present.
14 Never carry, drag, or suspend a tool by its cable as this causes loose connections and cable damage.

15 *Think* before and during use. Tools cannot be careless but their operators can. Most accidents are caused by simple carelessness.

Circular saw (Figure 12)

This is often known as a 'skill' saw and is used by the carpenter on site for a wide range of sawing operations. The saw is capable of cross-cutting, rip sawing, bevel-cutting and compound bevel-cutting.

Most types have either a 184 mm or 235 mm diameter blade. The normal specification for both sizes is:

	184 mm	235 mm
Diameter of blade	184 mm	235 mm
Weight	6.4 kg	7.4 kg
Number of load revolutions per minute of saw blade	4400	4000
Watts	1020	1350
Length	381 mm	381 mm
Maximum cutting capacity		
at 90 degrees	58 mm	84 mm
at 45 degrees	45 mm	62 mm

Operation of circular saw

Select and fit correct blade for work in hand (rip, cross-cut, combination or tungsten-tipped, etc.).

Adjust depth of cut so that the gullets of the teeth just clear the material to be cut.

Check blade guard is working properly. It should spring back and cover the blade when the saw is removed from the timber.

Set the saw to the required cutting angle. This is indicated by a pointer on the pivot slide.

Insert rip fence (if required) and set to the width required.

Note: When cutting sheet material or timber where the rip fence will not adjust to the required width, a straight batten can be temporarily fixed along the board to act as a guide for the sole plate of the saw to run against.

Check to ensure that all adjustment levers and thumbscrews are tight.

Ensure that the material to be cut is properly supported and securely fixed down.

Figure 12 *Circular saw*

Note: As the saw cuts from the bottom upwards, the face side of the material should be placed downwards. This ensures that any breaking out which may occur does not spoil the face of the material.

Plug the saw into a suitable power supply.

Rest the front of the saw on the material to be cut and pull the trigger to start the saw.

Allow the blade to reach its full speed before starting to cut. Feed the saw into the work smoothly and without using excess pressure.

Note: The blade guard will automatically retract as the saw is fed into the work.

If the saw binds in the work, ease it back until the blade runs free.

When the end of the cut is reached, remove the saw from the work, allowing the blade guard to spring back in place and then release the trigger.

Note: Do not release the trigger before the end of the cut has been reached.

Pocket cutting

This is a cut that starts and finishes within the length or width of a board or floor, etc. It is this cut that can be used when cutting traps for access to services in completed floors. When cutting pockets the following stages should be followed. This is in addition to the normal operating stages.

Mark the position of the pocket to be cut out.

If on a floor, check that the lines to be cut are free of nails, etc.

Adjust the depth of the cut so that the saw blade will penetrate the floor boards by less than 1 mm.

Note: If the blade is allowed to penetrate deeper there is a danger that the saw might cut into any services which may be notched into the tops of the joists, e.g. electric cables, water and gas pipes, etc.

Tack a batten at the end of the cut to act as a temporary stop.

Place the leading edge of the saw's sole plate on the work surface against the temporary stop (Figure 13).

Partially retract the blade guard using the lever and start the saw.

Allow the blade to obtain its full speed and gently lower the saw until its sole plate is flat on the work surface.

Release the trigger, allow the blade to stop, remove the saw, turn it around and complete the cut in the opposite direction to the corner.

Repeat the previous stages on the other three sides to complete the access trap.

Jig saw (Figure 14)

Jig saws are fairly widely used by both the carpenter on site and the joiner in the shop to cut and trim a wide range of materials, especially circular, shaped and pierced work.

The normal specification for a jig saw is:

Weight	2.1 kg
Number of strokes per minute	$\begin{cases} 2400 \text{ low speed} \\ 3000 \text{ high speed} \end{cases}$
Watts	350
Length	213 mm
Maximum cutting capacity:	
timber	up to 60 mm
mild steel	up to 6 mm
aluminium and other non-ferrous metals	up to 16 mm
plastics	up to 16 mm

Note: Different blades must be used for cutting these various materials.

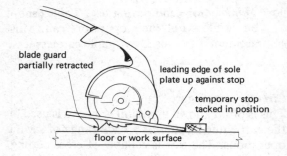

Figure 13 *Circular saw ready for pocket cutting*

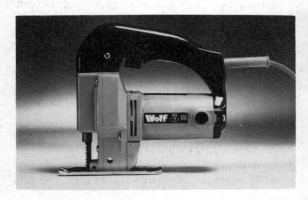

Figure 14 *Jig saw*

Operation of jig saw

Select the correct blade for the work in hand.

Select the correct speed, slow speed for curved work and high speed for straight cutting.

Ensure that the material to be cut is properly supported and securely fixed down.

Plug the saw into a suitable power supply.

Rest the front of the saw on the material to be cut and pull the trigger to start the saw.

When the blade has reached its full speed, steadily feed the saw into the work, but do not force it.

When the end of the cut is reached release the trigger, keeping the sole plate of the saw against the workpiece, but making sure the blade is not in contact.

Pocket cutting

Pocket cutting can also be carried out using the jig saw. It is especially useful for cutting out curved or shaped pockets, e.g. cutting sink holes in worktops and making router jigs, etc., as these can be accurately carried out freehand without the need for templates. The jig saw can also be used for pocket cutting in floors, although this is not to be recommended because of the possibility of cutting into services.

Note: Pocket cutting using a jig saw is carried out using a technique known as plunge cutting.

After setting the saw up and following the safety precautions as before, the stages to follow are:
Hold the saw over the line to be cut and tip forward until the front edge of the sole plate rests firmly on the workpiece (Figure 15 A).
With the blade clear of the work surface and keeping a firm grip on the saw, pull the trigger. Pivot the saw from the front edge so that the

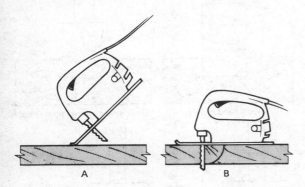

A   B

Figure 15   *Plunge cutting with a jig saw*

Figure 16   *Planer*

blade cuts into the surface until full penetration is made (Figure 15 B).
Proceed with normal cutting to complete the shape.

Note: If the pocket being cut is square or has sharp corners, it will be necessary to repeat the plunge cut along its other sides.

Planer (Figure 16)

The portable planer is used mainly for edging work, although it is also capable of chamfering and rebating. For example, on site, it is used for door hanging, etc., and in the shop for edging large sheet material that would be difficult to edge on the overhead planer. Surfacing and cleaning up can be carried out when required but this tends to leave ridges on surfaces which are wider than the length of the cutter. These ridges can be avoided if the corners of the cutters are rounded off.

Various sizes of planers are available, depending on the type of work being carried out. The model illustrated is medium size, a typical specification being:

Weight	4.9 kg
Cutter block r.p.m.	16,000
Watts	750
Length	388 mm
Width	176 mm
Planing depth	up to 3 mm
Rebate depth	up to 20 mm

Operation of planer

Check that the cutters are sharp and set correctly (see the manufacturer's instructions).
Adjust the fence to run along the edge of the work as a guide.
Connect to a suitable power supply.
Rest the front of the plane on the workpiece, ensuring that the cutters are not in contact with the timber.
Pull the trigger and allow cutters to gain speed.
Move the plane forward keeping pressure on the front knob.

Note: The depth of the cut can be altered by rotating this knob.

Continue planing, keeping pressure both down and up against the fence.

When completing the cut, ease the pressure off the front knob and increase the pressure on the back.

Note: This prevents the plane tipping forward causing the cutter to dig in when the end of the cut is reached.

Allow the cutters to stop before putting the plane down; otherwise the plane could take off on the revolving cutters.

Rebating and chamfering is carried out using a similar procedure. When surfacing, a number of overlapping strokes will be required.

Router (Figure 17)

This is a very versatile tool which is capable of performing a wide range of operations, including rebating, housing, grooving, moulding, slot mortising, edge trimming of plastic laminate, dovetailing and on most types, drilling and plunge cutting. Routers are available with various size motors, but a typical specification would be:

Weight	2.7 kg
Number of load r.p.m.	24,000
Watts	600

A wide range of cutters are available to suit most operations. These are held in the router by a tapered collet which grips the cutter shank as the locking ring is tightened. Figure 18 shows a range of router cutters for most purposes. High speed steel cutters are suitable but when working with abrasive timbers, laminates, plastics, plywood, chipboard and fibreboard, tungsten-tipped cutters should be used.

Figure 17   *Router*

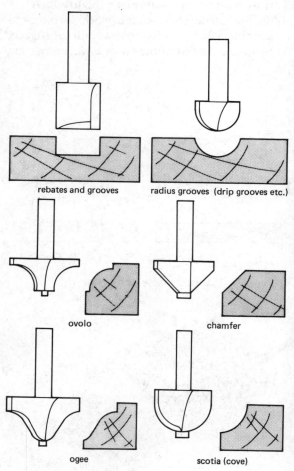

rebates and grooves   radius grooves (drip grooves etc.)

ovolo   chamfer

ogee   scotia (cove)

Figure 18   *Range of router cutters*

Operations of router

For most operations, once having set up the router, clamped the workpiece in position and connected it to the power supply, the work procedures consist of three basic stages which are shown in Figure 19.

1 Place the router on the workpiece ensuring that the cutter is clear. Taking a firm grip of the router, start the motor and allow it to obtain maximum speed. Plunge the router to the pre-set depth and lock.

   Note: For deep cuts, several passes will have to be made to achieve the required depth.

2 Applying a firm downward pressure move the router steadily forwards.

   Note: Routing too slowly will cause the cutter to overheat resulting in a poor finish and leaving burn marks on the work.

3 At the end of the cut release the lock which will cause the cutter to spring up clear of the work. Switch off the motor and allow the cutter to stop rotating before moving the router.

   Note: It is most important that the router is fed in the opposite direction to the rotation of the cutter. The cutter rotates clockwise when viewed from the top of the router (see Figure 20).

Drill stand

This is a useful accessory for the drills mentioned in *Carpentry and Joinery for Building Craft Students 1* and is used by many firms for drilling and light mortising.

Figure 21 shows the drill stand and drill in use.

Note: The stand is fitted with a retractable chuck and drill guard which must always be in position when drilling.

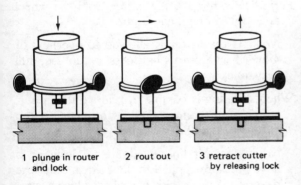

1 plunge in router and lock   2 rout out   3 retract cutter by releasing lock

Figure 19   *Router work procedure*

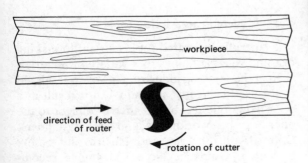

workpiece

direction of feed of router

rotation of cutter

Figure 20   *Direction of feed and cutter rotation*

Figure 21   *Drill stand*

Figure 22   *Drill stand used for mortising*

Figure 23   *Bench grinder*

Figure 22 shows the drill stand and drill being used for mortising. Various size chisels along with their augers are available for use in the drill stand.

Bench grinder (Figure 23)

Although this is not a woodworking tool as such, every craftsman needs to keep his tools sharp, so a bench-mounted grinder is normally installed in most workshops. The grinder and the mounting of its grinding wheel must comply with The Abrasive Wheels Regulations 1970 (SI 1970 No. 535), a copy of which is reproduced at the end of this chapter for reference purposes.

Operation of bench grinder

Assuming that the grinding wheel has been mounted by the appointed person (see regulations) and all guards are in position, adjust the tool rest to the required angle.
Put on a pair of goggles.

Start the grinder and allow the wheel to obtain its maximum speed.
Hold the cutter to be ground on the tool rest and offer the cutting edge to the revolving wheel.
Grind the cutter by moving it from side to side, while still keeping it flat against the tool rest.
Periodically remove the cutter from the wheel and cool by dipping in water.

Note: If the cutter is allowed to overheat or 'blue' it will lose its hardness and in use, dull very quickly.

When grinding is complete, remove the cutter, switch off machine and allow the wheel to stop before leaving the machine.

Note: Most grinding wheels are not designed to have pressure applied to their sides, therefore never grind on the side of a wheel which has not been specifically designed for that purpose.

Cartridge-operated fixing tools

The cartridge-operated tool is an aid to making fast and reliable fixings to a variety of materials used in the building industry. However, if this aid is not used correctly, not only can it result in a poor fixing but also be a source of danger to the operator, his workmates and any bystanders. Both BS 4078: 1966 and Health and Safety Executive Guidance Note PM14 give recommendations for the safe use and manufacture of cartridge-operated fixing tools. There are two different types of tool in use. These are direct-acting and indirect-acting.

Direct-acting tool (Figure 24)

In this type of tool the expanding gas from the detonated cartridge acts directly on the fastener, accelerating it from rest down the barrel to strike the base material at a velocity of up to 500 m/sec (metres per second). At no time are the fastener's propulsion or depth of penetration controlled. Should for any reason the base material be inconsistent, there is a danger that the fastener could through-penetrate or ricochet and cause untold damage in the surrounding area.

Direct-acting tools are also known as high velocity tools. They are operated by pulling a trigger which releases a spring to detonate the cartridge.

Indirect-acting tool (Figures 25 and 26)

This type of tool has a piston in its barrel. When the cartridge is detonated, the released gas acts on the piston, accelerating it from rest to drive the fastener into the base material at a maximum velocity of up to 100 m/sec. The piston is held captive in the tool and once the piston stops so will the fastener. This virtually eliminates the risk of through-penetration or ricochets, even if the base material is inconsistent. Indirect-acting tools are also known as low velocity tools. They may be operated in one of two ways, depending on the make and type of tool being used. The cartridge may be detonated by an externally applied blow. This blow is normally from a club hammer. Alternatively, the cartridge is detonated by a spring which is released when the trigger is pulled.

The club hammer detonated tool normally uses the contact piston principle which is illustrated in Figure 25. The drawback with this principle is the recoil experienced by the operator. This is because the only thing which ensures that it is the fastener which will penetrate the base material and not the tool being forced up from the material, is the pressure being applied by the operator and/or the club hammer.

The most modern type of trigger-operated tool

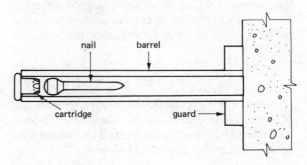

Figure 24   *Direct-acting, high velocity type*

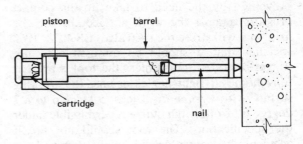

Figure 25   *Contact-piston principle (indirect-acting, low velocity type)*

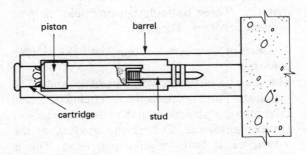

Figure 26   *Co-acting piston principle (indirect-acting, low velocity type)*

uses the co-acting piston principle where both the piston and the fastener travel down the barrel of the tool. This system reduces the level of recoil and is shown in Figure 26.

Indirect-acting low velocity tools are considered to be the safest type of cartridge-operated tool available. This is borne out by the fact that the company which produces a large number of the world's cartridge-operated tools only manufactures a range of indirect-acting low velocity types.

Tool safety devices
In order to achieve, as far as possible, the safe use of cartridge-operated tools, there are various hazards which must be prevented by careful tool design. These are described below.

Free flighting
This is the firing of a fastener into free air. This is prevented by the need to take up the contact pressure against the work surface, before the firing pin will strike the cartridge. BS 4078: 1966 specifies that it should be impossible to fire trigger-operated tools unless the tool is pressed fully home at right angles against the working surface with a force of at least 5 kg. Up to a 7 degree tilt from a right angle is permissible under the specification. The tool should not fire if accidentally dropped from a height of up to 3 m.

Ricochets
The deflection of the fastener within the base material leading to its free flighting out of the material. Three basic design principles help to prevent ricochets. These are:

The use of an indirect-acting low velocity type tool.

The use of a fastening with a ballistic point. The ballistic point prevents the nail being deflected by minor obstructions in the base material.

Double guidance. This is the guiding of the fastener at both its point and head. This is achieved at the point by a plastic or steel washer and at the head either by recessing the piston to take the head or making the head the same size as the barrel.

Through-penetration
This is the penetration of a fastener through thin or weak materials with enough energy to free flight and injure bystanders. This is virtually eliminated by using the indirect-acting low velocity type tool.

Accidental firing
This is caused either by dropping the tool or bumping it against a hard surface. It is prevented on trigger-operated tools by the contact pressure system and the trigger mechanism. The chance of accidently firing a hammer-operated tool is considered to be very remote. This is because the tool is designed to fire after a blow from a club hammer. Unless the tool is up against the working surface, the hammer blow will be absorbed by the movement in the operator's arm and therefore the cartridge is unlikely to fire. As the cartridge of a hammer-operated tool is fairly insensitive, it is unlikely to fire if accidently dropped. BS 4078: 1966 specifies that a tool should not fire if dropped from a height of up to 3 m. Some tools use a contact pressure of up to approximately 14 kg to comply with this specification.

Types of base material
A cartridge tool will provide a fixing in a wide range of building materials, but there are certain limitations and it is necessary for the operator to be aware of these in order to avoid wasted materials, damaged surfaces and accidents. The three main base materials which the operator meet are steel, concrete and brickwork.

Steel
Normal mild steel as used in the construction industry will accept a fastener with no problem and make a good fixing providing it is thicker than 4 mm.

When fixing to steel it is recommended that the following be avoided:

cartridge fixing into brittle steel, cast iron or other hard, cast or brittle metals;

cartridge fixing within 50 mm of a weld. This is because there may be a hardened zone in the vicinity of the weld.

The following checklist can be used as a guide when cartridge fixing to steel.

Minimum thickness of steel, 4 mm
Maximum penetration of fastener, 12 mm

Note: The strength of fixing decreases when the base steel exceeds 12 mm in thickness. The

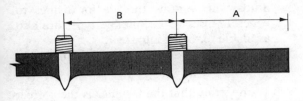

Figure 27 *Fixings in steel*

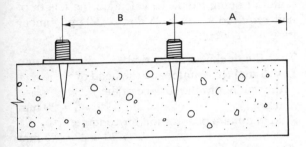

Figure 28 *Fixings in concrete*

maximum strength is obtained when the point of the fastener just breaks through the other side of the steel.

Minimum fixing distances for steel, as shown in Figure 27, are:

Edge distance (A). Minimum of 2.5 × shank diameter. Thus, where shank diameter is 4 mm, minimum edge distance is 10 mm (2.5 × 4).

Note: 13 mm is the minimum recommended distance.

Distance between fixings (B). Minimum of 6 × shank diameter. Thus where shank diameter is 4 mm, the minimum distance between fixings is 24 mm (6 × 4).

Concrete

The strength of fixings made into concrete varies with its compressive strength. The best fixings are made into concrete with a compressive strength of 20–40 N/mm^2 (newtons per square millimetre).

When fixing to concrete it is recommended that the following are avoided:

cartridge fixings to concrete outside the compressive strength range 10–60 N/mm^2;

any fixing near the reinforcing wires of prestressed concrete.

The following checklist can be used as a guide when cartridge fixing to concrete.

Minimum thickness of concrete should be twice the penetration depth.

Maximum penetration of fastener should be 22–32 mm depending on the properties of the concrete.

Minimum fixing distances for concrete (see Figure 28) are:

Edge distance (A). Minimum of between 50 mm and 100 mm depending on the properties of the concrete and the shape of the member, although 63 mm is the minimum recommended edge distance. Where the concrete is rendered or plastered this distance should be increased by twice the thickness of the rendering or plaster.

Distance between fixings (B). Minimum of twice the depth of penetration.

Brickwork

As with concrete, the strength of a fixing made into the brickwork varies with the type of brick and the compressive strength. When loads are to be imposed on fixings, trial fastenings should be made to test whether or not cartridge fixings are suitable.

When fixing to brickwork it is recommended that the following are avoided:

cartridge fixings into engineering or brittle bricks;

cartridge fixings into the mortar joint.

Note: If required, a fixing may be made in a mortar joint although there could be large differences in holding power owing to varying mortar strength.

The following checklist can be used as a guide when cartridge fixing to brickwork.

Maximum penetration of fastener should be between 30 mm and 50 mm depending on the type of brick.

Minimum fixing distances are the same as for concrete.

The best position for the fastener, if possible, should be in the centre of the brick face.

Cartridge fixings into hard or brittle material

These materials may not be suitable for cartridge fixing and any attempt at a cartridge fixing into such materials will result in an unsuccessful fixing and is likely to cause an accident.

When cartridge fixing into a suspect material the best procedure to follow is to carry out the hand hammer test. This is carried out by attempting to hand hammer a fastener into the material. It is not suitable for a cartridge fixing if any of the following occur.

The point of the fastener is blunted.

The fastener fails to penetrate at least 1.6 mm.

The surface of the material cracks, crazes or is damaged.

Fasteners

The BS 4078: 1966 which deals with the manufacture and use of cartridge tools, states that it is advisable to use only the fasteners manufactured by the tool manufacturer in their own tools. This is very important as only the manufacturer of the tool knows every aspect of the tool's operation and the force exerted on the fastening when the tool is being used. The use of another manufacturer's fastener could result in the fastener shattering instead of penetrating the base material, thereby producing a potentially dangerous situation.

Fastenings made by cartridge tools are of two types:

those where the object is fixed permanently, e.g. nailed;

those where the fastening must allow the object to be removed, in which case a threaded stud should be used.

Figure 29 illustrates the basic types of permanent and detachable fastener available.

1   A nail for fixings into concrete/brickwork and steel.

2   A nail for fixings into steel.

3,   Studs with various threads for fixings to

4   concrete/brickwork. Suitable types are also available for fixing into steel.

5   Eyelet pin for fixings into concrete and brick-work.

It is important that the fastener is the correct length for the work in hand. Length of fastener equals depth of penetration plus thickness of material being fixed. To calculate the length of nail required to fix a 25 mm × 50 mm timber batten to concrete:

Take the thickness of the timber   25 mm

Less 5 mm (to countersink the head of the nail below the surface of the timber) $25 - 5 = 20$ mm

Add minimum penetration for concrete, 22 mm $20 + 22 = 42$ mm

The required length of nail is   42 mm

Most cartridge tools require different pistons for driving nails and studs. It is important that the correct piston is used. When in doubt refer to the manufacturer's instructions before use.

Cartridges

The same recommendations as given for nails also applies to cartridges. Each box of cartridges carries certain information on its lid. This includes:

the tool manufacturer's name;

the size of the cartridge;

the strength of the cartridge;

the tool in which they may be used.

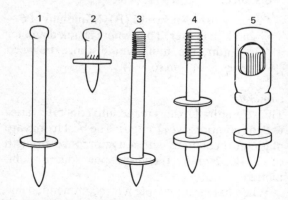

Figure 29   *Types of fasteners*

In order to identify the cartridge strength, each individual cartridge is colour-coded by a touch of colour on its crimped end and a code letter on its base. This colour-code is given in Table 2.

Table 2 Colour-coding of cartridges

Colour	Strength	Code letter
Brown	Extra low strength	EL
Green	Low strength	L
Yellow	Low/medium strength	LM
Blue	Medium strength	M
Red	Medium/high strength	MH
White	High strength	H
Black	Extra high strength	EH

Some cartridge tools use only one strength of cartridge. The required power level is obtained by simply adjusting a thumb-wheel on the side of the tool. The power adjustment of this type of tool works by varying the volume of the combustion chamber.

Safety in use

The person using a cartridge tool has a safety responsibility to the public at large, his workmates and himself.

The operator should be over eighteen years of age and fully trained in the safe use and maintenance of the tool being used. (Most cartridge tool manufacturers provide training and certificates for users of their products.) This is important, as each tool has different operation, maintenance, storage and mis-fire procedures. Before using, ensure you are familiar with these. If in doubt read the manufacturer's operating instructions or consult their technical representative for retraining.

It is recommended that when firing or maintaining a cartridge tool, the operator and any other person involved in the firing activities should use the following items of protective equipment:

suitable safety goggles;
suitable safety helmet;
suitable ear protectors (for use when firing in confined areas).

This equipment is normally available from the tool's manufacturer and in any case should be supplied by your employer.

The operator must ensure that the material into which he is fixing will take a cartridge fastener (remember, if in doubt, try the hand hammer test) and that he is using the correct piston/fastener/cartridge combination, as recommended by the tool's manufacturer.

When the strength of the material into which a fixing is being made is not known, a test fixing should be carried out in order to establish the required cartridge strength. Always make test fixings using the lowest strength cartridge first, increasing by one strength each time until the required fixing is achieved. As a general rule fixings into hard concrete or brickwork require minimum fastener penetration, whereas fixings into softer concrete or brickwork require maximum fastener penetration.

Safe working procedures

Safe working procedures are most important when using cartridge tools and these can never be over-emphasized. Before operating a tool, run through the following do's and don'ts checklist.

Do's

Do ensure the tool is in good repair (cleaned and serviced daily).
Do ensure you have had the correct training.
Do ensure you understand the misfire procedure (given in the manufacturer's handbook).
Do wear recommended safety equipment (goggles, helmet and ear protectors).
Do ensure the base material is suitable (try the hand hammer test).
Do ensure the tool is used at right angles to the fixing surface.
Do ensure the fixing surface is free from cracks and damage.
Do insert fixing device before inserting cartridge.
Do ensure correct pin, piston and cartridge combination is used.
Do ensure you understand the handling and storage of cartridges (stored in a metal box, in a secure store, to which only authorized persons have access).

Don'ts

Don't use a suspect tool. (If in doubt return to the manufacturer for overhaul).

Don't use a tool you have not been trained for. (Manufacturers provide on-site training for operators.)

Don't use force when loading a cartridge (it could detonate in your hand).

Don't load a cartridge before you need it.

Don't leave a loaded tool lying about.

Don't point the tool at any person.

Don't drive into brittle material.

Don't drive into very soft material.

Don't drive less than 63 mm from the edge of brick and concrete.

Don't drive less than 13 mm from the edge of steel.

Don't drive within 50 mm of a weld.

Don't drive into a damaged surface.

Don't drive where another fixing has failed.

Don't strip the tool without checking that it is unloaded.

Don't use the tool without recommended safety equipment.

Don't use other manufacturer's cartridges.

Don't use other manufacturer's fixing devices.

Figure 30 shows a general purpose cartridge tool that is suitable for all types of work. It operates using the co-acting piston principle and has incorporated into its design a variable power adjustment (enabling most fixings to be carried out using one strength of cartridge) and a silencer (which does away with the need to wear ear protectors).

Figure 30 *A general purpose cartridge tool and a similar model in use*

The Abrasive Wheels Regulations 1970

Factories Act 1961

SI 1970 No. 535

The Secretary of State:–

(*a*) by virtue of his powers under sections 17(3), 76 and 180(6) and (7) of the Factories Act 1961* and of all other powers enabling him in that behalf; and

(*b*) after publishing, pursuant to Schedule 4 to the said act of 1961, notice of the proposal to make the special Regulations and after the holding of an inquiry under that Schedule into objections made to the draft.

hereby makes the following Regulations of which all, with exception of Regulation 19, are special Regulations:–

Citation, commencement and revocation

1 (1) These Regulations may be cited as the Abrasive Wheels Regulations 1970 and shall come into operation on 2nd April 1971.

(2) Regulation 9 of the Grinding of Metals (Miscellaneous Industries) Regulations 1925† and Regulation 13 of the Grinding of Cutlery and Edge Tools Regulations 1925‡ are hereby revoked.

Interpretation

2 (1) The Interpretation Act 1899§ shall apply to the interpretation of these Regulations as it applies to the interpretation of an Act of Parliament and as if these Regulations and the Regulations hereby revoked were Acts of Parliament.

(2) For the purposes of these regulations, unless the context otherwise requires, the following expressions have the meanings hereby assigned to them respectively, that is to say:–

"abrasive wheel" means

(*a*) a wheel, cylinder, disc or cone which, whether or not any other material is comprised therein, consists of abrasive particles held together by mineral, metallic or organic bonds whether natural or artificial;

(*b*) a mounted wheel or point and a wheel or disc having in either case separate segments of abrasive material;

(*c*) a wheel or disc made in either case of metal, wood, cloth, felt, rubber or paper and having any surface consisting wholly or partly of abrasive material; and

(*d*) a wheel, disc or saw to any surface of any of which is attached a rim or segments consisting in either case of diamond abrasive particles.

and which is, or is intended to be, power driven and which is for use in any grinding or cutting operation;

"approved" means approved for the time being for the purposes of these Regulations by certificate of the Chief Inspector;

"factory" includes any place to which these Regulations apply;

"mounted wheel or point" means a wheel or point consisting in either case of abrasive particles held together by mineral, metallic or organic bonds whether natural or artificial and securely and permanently mounted on the end of a mandrel or quill;

"overhang" means in relation to a mounted wheel or point that part of the mandrel or quill which is exposed between the collet in which the mandrel or quill is held and the part of the abrasive material nearest to the said collet;

"principal Act" means the Factories Act 1961 as amended by or under any other Act.

Application and operation of Regulations

3 (1) These Regulations, other than Regulation 19, shall apply to any abrasive wheel used for any grinding or cutting operation in any of the following, that is to say, factories and any premises, places, processes, operations and works to which the provisions of Part IV of the principal Act with respect to special Regulations for safety and health are applied by any of the following provisions of that Act, namely, section 123 (which relates to electrical stations), section 124 (which relates to institutions), section 125 (which relates to certain dock premises and certain warehouses), section 126 (which relates to ships) and section 127 (which relates to building operations and works of engineering construction).

(2) In relation to abrasive wheels, the provisions of these Regulations are in substitution for the provisions of section 14(1) of the principal Act and accordingly the provisions of that subsection shall not apply in relation to any abrasive wheel.

(3) Regulation 19 shall apply to any abrasive wheel (other than an abrasive wheel or any of the kinds referred to in Regulation 4(1), (4) and (6)) and to any machine of the kind referred to in Regulation 7(1).

(4) Regulation 67(2) of the Shipbuilding and Ship-repairing Regulations 1960‖ and Regulation 42 of the Construction (General Provisions) Regulations 1961** shall not apply in relation to any abrasive wheel.

Exceptions

4 (1) Regulations 6, 7, 11 (*a*), and (*b*), 12 and 19 shall not apply to any abrasive wheel manufactured of metal, wood, cloth, felt, rubber or paper and having any surface consisting wholly or partly of abrasive material.

(2) Regulations 11(*a*) and (*b*) and 12 shall not apply to any abrasive wheel which consists wholly of abrasive particles held together by natural bonds.

(3) Regulation 6 shall not apply to any abrasive wheel having separate segments of abrasive material.

(4) Regulations 6, 7, 10(1), 11, 12, 18 and 19 shall not apply to any abrasive wheel which does not exceed 235 millimetres in diameter, is manufactured of cloth, felt, rubber or paper and has any surface consisting wholly or partly of abrasive material, when that abrasive wheel is used, or in the case of Regulation 19, is for use, in a portable machine.

(5) Regulations 7, 10(1), 11 and 12 shall not apply to any abrasive wheel when it is used for the grinding of glass.

(6) Regulations 6, 7, 12 and 19 shall not apply to any wheel, disc or saw being a wheel, disc or saw of a kind specified in Regulation 2(2)(*d*).

Exemptions

5 The Chief Inspector may (subject to such conditions, if any, as may be specified therein) by certificate in writing (which he may in his discretion revoke at any time) exempt from all or any of the requirements of these Regulations–

(*a*) any particular abrasive wheel or any type of abrasive wheel; or

(*b*) any machine or part of a machine or any class or description of machines or parts of machines; or

(*c*) any operation or process or any class or description of operations or processes,

if he is satisfied that the said requirements in respect of which the exemption is granted are impracticable or inappropriate or are not necessary for the protection of persons employed.

Speeds of abrasive wheels

6 (1) No abrasive wheel having a diameter of more than 55 millimetres shall be taken into use in any factory for the first time in that factory after the coming into operation of these Regulations unless the abrasive wheel or its washer is clearly marked with the maximum permissible speed in revolutions per minute specified by the manufacturer for that abrasive wheel.

(2) No abrasive wheel having a diameter of 55 millimetres or less shall be taken into use in any factory for the first time in that factory after the coming into operation of these Regulations unless there is kept permanently fixed in the room in which grinding is ordinarily carried out with that abrasive wheel a notice clearly stating the maximum permissible speed in revolutions per minute specified by the manufacturer for that abrasive wheel or for abrasive wheels of the class to which that abrasive wheel belongs and, in the case of mounted wheels and points, the overhang permissible at that speed:

Provided that when grinding with such an abrasive wheel is not ordinarily carried out in any one room the said notice shall be kept posted at a place and in a position where it may easily be read by persons employed in grinding with that abrasive wheel.

(3) No abrasive wheel shall be operated at a speed in excess of the maximum permissible speed in revolutions per minute specified in accordance with the foregoing provisions of this Regulation for that abrasive wheel:

Provided that where the diameter of an abrasive wheel has been reduced its said maximum permissible speed may be increased to that speed which bears the same proportion to the said maximum permissible speed as the original diameter of the abrasive wheel bears to its reduced diameter.

Speeds of spindles

7 (1) There shall be securely affixed to every power driven machine having any spindle on which an abrasive wheel is, or is intended to be, mounted, a notice specifying

(*a*) in the case of each such spindle (other than a spindle to which sub-paragraph (*b*) or (*c*) of this paragraph applies) its maximum working speed;

(*b*) in the case of any such spindle for which there are provided arrangements for operating the spindle at more than one specific working speed, each such speed; and

(*c*) in the case of any such spindle for which there are provided arrangements for operating the spindle at an infinite number of working speeds within a specified range, the maximum and minimum working speeds of the spindle.

(2) No such spindle shall while an abrasive wheel is mounted on it be operated at a speed in excess of the maximum working speed specified in accordance with the foregoing provisions of this Regulation for that spindle.

(3) The occupier shall, when so required by an inspector, provide him with all such facilities and information as are necessary to enable him to determine the working speed of any spindle, shaft, pulley, or other appliance, which is used to operate an abrasive wheel.

(4) The speed of every air driven spindle on which an abrasive wheel is mounted shall be controlled by a governor or other device so that the speed of the spindle does not at any time exceed the maximum working speed specified for that spindle in accordance with paragraph (1) of this Regulation.

(5) Every governor and other device used for controlling the speed of an air driven spindle on which an abrasive wheel is mounted shall be properly maintained.

Mounting
8 Every abrasive wheel shall be properly mounted.

Training and appointment of persons to mount abrasive wheels
9 (1) Except as provided in paragraphs (4) and (5) of this Regulation, no person shall mount any abrasive wheel unless he –

(*a*) has been trained in accordance with the schedule to these Regulations;

(*b*) is competent to carry out that duty; and

(*c*) has been appointed by the occupier of the factory to carry out that duty in respect of the class or description of abrasive wheel to which the abrasive wheel belongs; and every such appointment shall be made by a signed and dated entry in, or signed and dated certificate attached to, a register kept for the purposes of this Regulation.

(2) Particulars of the class or description of abrasive wheel to which any appointment made in accordance with paragraph (1)(*c*) of this Regulation relates shall be set out in the entry or certificate (as the case may be) of the appointment. Every person appointed under the said paragraph (1)(*c*) shall be furnished by the occupier with a copy of the entry or certificate of his appointment and of any entry revoking the same.

(3) Any appointment made under paragraph (1)(*c*) of this Regulation may be revoked by the occupier at any time by signed and dated entry in the said register.

(4) Paragraph (1) of this Regulation shall not apply to a person who is undergoing training in the work of mounting abrasive wheels and working under the immediate supervision of a competent person appointed under the said paragraph (1).

(5) Paragraph (1) of this Regulation shall not apply to any person who mounts any mounted wheel or point.

Provision of guards
10 (1) Except as provided in paragraph (2) of this Regulation, a guard shall be provided and kept in position at every abrasive wheel in motion.

(2) Paragraph (1) of this Regulation shall not apply to an abrasive wheel where, by reason of the work being done thereat, or of the work which is ordinarily done thereat (or, in the case of a new wheel, is intended ordinarily to be done thereat), or the nature of the wheel, the use of a guard is impracticable.

Construction, maintenance, etc., of guards
11 Every guard provided in pursuance of these Regulations shall –

(*a*) so far as is reasonably practicable, be of such a design and so constructed as to contain every part of the abrasive wheel in the event of any fracture of the abrasive wheel or of any part thereof occurring while the abrasive wheel is in motion;

(*b*) be properly maintained and so secured as to prevent its displacement in the event of any such fracture as aforesaid; and

(*c*) enclose the whole of the abrasive wheel except such part thereof as is necessarily exposed for the purpose of any work being done at that abrasive wheel or, where a guard which is not adjustable is used, for the purpose of the work which is ordinarily done thereat (or, in the case of a new abrasive wheel, is intended ordinarily to be done thereat).

Tapered wheels and protection flanges

12 Where the work which is ordinarily done (or, in the case of a new abrasive wheel, is intended ordinarily to be done) at any abrasive wheel requires that the exposed arc of the wheel shall exceed 180 degrees measured at the centre of the wheel then, where practicable, the wheel used shall be tapered from its centre towards its periphery by at least 6 per cent on each side and shall be mounted between suitable protection flanges.

(2) Protection flanges between which any abrasive wheel is mounted in accordance with this Regulation shall be of substantial construction and properly maintained and shall have the same degree of taper as the wheel and shall –

(*a*) in the case of a wheel of 300 millimetres or less in diameter, be of a diameter equal to at least half the diameter of the wheel;

(*b*) in the case of a wheel of more than 300 millimetres but not exceeding 750 millimetres in diameter, be of a diameter equal to at least the diameter of the wheel less 150 millimetres; and

(*c*) in the case of a wheel of more than 750 millimetres in diameter, be of a diameter equal to at least the diameter of the wheel less 200 millimetres.

Selection of abrasive wheels

13 All practicable steps shall be taken to ensure that any abrasive wheel used is suitable for the work for which it is used to the extent necessary to reduce the risk of injury to persons employed.

Machine controls

14 No abrasive wheel shall be used in a machine unless the said machine is provided with an efficient device or efficient devices for starting and cutting off, the power to the machine and the control or controls of the device or devices shall be in such a position and of such design and construction as to be readily and conveniently operated by the person operating the machine.

Rests

15 (1) Where at any abrasive wheel there is a rest for supporting a workpiece that rest shall at all times while the wheel is in motion be

(*a*) properly secured; and

(*b*) adjusted so as to be as close as practicable to the exposed part of the abrasive wheel.

(2) Every such rest as aforesaid shall be of substantial construction and properly maintained.

Cautionary notice

16 The approved cautionary notice as to the dangers arising from the use of abrasive wheels and the precautions to be observed shall be affixed in every room in which grinding or cutting by means of abrasive wheels is ordinarily carried out, or, where such grinding or cutting is not ordinarily carried out in a room, at a place and in such a position where it may be easily read by persons employed in grinding or cutting.

Condition of floors

17 (1) The floor immediately surrounding every fixed machine on which an abrasive wheel is, or is intended to be, mounted shall be maintained in good and even condition and shall, so far as is practicable, be kept clear of loose material and prevented from becoming slippery.

(2) All reasonably practicable steps shall be taken to ensure that the floor of any room or place in which any portable machine on which an abrasive wheel is mounted is used in good and even condition, is kept clear of loose material and is prevented from becoming slippery.

Duties of employed persons

18 (1) No employed person using an abrasive

wheel shall wilfully misuse or remove any guard, or wilfully misuse any protection flanges or other appliance provided in pursuance of these Regulations or any rest for a workpiece.

(2) Every employed person shall make full and proper use of guards, protection flanges and other appliances provided in pursuance of these Regulations and of rests for workpieces and if he discovers any defect in the same shall forthwith report such defect to the occupier, manager or other appropriate person.

Sale or hire of machinery

19 The provisions of section 17(2) of the principal Act (which prohibits the sale or letting on hire of certain machines which do not comply with the requirements of that section) shall extend to –

(*a*) any abrasive wheel to which this Regulation applies having a diameter of more than 55 millimetres which is for use in a factory and which is not marked in the manner required by Regulation 6(1);

and

(*b*) any machine supplied with its prime mover as a unit which is for use in a factory and is of a kind specified in Regulation 7(1) which does not comply with the requirements of that paragraph.

Signed by order of the Secretary of State.
1st April 1970

Harold Walker
Parliamentary Under Secretary of State
Department of Employment and Productivity

Regulation 9
SCHEDULE
Particulars of training required by paragraph (1) of Regulation 9
The training shall include suitable and sufficient instruction in the following matters in relation to each class or description of abrasive wheel in respect of which it is proposed to appoint the person being trained, that is to say –
(1) Approved advisory literature relating to the mounting of abrasive wheels;
(2) Hazards arising from the use of abrasive wheels and precautions which should be observed;
(3) Methods of marking abrasive wheels as to type and speed;

(4) Methods of storing, handling and transporting abrasive wheels;
(5) Methods of inspecting and testing abrasive wheels to check for damage;
(6) The functions of all components used with abrasive wheels, including flanges, washers, bushes and nuts used in mounting and including knowledge of the correct and incorrect methods of assembling all components and correct balancing of abrasive wheels;
(7) The proper method of dressing an abrasive wheel;
(8) The adjustment of the rest of an abrasive wheel;
(9) The requirements of these Regulations.

EXPLANATORY NOTE
(This Note is not part of the Regulations.)

These Regulations impose requirements in relation to abrasive wheels used in factories and in other premises and places to which the Factories Act 1961 applies. As respects abrasive wheels, the Regulations are in substitution for section 14(1) of the Factories Act 1961, for Regulation 67(2) of the Shipbuilding and Ship-repairing Regulations 1960 and for Regulation 42 of the Construction (General Provisions) Regulations 1961 (all of which require that dangerous parts of machinery shall be securely fenced).

The Regulations provide for the maximum permissible speeds of abrasive wheels to be specified and for the control of such speeds; for the proper mounting of abrasive wheels; for the training and appointment of persons permitted to mount abrasive wheels; for the provision and maintenance of guards and protection flanges for abrasive wheels; for the controls to be provided for machines in which abrasive wheels are used; for the securing and adjustment of rests for workpieces at abrasive wheels; for the affixing of cautionary notices as to the dangers from the use of abrasive wheels and the precautions to be observed; and for the condition of floors where there are machines on which abrasive wheels are mounted.

The Regulations also prohibit the sale or letting on hire for use in a factory of certain abrasive wheels which are not marked with their maximum permissible speeds and of certain machines on which abrasive wheels are or are intended to be mounted to which the notice as to working speeds is not affixed as required by the Regulations.

* 1961 c. 34.
† S.R. & O. 1925/904 (Rev. VII, p. 328: 1925, p. 356).
‡ S.R. & O. 1925/1089 (Rev. VII, p. 323: 1925, p. 362).
§ 1889 c. 63.
‖ S.I. 1960/1932 (1960 II, p. 1427).
** S.I. 1961/1580 (1961 I, p. 3207).

 Health & Safety Executive

Self-assessment questions

1 Which mould would the router cutter shown in Figure 31 make?
   (a) scotia
   (b) ogee
   (c) ovolo
   (d) chamfer

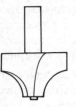

Figure 31

2 Which of the following operations requires the use of special guards when being worked on the surface planer?
   (a) surfacing
   (b) edging
   (c) levelling
   (d) rebating

3 An access trap is to be cut in an existing timber floor. Which of the following tools would be most suitable?
   (a) circular saw
   (b) jig saw
   (c) dimension saw
   (d) router

4 Before using a cartridge-operated fixing tool the operator should:
   (a) study The Woodworking Machines Regulations
   (b) be over sixteen years of age
   (c) be fully trained in its operation
   (d) make sure that the tool is fully loaded

5 When surfacing it is found that the timber will not feed on to the out-feed table. This is most probably caused by:
   (a) the out-feed table being set too high
   (b) the out-feed table being set too low
   (c) the out-feed roller being incorrectly set
   (d) dull cutters

6 Which machine can be positioned in the timber store to avoid bringing long lengths of timber into the machine shop?
   (a) rip saw
   (b) cross-cut saw
   (c) band saw
   (d) dimension saw

7 Two of the following statements are incorrect.
   (1) Routing too slowly causes burn marks on the timber.
   (2) Grinding wheels can only be mounted by an appointed person.
   (3) Always start and stop a power tool under load.
   (4) Jig saws cannot be used for plunge cutting.

   Which are they?
   (a) 1 and 2
   (b) 3 and 4
   (c) 4 and 2
   (d) 3 and 1

8 One cause of a mortising machine chisel overheating is:
   (a) auger turning too fast
   (b) timber not clamped correctly
   (c) chisel not square to fence
   (d) not enough clearance between chisel and auger

9 When preparing a batch of timber, the following machines were used:
   (1) mortiser
   (2) thicknesser
   (3) cross-cut saw
   (4) surface planer
   (5) rip saw
   (6) tenoner

   The correct sequence of use is:
   (a) 3, 5, 4, 2, 6, 1
   (b) 5, 3, 4, 2, 6, 1
   (c) 3, 5, 4, 2, 1, 6
   (d) 3, 5, 2, 4, 1, 6

10 Only two of the following statements con-
    cerning cartridge-operated fixing tools are
    correct.
    (1) When fixing to steel do not fix within 50
        mm of a weld.
    (2) A red cartridge is classed as low
        strength.
    (3) The maximum depth of fastener pene-
        tration in steel is 22 mm.
    (4) Indirect-acting, low velocity tools are
        considered to be the safest type.

    Which are they?
    (a) 4 and 3
    (b) 1 and 2
    (c) 3 and 2
    (d) 1 and 4

The answers to the self-assessment questions can
be found at the end of this book on page 185.

chapter 2

Materials

After reading this chapter the student should be able to:

1 Sketch the cellular structure and general cross features of softwoods and hardwoods.

2 State the main factors which affect the strength of timber.

3 State how the properties of timber may affect the cutting edge of tools.

4 Describe how timber burns and state a method of increasing its fire resistance.

5 Describe the main species of wood-boring insects and procedures to be followed for their prevention and eradication.

6 Recognize and select suitable ironmongery for a given purpose.

Softwoods and hardwoods

Apart from any general identifying characteristics, softwoods and hardwoods have a different cellular structure. These structures were outlined in *Carpentry and Joinery for Building Craft Students 1*.

Softwoods contain: tracheids (to conduct sap and give mechanical strength); and parenchyma (for food storage). Groups of parenchyma are called rays.

Hardwoods contain: pores (to conduct sap); fibres (for mechanical strength); and parenchyma (for food storage).

Note: Rays in hardwoods are normally much larger than those in softwoods.

Figure 32 illustrates these various types of cell.

Note: Both softwood and hardwood cells contain pits through which sap passes from one cell to the next. These pits are thin areas in the cell walls and they are known as simple pits or bordered pits depending on their type.

Although the cross features of softwoods and hardwoods vary from type to type, typical magnified softwood and hardwood cubes are shown in Figure 33. From these it can be seen why various types of grainings can be seen on timber

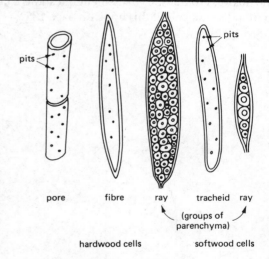

Figure 32   *Types of cells found in wood*

when different methods of conversion are used (tangential as opposed to radial).

Figure 34 shows a piece of timber to indicate the three different surfaces of the cubes shown in Figure 33.

Strength of timber

All timbers have their own particular strength. Some are stronger in tension, others in compres-

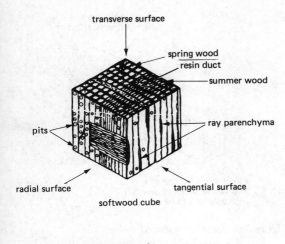

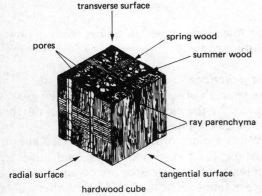

Figure 33   *Magnified timber cubes*

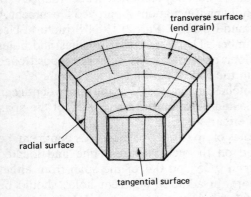

Figure 34   *Types of cut surfaces*

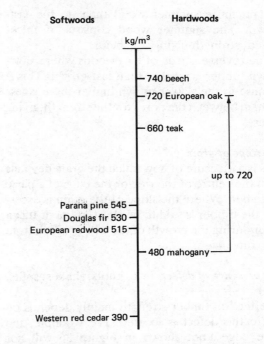

Figure 35   *Densities of some common timbers*

sion, while others have good abrasive strength (hard-wearing surface).

In general, the heavier or denser a timber is, the stronger it will be. The average density of a number of common building timbers is shown in Figure 35.

Note: Density is measured in kilograms per cubic metre (kg/m^3).

This statement, while being true, must be qualified by consideration of the following factors, which also influence the strength of timber:

the rate of growth;
the slope of grain;
the presence of defects;
the moisture content;
bad practices.

The rate of growth
Slow-grown softwoods are stronger than fast-grown. This is because the slow-grown timbers

contain more summer wood than do the fast-grown. The summer wood consists of thick-walled, strength-giving, tracheids.

The reverse is true of hardwoods where slow-grown timber is weaker than fast-grown. This is because in the slower-grown timber there is less room in between the pores for the strength-giving fibres.

The slope of grain

This is a measure of how much the grain deviates from the centre of the tree or the edge of a piece of timber. Where the slope of the grain is excessive the timber is said to be short-grained. It can occur during the growth of the tree or result from bad conversion.

The presence of defects (e.g. knots, shakes, splits, etc.)

Its effect on timber strength mainly depends on where the defect is located. For example, the large edge knot shown in Figure 36 will not greatly affect the timber strength, but if the joist was laid over the other way so that the knot was on the underside, the strength of the joist would be greatly reduced and could possibly result in the joist breaking under the load.

The moisture content

The strength and stiffness of timber increases as the moisture content decreases. Therefore timber with a high moisture content is weaker

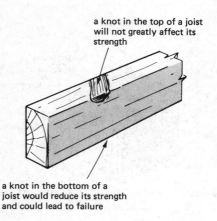

a knot in the top of a joist will not greatly affect its strength

a knot in the bottom of a joist would reduce its strength and could lead to failure

Figure 36   *Strength reducing knots*

than the same type of timber with a lower moisture content.

Bad practices

The strength of structural timber can be greatly reduced by the incorrect positioning of notches and holes for pipes and cables.

When a piece of timber is supported at both ends, e.g. floor joists and beams, and subjected to a load, internal stresses are set up within the piece of timber. The top half of the timber will be in compression and the bottom half in tension. The stresses along the centre line of the joist will be minimal and this is therefore known as the neutral stress line. To avoid reducing the strength of structural timbers, notches for pipes and holes for cables must be positioned in accordance with the Building Regulations Approved Document A (B6) and BS 5268: Part 2: 1984 Structural Use of Timber. These state that notches and holes for floor and roof joists should be positioned within the following limits (see Figure 37).

Notches of up to 0.125 of the joist's depth can be located between 0.07 and 0.25 of the span from either support.

Holes of up to 0.25 of the joist's depth can be drilled on the neutral stress line and located between 0.25 and 0.4 of the span from either support. In addition adjacent holes should be separated by at least three times their diameter (centre to centre).

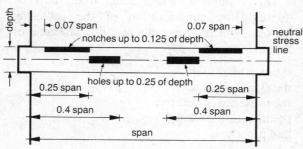

Figure 37   *Positions for notches and holes*

Example Permissible positions and sizes of notches and holes for a 200 mm deep joist spanning 4 m are:

Notches: up to 25 mm deep and positioned between 280 mm and 1 m in from each end of the joist.

Holes: up to 50 mm in diameter and positioned between 1 m and 1.6 m in from each end of the joist.

Note: No cutting is permitted adjacent to the supports as this is the position of maximum shear stress. Likewise no cutting is permitted in mid span as this is the area of maximum bending (combination of compression and tension).

The properties of timber and their effect on cutting tools

Many traditional commercial timbers can be machined with very little blunting affect on the machine cutters. However, as many timbers are becoming increasingly rare and more expensive, substitute timbers are being used, e.g. iroko for teak and utile, obeche, luan, etc., for mahogany.

Unfortunately many of these substitute timbers present problems when machining by frequently blunting the cutters. This is because they have interlocked grains and often contain abrasive deposits in their cells, absorbed by the roots during the tree's growth.

In order to overcome these problems it is advisable to use tungsten-tipped saws and cutters.

The machining of preservative-treated timber and timber treated to resist fire, also tends to quickly blunt the cutters. This can be overcome by machining the timber before it is treated. This also avoids machining into the treated areas and reducing the depth of penetration.

Fire protection of timber

When timber is exposed to a flame, its temperature will not increase above 100 degrees until the majority of its moisture has evaporated. This causes a check in the spread of flame. When all of the moisture has been dried out of the timber, the temperature will rise to approximately 300 degrees centigrade, causing a chemical change to take place. Inflammable gases are given off which immediately ignite, causing the timber to burn and gradually disintegrate forming charcoal.

No amount of treatment can make timber completely fireproof, but treatment can be given to increase the timber's resistance to ignition and, to a large extent, stop its active participation in a fire. This treatment is known as a fire resisting or fire retarding treatment. It consists of treating the timber with a fire resisting chemical. The main fire resisting chemicals are: diammonium phosphate; monammonium phosphate; or a mixture of one of these with ammonium sulphate, ammonium chloride, zinc chloride and boric acid.

The application of these fire retardants can be carried out using similar methods to those used for the preservative treatment of timber, e.g. brushing, spraying, dipping, steeping and pressure impregnation, the latter being considered the most effective.

Wood-boring insects

The decay of building timbers can be caused by an attack of:

wood-destroying fungi, e.g. dry rot, wet rot, etc.
(covered in *Carpentry and Joinery for Building Craft Students 1*); and/or
wood-boring insects.

The majority of damage done to building timber in the British Isles can be attributed to five species of insect or woodworm as they are commonly called. These are shown in Figure 38.

In addition to these five main types of wood-boring insects, several other species, such as the bark borer, the pinhole borer and the wharf borer may occasionally be found in building timbers, although they are only normally found in forests or timber yards and, in the case of the wharf borer, in water-logged timber.

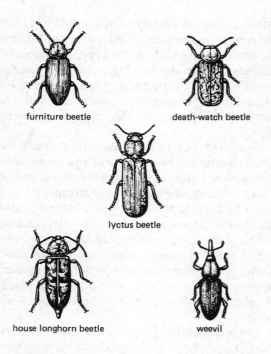

furniture beetle

death-watch beetle

lyctus beetle

house longhorn beetle

weevil

Figure 38   *Common species of wood-boring insects*

Recognition
It is easy to distinguish between an attack of wood-boring insects and other forms of timber decay by the presence of their characteristic flight holes which appear on the surface. Also, when a thorough inspection is made below the surface of the timber, the tunnels or galleries bored by the larvae will be found. The adult beetles of the different species can be readily identified but, as these only live for a short period in the summer, the identification of the species is generally carried out by a diagnosis of the flight holes, bore dust and the type and location of the timber attacked.

Life cycle
The life cycle of all the wood-boring insects is a fairly complex process, but it can be divided up into four distinct stages.

Stage 1: eggs   (Figure 39)
The female insect lays eggs during the summer months, usually on the end grain or in cracks and

shakes of the timber which afford the eggs a certain amount of protection until they hatch.

Stage 2: larvae   (Figure 40)
The eggs hatch into larvae, or woodworm, between two and eight weeks after being laid. It is at this stage that damage to the timber is done. The larvae immediately start to bore into and eat the timber. The insects, while boring, digest the wood and excrete it in variously shaped pellets or bore dust, which is often used to identify the particular species of insect that is attacking the timber. The destructive stage can last between six months and ten years, according to the species.

Stage 3: pupae   (Figure 41)
During the early spring, the larva hollows out a pupal chamber near the surface of the timber, in

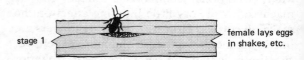

stage 1

female lays eggs
in shakes, etc.

Figure 39   *Eggs*

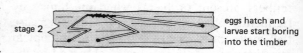

stage 2

eggs hatch and
larvae start boring
into the timber

Figure 40   *Larvae*

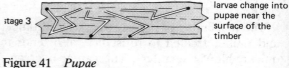

stage 3

larvae change into
pupae near the
surface of the
timber

Figure 41   *Pupae*

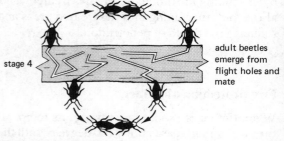

stage 4

adult beetles
emerge from
flight holes and
mate

Figure 42   *Adult insects*

which it can change into a pupa or chrysalis. The pupa remains inactive for a short period of time in a mummified state. It is during this period that it undergoes the transformation into an adult insect.

Stage 4: adult insects   (Figure 42)
Once the transformation is complete, the insect bites its way out of the timber, leaving its characteristic flight hole. This is often the first external sign of an attack.

Once the insect has emerged from the timber, it is an adult and capable of flying. The adult insect's sole purpose is to mate. This usually takes place within twenty-four hours. Very soon after mating, the male insect will die, while the female will search for a suitable place in which to lay her eggs, thus completing one life cycle and starting another. The female insect will also die, normally within fourteen days.

Identification
The chart shown in Table 3 outlines the main identifying characteristics of the various species of wood-boring insects and also gives the location and type of timber mainly attacked.

Table 3   **Characteristics of wood-boring insects**

Species	Actual size	Bore dust	Location and timber attacked
Furniture beetle (*Anobium punctatum*) This is the most common wood-boring insect in the British Isles. Its life cycle is usually two to three years, with adult beetles emerging during the period between May and September. After mating the females usually lay between twenty and forty eggs each.	beetle flight holes	Small, gritty pellets which are egg-shaped under magnification	Attacks both hardwoods and softwoods, although heartwood is often immune. Commonly causes a considerable amount of damage in structural timber, floorboards, joists, rafters and furniture
Death-watch beetle (*Xestobium rufovillosum*) Rarely found in modern houses, its attack being mainly restricted to old damp buildings, normally of several hundred years old, e.g. old churches and historic buildings. Named the death-watch because of its association with churches and the characteristic hammering noise that the adults make by hitting their heads against the timber. This hammering is in fact the adult's mating call. Its life cycle is between four and ten years, with adult beetles emerging during the period between March and June. Females normally lay between forty and seventy eggs each.		Coarse, gritty, bun-shaped pellets	Attacks old oak and other hardwoods. Can occasionally be found in softwoods near infested hardwoods. Mainly found in large-sectioned structural timber in association with a fungal attack

Species	Actual size	Bore dust	Location and timber attacked
Lyctus or powder-post beetle In the British Isles there are four beetles in this group which attack timber. The most common is *Lyctus brunneus*. This species is rarely found in buildings, as it attacks mainly recently felled timber before it has been seasoned. Therefore it is only usually found in timber yards and storage sheds. Its life cycle is between one and two years, but is often less in hot surroundings. Adult beetles emerge during the period between May and September. Females normally lay 70–220 eggs each.		Very fine and powdery	Attacks the sapwood of certain hardwoods, e.g. oak, ash, elm, walnut, etc., normally before seasoning. But it has been known to attack recently seasoned timber. An attack is considered unlikely in timber over ten to fifteen years old
House longhorn beetle (*Hylotrupes bajulus*) This is by far the largest wood-boring insect found in the British Isles. It is also known as the Camberley beetle for its attacks are mainly concentrated around Camberley and the surrounding Surrey and Hampshire areas. Its life cycle is normally between three and ten years, but can be longer. The adult beetles emerge during the period between July and September, with females laying up to 200 eggs each.		Barrel-shaped pellets mixed with fine dust	Attacks the sapwood of softwoods, mainly in the roof spaces, e.g. rafters, joists and wall plates, etc. Owing to its size and long life cycle, very often complete collapse is the first sign of an attack by this species. Complete replacement of timber is normally required
Weevils (*Euophryum confine* and *Pentarthrum huttoni*) These are mainly found in timber which is damp or subject to a fungal attack. Unlike other wood-boring insects, the adult weevils as well as the larvae bore into the timber and cause damage. Its life cycle is very short, between six and nine months. Two life cycles in one year is not uncommon. Adult beetles can be seen for most of the year. Females lay about twenty-five eggs each.		Small, gritty egg-shaped pellets, similar to bore dust of furniture beetles but smaller	Attacks both damp or decayed hardwoods and softwoods, Often found around sinks, baths, toilets and in cellars

Prevention

The wood-boring insects feed on the cellulose and starch which is contained in all timber, both heartwood and sapwood, although sapwood is usually more susceptible to insect attacks. The only sure way of preventing an attack is to poison the food supply by pressure-treating the timber, before it is installed into the building, with a suitable preservative.

Note: Various types and methods of timber preservation are available. These were covered in *Carpentry and Joinery for Building Craft Students 1*.

Eradication

By following the stages in the order given, an attack of wood-boring insects can be successfully eradicated.

Stage 1 Open up affected area, e.g. take up floorboards or remove panelling. Carefully examine all structural timber.

Stage 2 Remove and burn all badly affected timber.

Stage 3 Strip off any surface coating or finish on the timber, e.g. paint, polish or varnish.

Note: This is because the fluid used to eradicate the woodworm will not penetrate the surface coating.

Stage 4 Thoroughly brush the timber in order to remove from its surface all dirt and dust.

Stage 5 Replace all timber which has been taken out with properly seasoned timber that has been treated with two or three coats of woodworm preservative or, alternatively, with timber that has been pressure-impregnated with a preservative.

Note: All fresh surfaces which have been exposed by cutting or drilling, must also be treated with a preservative.

Stage 6 Apply a proprietary woodworm killer, by brush or spray, to all timber, even that which is apparently unaffected. Pay particular attention to joints, end grain and flight holes. Apply a second coat of the fluid as soon as the first has been absorbed.

Note: Floorboards must be taken up at intervals to allow thorough coverage of the joists and the underside of the floorboards. Care must be taken to avoid the staining of plaster particularly when treating the ceiling joists and rafters in the loft.

Stage 7 In most cases it is possible to completely eradicate an attack by one thorough treatment as outlined in stages 1 to 6, but to be completely sure inspections for fresh flight holes should be made for several successive summers. If fresh holes are found re-treat timber with a woodworm killer.

Furniture

When timbers inside a building have been attacked by a wood-boring insect, it is almost certain that the furniture will also be affected. Therefore, to successfully eradicate the attack, the furniture must also be treated. This can be done by following the stages in the order given.

Stage 1 Remove all dirt and dust, then inject a proprietary woodworm killer into the flight holes. A special aerosol can with a tube, or nozzled injector bottles are available for this purpose.

Stage 2 Apply two coats of a proprietary woodworm killer to all unfinished surfaces, e.g. all surfaces which are not painted, polished or varnished.

Stage 3 Make inspections for fresh flight holes for several successive summers. Repeat if required.

Ironmongery

The majority of ironmongery can be classified into three groups, these being:

fixing devices;
fittings which allow movement;
fittings which give security.

Note: Other items of ironmongery are available and can be listed under miscellaneous, e.g. letter plates, finger plates, door knockers and coat hooks, etc.

Specialist fixing devices

As well as the standard range of fixing devices,
e.g. nails, screws and plugs, etc., which were
covered in *Carpentry and Joinery for Building
Craft Students 1*, there is a wide range of specialist
fixing devices produced by many manufacturers.
The chart shown in Table 4 illustrates a typical
range of suitable fixing devices and installation
procedures for a number of specific applications.

Minimum spacing for anchors

As most expanding anchors compress their base
material (concrete, brickwork, etc.), when expanding an allowance must be made for the
stresses which this sets up. Therefore, in order to
prevent failure of the anchor and damage to the
base material, the minimum spacing between
adjacent anchors or between the anchor and the
edge of the structure must be twice the length of
the anchor.

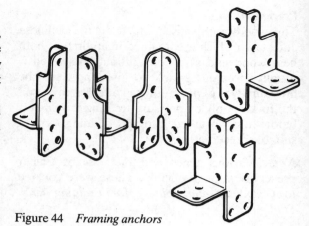

Figure 44   *Framing anchors*

Joint substitutes and other metalwork

The use of a wide range of joint substitutes and
other metalwork is rapidly increasing. This is
because their use offers an economic alternative
to the traditional methods of jointing, resulting in
a saving of both labour and material costs.

Joist hangers (Figure 43)

These are available in a wide variety of types and
sizes, to suit all fixing applications. A and B are
used for connecting joists at right angles to one

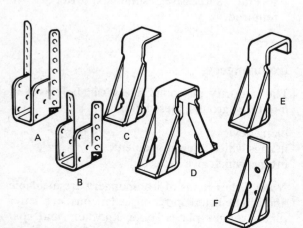

Figure 43   *Joist hangers*

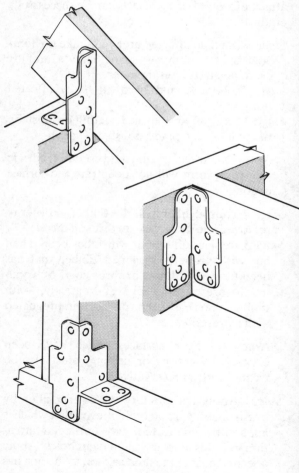

Figure 45   *Uses of framing anchors*

Table 4

Application	Suitable fixing device	Installation procedure
Light duty fixing in thin material, e.g. plasterboard ceilings and walls, hollow core doors and cavity blocks, etc.	Nylon toggle anchor *Note:* This type of anchor can also be used as a normal plug in thicker materials.	1 Drill hole through material and fold anchor 2 Insert anchor into hole and tap flush with material 3 Expand anchor using toggle key 4 Insert wood screw or self-tapping screw and tighten
Fixing mineral wool, glass wool or expanded polystyrene insulation to brickwork, concrete or timber, etc.	Insulation fastener (made from polypropylene)	1 Drill hole through insulation into base material 2 Insert fastener into hole and gently tap home
Rapid plug and screw through fixings into brickwork, concrete, etc.	Hamma screw (combined nylon plug and zinc plated screw)	1 With item to be fixed in position, drill through item into base material 2 Insert hamma screw into hole 3 Drive hamma screw home with a sharp blow from a hammer. *Note:* The hamma screw can be removed with a screwdriver if required
Fixings for suspended ceilings and other items hanging from concrete ceilings	Steel ceiling suspension anchor	1 Drill hole in concrete ceiling 2 Gently tap anchor into hole 3 Expand anchor by giving the ring bolt a sharp pull with a claw hammer

Applications	Suitable fixing device	Installation procedure	
Medium to heavy duty through-fixing to concrete of machinery door frames and steel sections, etc.	Zinc-plated stud anchor	1 Position item to be fixed and drill through fixing holes into concrete 2 Remove dust from hole using blow-out bulb 3 Insert anchor into hole and gently tap home 4 Expand anchor by tightening nut	
Fixing door and window frames that have not been 'built in', to concrete, brickwork or blockwork	Galvanized steel sleeve expansion/ frame anchor	1 With frame in position drill hole through frame and into wall 2 Insert anchor and tap through frame into wall with setting tool 3 Adjust position of frame if required and tighten screw *Note:* Using this method there is no need for any packing between the wall and frame	
Medium to heavy duty bolt fixing of machinery and steel sections, etc. to concrete and solid brickwork	Steel expansion anchor	1 Drill hole in base material. Remove dust from hole using blow-out bulb 2 Insert anchor into hole and tap home using setting tool. This expands anchor which will then be ready to accept a suitable bolt	
Heavy duty through-fixing of machinery and structural steelwork, etc. to concrete	Heavy duty steel expansion anchor	1 With item in position, drill through fixing holes into concrete. Remove dust from hole using blow-out bulb 2 Insert anchor into hole and tap home 3 Expand anchor by tightening bolt	

Applications	Suitable fixing device	Installation procedure	
Self-drilling, medium/heavy duty bolt for fixing machinery and steel sections, etc. to concrete	Self-drilling steel expansion anchor	1 Insert anchor into a rotary hammer drill and bore into concrete. Remove dust from hole using a blow-out bulb 2 Place taper plug into anchor 3 Insert anchor into hole and drive home using tool. This will expand plug 4 Move tool sharply downwards to snap off anchor. The anchor will then be ready to accept a suitable bolt	
Heavy duty fixings into concrete, especially when subject to vibration	Chemical resin anchor	1 Drill hole into concrete and clean out using blow-out bulb. Insert resin cartridge 2 Using a rotary hammer drill and adaptor, drive anchor rod into resin cartridge 3 Remove tool and then adaptor 4 Allow resin to harden before using anchor. This takes between ten minutes at 20 degrees and over, and up to five hours at −5 degrees	

another, e.g. when trimming around stairwells. Types C, D, E and F are used for connecting joists to walls and beams. This is an alternative to 'building in' to the wall the ends of the joists themselves.

Framing anchors (Figure 44)
These are available in three types which can be either left or right handed and are suitable for a wide range of applications. Figure 45 shows framing anchors being used for rafter to wall plate fixings, stud to sole plate fixings and trimmed joist to trimmer fixings.

Truss clip (Figure 46)
This is a purpose-made clip that ensures a positive fixing between trussed rafters and the wall plate.

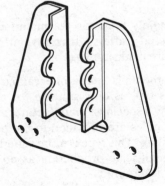

Figure 46   *Truss clip*

Steel straps (Figure 47)
These come in a wide range of shapes and sizes for particular applications. Their uses include anchoring wall plates to walls, holding down flat

roof joists and use as lateral restraint straps to
anchor floors and roofs to the wall.

Timber connectors for use with bolts (Figure 48)
There are three main types of timber connectors
for use with bolts:

double- or single-toothed plates;
split ring;
shear plate.

All three have the same purpose which is to
increase the strength of overlapping joints, either
timber to timber or timber to metal. The double-
toothed plate and the split ring are used for
timber to timber connections, e.g. for making
bolted roof trusses and joining two joists together
to make a beam. The single-toothed plate and the
shear plate are both used for timber to metal
connections, e.g. bolting timber to steel section.

Note: The double- and single-toothed plate
connectors have an advantage over the split ring
and shear plate connectors so far as their installation is concerned. This is because the toothed
plate connectors are embedded into the timber
when the bolt is tightened, unlike the split ring
and shear connectors which require the use of
special sinking and grooving tools.

Nail plates (Figure 49)
These are mainly used for the manufacture of
modern trussed rafters, trussed purlins and
beams, and are made in two types:

those where the nails are an integral part of the
  plate. This type is only suitable for machine
  assembly by a specialist manufacturer; and
those where holes are provided in the plate for
  normal nailing. This type is more suited for site
  use and small-scale production as no special
  machinery is required.

Steel joist struts (Figure 50)
These can be used as an alternative to timber
herring-bone strutting for stiffening floor and flat
roof joists. They are available in a wide range of
sizes to suit various joist depths and spacings.
Figure 51 shows steel joist struts in position.

Figure 47   *Steel straps*

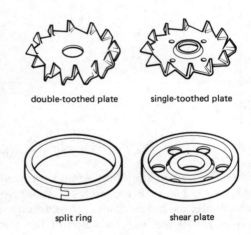

double-toothed plate   single-toothed plate

split ring   shear plate

Figure 48   *Timber connectors*

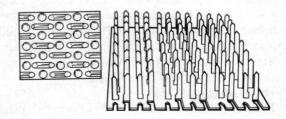

Figure 49   *Nail plates*

Figure 50   *Steel joist strut*

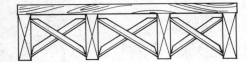

Figure 51   *Steel joist struts in use*

Figure 52   *Corrugated fastener*

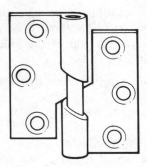

Figure 53   *Rising butt*

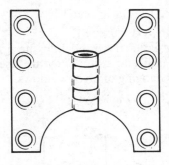

Figure 54   *Parliament hinge*

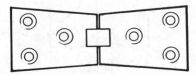

Figure 55   *Counter flap*

Corrugated fasteners (Figure 52)
These are also known as wrinkle or corrugated nails. They can be used to reinforce butt joints and mitre joints of simple framing, e.g. hollow core flush door construction.

Fittings which allow movement

Rising butt (Figure 53)
Rising butts are designed to lift the door as it opens in order to clear any obstructions, e.g. mats and rugs. The use of these butts also gives the door some degree of self-closing.

Parliament hinge (Figure 54)
The extended knuckle on this type of hinge enables the door to clear deep architraves, etc. and fold back against the wall.

Counter flap hinge (Figure 55)
This hinge, as its name implies, is for use on counters. It is made from brass and sunk flush with the face of the counter top.

Double and single action spring hinges   (Figure 56)
These are designed to make a door self-closing. They are similar to the butt hinge except for their large knuckles that contain the springs. These

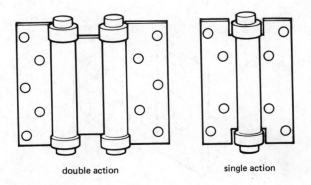

double action   single action

Figure 56   *Spring hinges*

springs can be adjusted to give the required closing action by using a 'tommy bar' and moving the small pin at the top of the knuckle into a different hole.

Note: Double action means that the door can swing both ways. Single action means that the door can swing one way only.

Flush hinge (Figure 57)
These can be used in the same way as butt hinges on both cupboard and full size doors, but this type has the advantage that they do not require 'sinking in'.

Window pivot (Figure 58)
These pivots are recessed into the edge of the window jamb and stile. They are used for the concealed hanging of pivot windows.

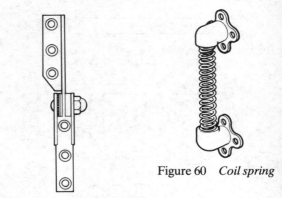

Figure 60   *Coil spring*

Figure 59   *Friction pivot hinge*

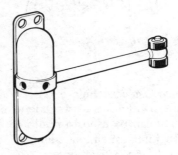

Figure 61   *Door spring*

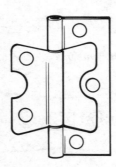

Figure 57   *Flush hinge*

Friction pivot hinge (Figure 59)
This is a modern type of hinge used for hanging pivot windows. It screws onto the face of the window and also contains a friction action, enabling the window to remain open in any position.

Coil spring (Figure 60)
This is mainly used for gates and ledged and braced doors, in order to make them self-closing. It is fixed onto the back face of the door and frame and can be adjusted to the required tension.

Door spring (Figure 61)
This is a self-closing spring for internal use. The unit itself fixes onto the door frame while the arm, which can be adjusted to give the desired closing action applies the pressure to the door. A concealed type of door closer is also available which sinks into the edge of the door and frame.

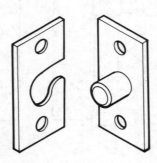

Figure 58   *Window pivot*

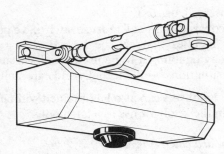

Figure 62   *Overhead door closer*

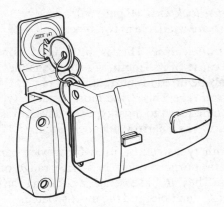

Figure 63   *Cylinder rim latch*

Overhead door closers (Figure 62)

These are mainly used in offices, shops and industrial premises to give their normally larger and heavier doors a controlled self-closing action, and also to enable the door to be held in the open position when required. Certain types of closer are fitted with a temperature-sensitive device that automatically closes the door from the held-open position in the event of a fire.

Fittings which give security

Cylinder rim latch (Figure 63)

Cylinder rim latches are mainly used for entrance doors to domestic property but, as they are only a latch, provide little security on their own. When fitted, the door can be opened from the outside with the use of a key and from the inside by turning the handle. Some types have a double locking facility which improves its security.

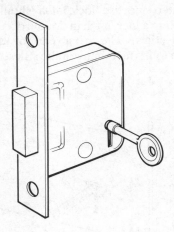

Figure 64   *Mortise deadlock*

Mortise deadlock (Figure 64)

This provides a straightforward key-operated locking action and is often used to provide additional security on entrance doors where cylinder rim latches are fitted. They are also used on doors where simple security is required, e.g. storerooms.

Mortise latch (Figure 65)

This is used mainly for internal doors that do not require locking. The latch which holds the door in the closed position can be operated from either side of the door by turning the handle.

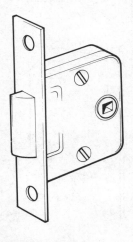

Figure 65   *Mortise latch*

Mortise lock/latch (Figure 66)
These are available in two types:

Horizontal type This is little used nowadays because of its length, which means that it can only be fitted to substantial doors.
Vertical type This is the more modern type and can be fitted to most types of doors. It is often known as a narrow stile lock/latch.

Both types can be used for a wide range of general purpose doors in a wide range of locations. They are, in essence, a combination of the mortise deadlock and the mortise latch.

Rebated mortise lock/latch (Figure 67)
A rebated mortise lock/latch should be used when fixing a lock/latch in double doors that have rebated stiles. The front end of this lock is cranked to fit the rebate on the stiles.

Knobset (Figure 68)
This consists of a small mortise latch and a pair of knob handles that can be locked with a key. Thereby enabling it to be used as a lock/latch in most situations both internally and externally.

Note: Knobsets can also be obtained without the lock in the knob for use as a latch only.

Cupboard catch (Figure 69)
There are many types of cupboard catches available ranging from ball or roller-operated to magnetic catches. The type illustrated is a double ball action catch which is normally made from brass.

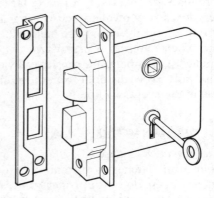

Figure 67   *Rebated mortise lock/latch*

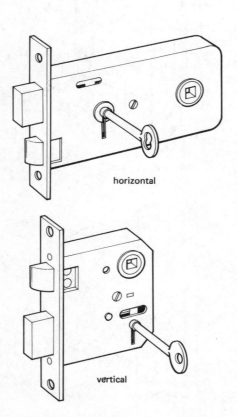

Figure 66   *Mortise lock/latches*

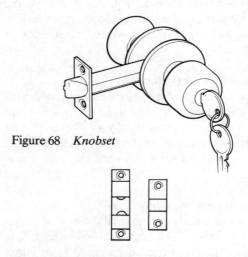

Figure 68   *Knobset*

Figure 69   *Double ball cupboard catch*

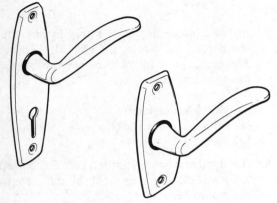

Figure 70   *Lever furniture*

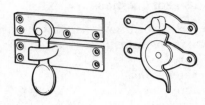

Figure 71   *Sash fasteners*

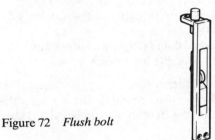

Figure 72   *Flush bolt*

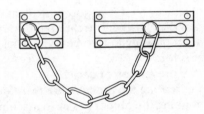

Figure 73   *Security chain*

Figure 74   *Door holder*

Lever furniture (Figure 70)
A wide range of different patterns are available for use with mortise latches and mortise lock/ latches.

Note: Knob furniture and keyhole escutcheon plates are normally used for horizontal mortise lock/latches.

Sash fasteners (Figure 71)
These are available in a number of types and are used to hold the meeting rails of a sash window together, thereby securing the sashes in a closed position.

Flush bolt (Figure 72)
As this is a flush-fitting bolt, it requires sinking in to the timber. It is used for better quality work on the inside of external doors to provide additional security and also on double doors and french windows to bolt one door in the closed position. Two bolts are normally used, one at the top of the door and the other at the bottom.

Security chain (Figure 73)
This can be fixed on front entrance doors, the slide to the door and the chain to the frame. When the chain is inserted into the slide, the door will only open a limited amount until the identity of a caller is checked.

Note: The chain can only be inserted or removed with the door in the closed position.

Door holders (Figure 74)
This is a foot-operated holder that holds doors and gates in the open position. It is particularly useful for holding side-hung garage doors open while driving into or out of the garage.

Self-assessment questions

1 The cells which give hardwood its mechanical strength are the:
  (a) pores
  (b) parenchyma
  (c) fibres
  (d) tracheids

2 Slow-grown softwoods are in general:
  (a) stronger than fast-grown softwoods
  (b) the same strength as fast-grown softwoods
  (c) weaker than fast-grown softwoods
  (d) only suitable for joinery work

3 A pipe requires notching into the tops of 200 mm deep joists towards their ends, the maximum depth of these notches should be:
  (a) 35 mm
  (b) 20 mm
  (c) 25 mm
  (d) 50 mm

4 A specification for a job states that only timber that has been treated with monammonium phosphate is to be used. This treatment is for:
  (a) the prevention of decay
  (b) increasing the timber's fire resistance
  (c) making the timber easier to machine
  (d) killing death-watch beetles

5 Which one of the following timbers has the lowest density?
  (a) Parana pine
  (b) European oak
  (c) European redwood
  (d) Western red cedar

6 The presence of small holes in the surface of timber that has been attacked by wood-boring insects indicates:
  (a) the timber is no longer infested
  (b) the larvae have bored into the timber
  (c) adult beetles have emerged
  (d) the larvae have changed into pupae

7 Insect damage has been found in the softwood roof timbers of a Camberley house. The insect most likely to be responsible for the attack would be:
  (a) *Lyctus* beetle
  (b) death-watch beetle
  (c) house longhorn beetle
  (d) weevils

8 A ledged and braced garden gate is required to be self-closing. The most suitable item to use would be:
  (a) a coil spring
  (b) a rising butt
  (c) an overhead closer
  (d) a door spring

9 A machine is to be bolted onto a concrete wall. The bolts will be subject to a lot of vibration. Which is the most suitable fixing device to use?
  (a) steel expansion anchor
  (b) self-drilling anchor
  (c) nylon plug and large screw
  (d) chemical resin anchor

10 The item shown in Figure 75 is used for:
  (a) fixing roof trusses to the wall plate
  (b) fixing trimmed joists to the trimmer
  (c) supporting the ends of joists
  (d) joining timbers when making trussed rafters

Figure 75

chapter 3

Scaffolding

After reading this chapter the student should be able to:

1 List the main requirements for the construction and use of scaffolds and ladders.

2 Identify the various types of scaffold fittings and equipment.

3 State the responsibilities of a site safety supervisor with regard to scaffolding.

4 Define putlog scaffold; independent scaffold; trestle scaffold; and tower scaffold.

5 List the correct sequence of erection and dismantling of a putlog scaffold and an independent scaffold.

6 State the main requirements of scaffold boards and pole ladders.

A scaffold can be defined as a temporary structure which is used in order to carry out certain building operations. It should provide a safe means of access to heights and a safe working platform.

Scaffolding should only normally be erected and dismantled by a trained scaffolder, although occasionally it may be necessary for a craftsman to erect or dismantle his own simple scaffolding of one or two lifts in height. It is therefore essential that the craftsman has an understanding of scaffolding principles, types, materials, erection and dismantling.

The following official publications deal with scaffolding and they are recommended for further reading.

The Construction Regulations, 1966: Working Places.
BS 1139, 1964: Metal Scaffolding.
BS CP 97, Part 1, 1967: Metal Scaffolding.

Materials

All scaffolding materials must conform to the specifications laid down in BS 1139, 1964: Metal Scaffolding.

Scaffold tubes
These may be of either tubular steel or tubular aluminium. Both types have an outside diameter of 48 mm and are dimensionally fully interchangeable. However, this is not recommended as aluminium tubes deflect more than the tubes made from steel under the same loading conditions.

Fittings
Scaffold fittings may be manufactured from either steel or aluminium. They are both normally suitable for use with steel and aluminium tubes, unless the manufacturer or supplier states a specific use. The main fittings used for scaffolding are described below:

Double coupler (Figure 76) A one piece coupler which connects two scaffold tubes together at right angles.

Figure 76 *Double coupler*

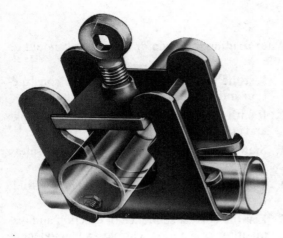

Figure 77   *Universal coupler*

Figure 78   *Swivel coupler*

Universal coupler (Figure 77) Can connect two scaffold tubes together at right angles or parallel to each other.

Swivel coupler (Figure 78) A one piece coupler which connects two scaffold tubes together at any angle.

Putlog coupler (Figure 79) A one piece coupler used solely for connecting putlogs and transoms to ledgers.

Joint pin (Figure 80) An internal fitting which expands and grips against the wall of the tube. It is used for joining two vertical scaffold tubes end to end.

Sleeve coupler (Figure 81) An external fitting used for joining two horizontal or bracing scaffold tubes end to end.

Base plate (Figure 82) A steel plate 150 mm square with integral spigot. It is used for distributing loads from standards and has fixing holes for nailing to sole plates.

Adjustable base plate (Figure 83) A base plate for use on uneven ground. It incorporates a robust screw thread which provides a 230 mm range of adjustment.

Reveal pin (Figure 84) For inserting into the end of a scaffold tube. When adjusted it will form a rigid horizontal or vertical member in any suitable aperture, e.g. window reveal.

Putlog end (Figure 85) Attached over the end of a scaffold tube to convert it into a putlog.

Guard board clip (Figure 86) This securely connects the guard board or toe board to a scaffold standard.

Gin wheel incorporates a 50 mm diameter swivel ring at the top which completely encircles the tube for maximum safety. It is used for raising and lowering equipment on the scaffold.

Scaffold boards

These should comply with the recommendations given in BS 2482: 1970.

The following are the main considerations for scaffold boards.

They are best made from spruce, fir, redwood or whitewood.

They should be free from any defects, such as splits, checks, shakes or damage which could affect their strength.

Their dimensions should be 38 mm × 225 mm in section and not exceed 4.8 m in length.

In order to prevent the ends from splitting, they should be bound with 25 mm × 0.9 mm galvanized or sheradized hoop iron, which extends along each edge at least 150 mm. These hoop irons should be fixed with 30 mm large head, clout nails. A minimum of two on each edge and two on the end (six fixings for each hoop iron).

Each board should be of such a strength, that it can support a uniformly distributed load of 6.7 kN/m², when supported at 1.2 m centres.

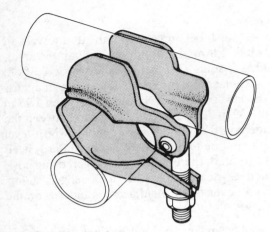

Figure 79   *Putlog coupler*

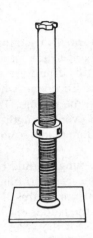

Figure 83   *Adjustable base plate*

Figure 80   *Joint pin*

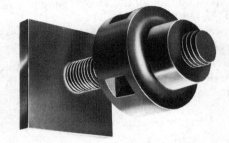

Figure 84   *Reveal pin*

Figure 81   *Sleeve coupler*

Figure 85   *Putlog end*

Figure 82   *Base plate*

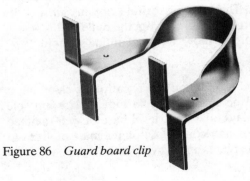

Figure 86   *Guard board clip*

Ladders

Pole ladders are normally used for access to scaffolds and are available in a range of sizes from 3.5 m to 10 m in length. These are normally made from one piece of European whitewood which has been cut down the middle. This is to ensure the ladder has an even strength and flexibility. The rungs are either made from oak, birch or hickory.

The ends of the rungs should be glued with a synthetic resin adhesive into blind holes in the stiles, spaced at 250 mm centres. The rungs at the top and bottom of the ladder must be at least 100 mm from the ends of the stiles. Steel tie rods should be fitted at intervals of not more than nine rungs apart and under the second rung from each end of the ladder.

Before use, all ladders should be protected with a coat of clear exterior quality varnish. They should never be painted as this may conceal potentially dangerous damage or defects in the ladder.

Types of scaffolding

Basically there are two main types of scaffolding in general use: putlog scaffolds; and independent scaffolds.

Putlog scaffolds

These are often known as either a bricklayer's scaffold or a single scaffold. This is because they are normally used when constructing new brick buildings. They consist of a single row of vertical standards which are connected together by horizontal ledgers. Putlogs are coupled to the ledgers and are built into the wall as the brickwork proceeds. This type of scaffold obtains most of its support and stability from the building.

Figure 87 shows a typical putlog scaffold.

Base

A good foundation for a scaffold is essential, it should be made using 38 mm × 225 mm sole plates laid on a firm, level base of well-rammed earth or hardcore. Base plates must be fixed to the sole plates under every standard.

Standards

These must be erected plumb at intervals of between 1.8 m and 2.4 m depending on the intended loading. For a five-board wide scaffold the distance from the centre line of the standards to the face of the wall should be between 1.27 m and 1.32 m. This allows a small gap between the inside board and the wall to enable a spirit level or plumb line to be used. Where standards need to be jointed, these should be staggered and positioned as near as possible to a ledger. Joints should never occur in adjacent standards on the same lift.

Note: The maximum load per bay (in between two standards) depends on the spacing of the standards and is as follows:

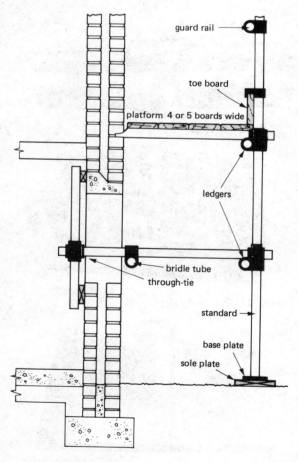

Figure 87   *Putlog scaffold*

With the standards at 1.8 m centres, the maximum load is 610 kg. This is approximately equal to one man, a spot board full of mortar and 180 bricks.

With the standards at 2.4 m centres, the maximum load is 530 kg. This is approximately equal to one man, a spot board full of mortar and 150 bricks.

Where two men are required to work in one bay at the same time, the weight of the materials should be reduced accordingly.

Ledgers

These should be horizontally level and connected on the inside of the standards with right angle couplers. The spacing between ledgers varies with the height of the lift. A spacing of 1.35 m is found to be the most convenient height for bricklayers to build a wall before moving up to the next lift. Joints in ledgers should be staggered and never occur in adjacent standards in the same bay

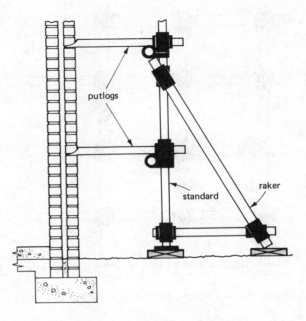

Figure 88 *Scaffold with temporary rakers*

Putlogs

When using 38 mm × 225 mm scaffold boards, the putlogs should be coupled to the ledgers at centres of not more than 1.2 m. Each standard should have a putlog as close as possible to it and in any case not more than 300 mm away from it.

Double putlogs are required where the scaffold boards are butted together. These must be placed so that no board overhangs more than 150 mm or less than 50 mm.

Where a putlog is required opposite an opening in the building, a bridle tube should be clamped with right angle couplers to the underside of the putlogs adjacent to the opening. The intermediate putlog can then be fixed to the ledger and bridle using right angle couplers.

Tying into building

This is most important as putlogs can easily work loose in green (newly laid) brickwork. All ties should be of the through type, as shown in Figure 87 and placed on each alternate lift, at intervals of not more than 6 m. All couplers used for tying should be right angle couplers and the ties should be next to, or as close as possible to, the inter-

section of a standard and ledger. Until the ties become effective, temporary rakers, as shown in Figure 88, should be fixed to each alternate standard, in order to stabilize the scaffold.

Bracing

The bracing of putlog scaffolds can be either one of two types, as shown in Figure 89.

Longitudinal bracing which is fixed to the standards at an angle of approximately 45 degrees and at 30 m intervals in a V or Λ shaped pattern.

Zigzag bracing which is fixed to the standards in the end bays and at intervals of 30 m.

Working platform

The working platform should be at least four and not more than five 38 mm × 225 mm scaffold boards in width. Each board should normally have at least three supports in order to prevent undue sagging. Where there is a danger of high winds the scaffold boards should be clipped down to putlogs.

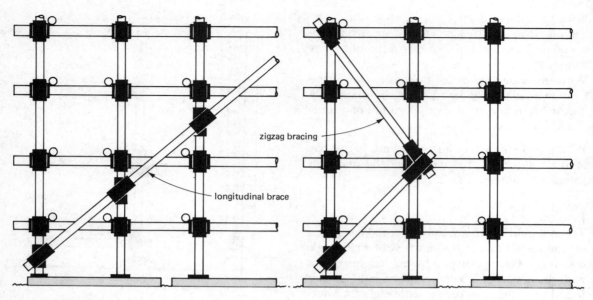

Figure 89   *Alternative methods of bracing*

Guard rails and toe boards

These must be fitted to all working platforms where it is possible for a person or materials to fall 1.98 m or more.

Guard rails and toe boards should be fixed to the inside of the standards along the outside edge and the ends of the working platform and should be not less than 0.92 m and not more than 1.155 m.

Toe boards must rise at least 155 mm above the working platform and the distance between the

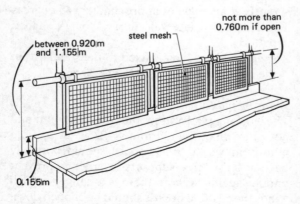

Figure 90   *Guarding to side of scaffold*

top edge of the toe board and the underside of the guard must not exceed 0.76 m. Where materials are stacked on a scaffold the use of wire mesh panels is recommended, as shown in Figure 90.

Ladder access

The ladder should be set at a working angle of 75 degrees. This is a slope of four vertical to one horizontal (Figure 91). The stiles of the ladder should stand on a firm base and be securely held at the top and bottom to prevent sideways or outward movement. The top of the ladder must rise at least 1.07 m above the landing point, with the stepping-off rung level or just above this point. Where ladders are required to rise more than 9 m, a properly guarded intermediate landing stage must be provided.

Note: Ladders should be boarded over to prevent access after working hours.

Limitations

Putlog scaffolds should never have at any time more than one working platform and its height is restricted to a maximum of 45 m, although in practice the height is reduced to 30 m.

Inspection

Each scaffold must be inspected by an experienced, competent person. This is normally the responsibility of the site safety supervisor and the inspection should be carried out as follows:

after erection, before the scaffold is used;
at least once every seven days;
after cold weather, heavy rainfall or high winds.

Each inspection must be recorded in a scaffold register which is kept on site. The safety supervisor should be looking at a number of different points to ensure that the scaffold complies with the regulations.

Erection of a putlog scaffold

Compact base and lay sole plate in required position.
Fix base plates to sole plate in correct position.
Set up standards on base plates.

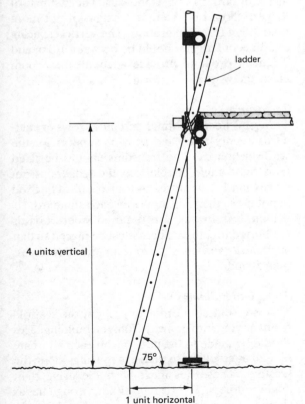

Figure 91 *Ladder access*

Fix ledgers to standards at first lift height.
Next to each standards fix a putlog, its flat end should be fully inserted into the brick course.
Fix intermediate putlogs.

Note: Maximum safe span of 38 mm × 225 mm scaffold boards is 1.5 m.

Tie in scaffold and fix longitudinal or zigzag bracing. Fix temporary raker until tying is effective.
Board out working platform.
Fix rails, toe boards and wire mesh panels.
Erect access ladder.

Note: The standards should be plumbed. Ledgers and putlogs to be levelled and all fittings tightened as the work proceeds.

Dismantling

The dismantling procedure is the reverse of the erection procedure. Points to note are:

Move the materials and waste off the scaffold before dismantling.
Nothing should be thrown from a scaffold. It should be properly lowered.
When erecting, altering or dismantling a scaffold, access to it must be blocked and a warning notice displayed, stating that the scaffold *must not be used*.
All tubes and fittings should be cleaned, sorted and stored after use.

Note: Bent tubes should be returned to the supplier for straightening.

Scaffold boards and ladders should be checked for damage, including twist, splits, decay and loose or broken rungs. If found to be defective they should be discarded.

Independent scaffolds

These are sometimes called double scaffolds as they are constructed using a double row of standards. This type of scaffold carries its own weight and the full weight of all loads imposed upon it, but it is not completely independent. It must be suitably tied to the building for stability.

Figure 92 shows a typical, general purpose, independent scaffold.

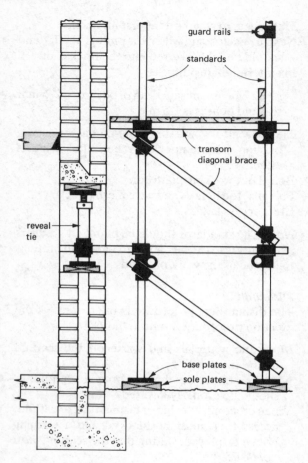

Figure 92   *Independent scaffold*

Base
This is the same as for the putlog scaffold except that two rows of sole plates should be laid to accommodate both the inner and outer row of standards.

Standards
These must be placed on steel base plates and erected plumb, at intervals of between 2.1 m and 2.4 m, depending on its intended loading.

The inner row of standards should be placed about 325 mm from the building. This is to allow the use of one 38 mm × 225 mm scaffold board against the wall, and still provide a working clearance for plumbing and levelling.

The outer row of standards are placed opposite and approximately 1 m from the inner row of standards. This allows for four 38 mm × 225 mm scaffold boards to be used.

Where joints are required in standards, these must be staggered, in the same manner as putlog scaffold standards.

Note: The maximum load per bay depends on the spacing of the standards and is approximately as follows:

With standards at 2.1 m centres, 460 kg (one man, spot board full of mortar and 130 bricks);
With standards at 2.4 m centres, 425 kg (one man, spot board full of mortar and 110 bricks).

Where two men are required to work in one bay the number of bricks should be reduced by forty.

Ledgers
These are fixed with right angle couplers to the inside of both rows of standards. The first pair of ledgers should be fixed at a height of not more than 2.6 m from the ground. The vertical spacing of adjacent ledgers should be between 1.8 m and 2.1 m in order to provide adequate headroom along the working platform.

Transoms
Transoms keep the inner and outer rows of standards evenly apart and provide support for the scaffold boards. The transoms should be fixed with right angle couplers to the ledgers at not more than 1.2 m centres. A transom must be fixed at not more than 300 mm from each standard.

Double transoms are required where boards are butted together. These must be placed so that no board overhangs more than 150 mm or less than 50 mm.

Tying into buildings
This is essential in order to prevent the scaffold from moving into or away from the building. Ties should be made to the building on each alternate lift and at not at more than 6 m spacings along the scaffold. These ties must be made using right angle couplers. They can be either through ties as shown in Figure 88 or reveal ties as shown in Figure 92 provided that where reveal ties are

used, they do not exceed 50 per cent of the total number of ties and are evenly distributed with through ties throughout the whole scaffold area.

Bracing
The use of bracing stiffens the structure and on independent scaffolds must take two forms.

Longitudinal or zigzag bracing The same as that used for putlog scaffolds.

Diagonal bracing These are fixed diagonally to each alternate pair of standards at right angles to the building. They may be fixed either parallel to each other or in a zigzag pattern. Whichever method is used, the bracing should continue the full height of the scaffold.

Note: Bracings should be fixed wherever possible using right angle couplers, although in many situations this is not possible. Therefore the use of swivel couplers is permitted.

Working platforms
These should be not more than five 38 mm × 225 mm scaffold boards wide. One board can be placed between the inner row and the building if required. Each board must have at least three supports and be clipped down where there is a danger of high winds lifting them.

Guard rails and toe boards
The same applies as for putlog scaffolds. Guard rails and toe boards are also required on the inside of the scaffold in the following circumstances:

where the gap between the scaffold and the inside of an existing building exceeds 300 mm;
where the scaffold rises above a building;
where recesses occur in the building.

Ladder access
The same applies as for putlog scaffolds.

Limitations
General purpose independent scaffolds may have up to four working platforms in use at any one time and may extend up to a maximum height of 45 m.

Inspection
The same applies as for putlog scaffolds.

Erection and dismantling of an independent scaffold
This is very similar to the method used for putlog scaffolds except with the addition of an inner row of standards and the diagonal bracing.

Trestle and tower scaffolds
Figure 93 shows a folding trestle scaffold that can be used for work up to about 4.5 m in height. It consists of a pair of trestles with a lightweight staging board forming the working platform. The platform must overhang the trestles at either end by at least 50 mm, but not more than four times its thickness.

Figure 94 shows a tower scaffold that is suitable for both internal and external use for work up to about 6 m in height. For work above this height the tower should be tied into the building or be fitted with counterweights to stabilize it. When the tower is fitted with castors, these should incorporate brakes which lock the wheels. The height is also limited according to the size of the tower's base. For internal use the maximum height should not exceed 3½ times the shorter base dimension. For external use the height is restricted to three times this dimension.

Figure 93   *Trestle scaffold*

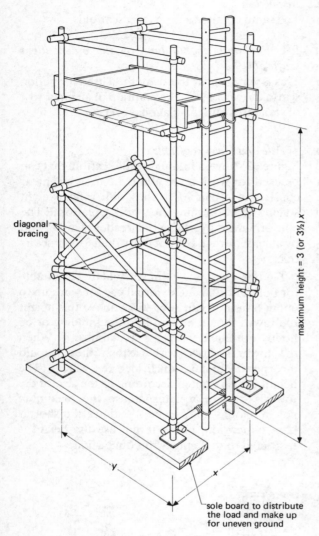

diagonal
bracing

maximum height = 3 (or 3½) x

sole board to distribute
the load and make up
for uneven ground

Figure 94   *Tower scaffold*

Note: A tower scaffold must only be used on firm level ground and mobile towers must never be moved while men or equipment are on it.

Self-assessment questions

1 On an independent scaffold the first row of ledgers should be placed above the ground at a distance of not more than:
   (a) 2.4 m
   (b) 1.8 m
   (c) 2.6 m
   (d) 2.1 m

2 Assuming normal weather conditions scaffolding should be inspected at least:
   (a) every day
   (b) every seven days
   (c) every fourteen days
   (d) before it is dismantled

3 Handrails must be fixed to all working platforms where it is possible for a person or materials to fall:
   (a) 1 m or more in height
   (b) 0.98 m or more in height
   (c) 1.98 m or more in height
   (d) 2.5 m or more in height

4 The distance between the handrail and the working platform should be between:
   (a) 1 m and 1.5 m
   (b) 0.9 m and 1.2 m
   (c) 1 m and 1.15 m
   (d) 0.92 and 1.155 m

5 Putlog scaffolds must be tied in to the building at 6 m intervals using:
   (a) through ties
   (b) reveal ties
   (c) 50 per cent through ties and 50 per cent reveal ties
   (d) zigzag ties

6 Longitudinal bracing should be fixed at an angle of approximately:
   (a) 25 degrees
   (b) 30 degrees
   (c) 45 degrees
   (d) 60 degrees

7   Ladders should be fixed to the scaffold at a
    working angle of:
    (a) 60 degrees
    (b) 45 degrees
    (c) 90 degrees
    (d) 75 degrees

8   The following items have to be fixed when
    erecting a putlog scaffold: (1) base plates
    (2) putlogs (3) ledgers (4) bracings
    (5) standards

    The correct sequence of erection is
    (a) 1, 5, 3, 2, 4
    (b) 2, 5, 4, 1, 3
    (c) 1, 5, 2, 4, 3
    (d) 5, 2, 4, 3, 1

9   The scaffold fitting shown in Figure 95 is a:
    (a) right angle coupler
    (b) putlog coupler
    (c) sleeve coupler
    (d) joint pin

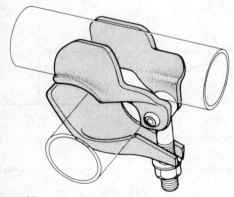

Figure 95

10 Scaffold boards on a working platform must
    overhang the transom. The minimum and
    maximum permitted overhang is:
    (a) 50 mm to 150 mm
    (b) 25 mm to 50 mm
    (c) 150 mm to 250 mm
    (d) 50 mm to 100 mm

chapter 4

Site setting out and levelling

After reading this chapter the student should be able to:

1 List the sequence of operations used to set out a simple building.

2 Describe three methods which can be used to set out right angles.

3 Recognize and state the significance of an ordnance bench mark.

4 Describe four methods which can be used to transfer levels.

5 Describe the use of boning rods.

Setting out a building

The carpenter is not normally expected to set out a building, except on very small sites, where the foreman carpenter or even the carpenter may be asked to carry out this work.

On most building sites the actual setting out of a building is done by the general foreman, but very often the carpenter is asked to assist him in this task. Therefore an understanding of the basic setting out principles is essential.

The setting out of the building can be divided into two distinct operations:

establishing the position of the building and setting up profile boards;

establishing a datum peg and transferring the required levels to various positions.

Establishing the position

To establish the position of the building the following procedure can be adopted (Figure 96).

All setting out is done from the building line. This will be indicated on the block plan and its position is decided by the local authority. The line is established by driving in 50 mm × 50 mm softwood pegs A and B on the side boundaries at the correct distance from, and parallel to, the centre line of the road. A nail in the top of the peg indicates the exact position of the line (see Figure 97). Strain a line between these two nails.

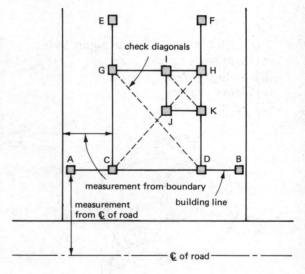

Figure 96   *Setting out a building*

Drive two pegs C and D along the building line to indicate the front corners of the building. The position of the building in relation to the side boundaries will be indicated on the architect's drawings. Drive nails into the tops of the pegs to indicate the exact position of the corners on the building line.

Set out lines at right angles to pegs C and D and establish pegs E and F. Drive nails into the tops of pegs E and F to indicate the exact positions and tension lines between the four pegs.

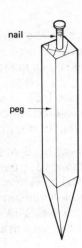

Figure 97
Setting out peg

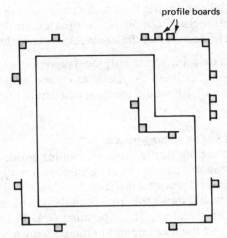

Figure 98   *Layout of profile boards*

Note: The right angles can be set up using any one of three main methods: using a builder's square; using Pythagoras's 3:4:5 rule; using an optical square. The first two methods were dealt with in *Carpentry and Joinery for Building Craft Students 1*. The third method is covered later in this chapter.

Measure along lines C E and D F to establish pegs G and H in the far corners of the building. It is advisable at this stage to check the diagonals CH and DG. If these diagonals measure the same, the building must be square and the setting out can continue. When the diagonals are not the same, a check must be made through the previous stages to discover and rectify the inaccuracy before proceeding to the next stage.

Peg out the positions of offset I, J and K. Check the smaller diagonals which have been formed, to ensure accuracy.

Set up profile boards just clear of the trench runs at all of the corners and wall intersections of the building. Transfer positions of setting out lines to the profile boards (see Figure 98).

Note: Profile boards consist of 50 mm × 50 mm softwood pegs driven into the ground, on to which a 25 mm × 150 mm board has been fixed.

Four nails are driven into the top of each profile board to indicate the edges of the foundation trench and the edges of the brickwork.

Note: An alternative, which is sometimes used

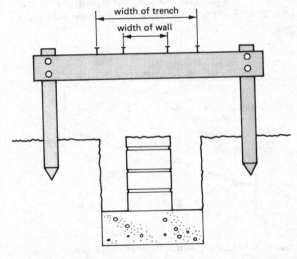

Figure 99   *Profile board in relation to trench and brickwork*

instead of the nails is to mark the positions on top of the profile boards with four saw cuts. Figure 99 shows a profile board in relation to the trench and brickwork.

Lines can be strained between the nails on the profiles to indicate the exact positions for the excavators and bricklayers.

Note: Where the trenches are excavated by machine, the position of the trench should be marked by sprinkling sand on the ground directly under the lines to indicate the sides of the trenches. The lines are then taken down and replaced after the excavation is complete.

It is advisable to use only steel tapes for setting out work, as linen or plastic tapes are liable to stretch and this would result in inaccurate setting out.

Setting out on sloping ground

Where setting out is done on sloping ground a measurement parallel to the ground will not give the correct horizontal distance.

Figure 100 shows the correct method to be used for short distances. The tape must be held horizontal and the measurement plumbed down onto a peg.

Note: A straight edge and level or plumb bob and line may be used for plumbing down onto the peg.

For longer distances the horizontal measurement should be divided and marked out in a number of stages as shown in Figure 101.

The site square (Figure 102)

This is a useful optical instrument for setting out right angles. It consists of two main parts:

Part 1 The cylindrical head which contains two telescopes permanently mounted at right angles (90 degrees) to each other. Both of the telescopes can be individually adjusted vertically both up and down. This gives the instrument a range of between 2 m and 90 m.

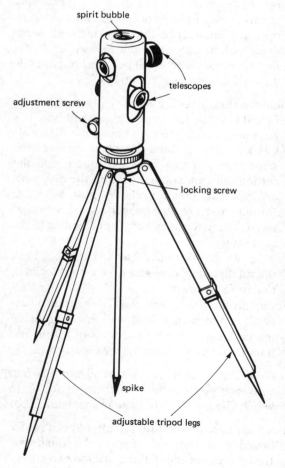

Figure 102   *Site square*

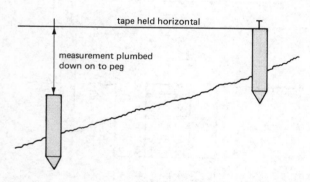

Figure 100   *Taking short distance measurements*

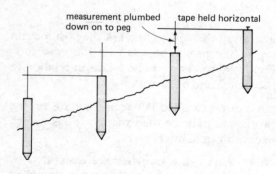

Figure 101   *Taking long distance measurements*

Part 2 The tripod, with adjustable sliding legs, and a datum rod, the end of which contains a spike. The spike is pointed at one end to set up over a given position or mark. The other end of the spike is hollowed out to fit over the end of a nail.

Setting up the instrument

The correct procedure is as follows:

Set up tripod; ensure all bolts and adjustable nuts are tight.

Place tripod over the corner peg of the building and extend the spike to fit over the nail in the top of the peg.

Carefully screw the instrument onto tripod and line lower telescope along the front building line.

Adjust tripod legs so that the spirit bubble on top of the cylindrical head is in a central position. Tighten all tripod adjusting nuts and recheck the spirit bubble. The instrument is now set up and ready for use.

Method of use

This is illustrated in Figure 103.

Set up the instrument over corner peg A.

Sight through lower telescope towards peg B. This is the furthest front corner of the building.

Adjust the fine setting screw and tilt the telescope until the spot on view is seen through it. See

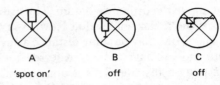

| A | B | C |
| 'spot on' | off | off |

Figure 104   *View through site square*

Figure 104(a). The view through the telescope shown in Figure 104(b) and (c) are off the mark and the telescope requires further adjustment to obtain the spot on view.

Measure distance required to peg C. Sight through top telescope taking care not to move the instrument. Direct your assistant to move peg C sideways until the spot on view is seen through the telescope. Pegs BAC now form a right angle.

The fourth corner peg of the building is located by resetting the instrument over either peg B or C and repeating the previous stages.

Note: It is good practice to measure the diagonals in order to check the accuracy of the setting out.

Establishing a datum peg

A datum peg is a timber or steel peg, driven into the ground to a suitable level and then set in concrete (see Figure 105).

In order to establish the value of the datum peg one must refer it back to an ordnance bench mark (OBM). OBMs are to be found cut into the walls of churches and public buildings. An OBM is illustrated in Figure 106. The level value of an OBM can be obtained from the relevant Ordnance Survey map, or from the local planning

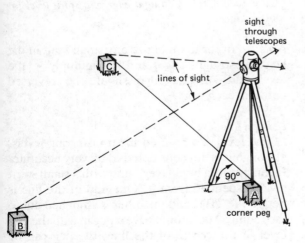

Figure 103   *Using a site square*

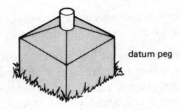

Figure 105   *Datum peg*

authorities office. The level given will be a fixed height above the ordnance datum. The ordnance datum is the mean sea level at Newlyn in Cornwall. The OBM may be some distance away from the site and will have to be transferred back to a datum peg on the site. This is done by taking a series of flying levels from the OBM back to the site datum peg, using an optical levelling instrument and staff.

Note: The site datum peg is also known as a temporary bench mark (TBM).

Levels can be transferred to the required positions on site in a number of ways:

using a water level (this was covered in *Carpentry and Joinery for Building Craft Students 1*);
using a straight edge and level;
using a line level;
using a Cowley automatic level.

Note: A dumpy level may also be used for levelling operations but its use is beyond the scope of this chapter.

Using a straight edge and level

The straight edge and level is a very simple method, it can be used for most levelling operations. Figure 107 shows the straight edge and level being used to transfer a level from the TBM.

For transferring levels over distances shorter than the straight edge (up to 3 m), drive a 50 mm × 50 mm softwood peg in the required position. Rest the straight edge and level on top of the TBM and peg. Drive the peg into the ground until a horizontal level is achieved. Check for accuracy by first reversing the level on the straight edge and then reversing the straight edge on the TBM and peg. If the bubble in the level alters during these checks either the level is faulty or the straight edge is not parallel.

Note: In order to prevent any damage to the level it should be removed while driving in the pegs.

When transferring levels over greater distances the procedure to be used is similar, except that additional pegs are driven into the ground at up to 3 m intervals and levelled from the previous peg (see Figure 108).

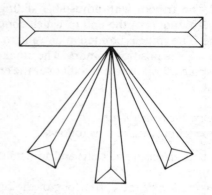

Figure 106   *Ordnance bench mark*

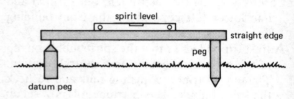

Figure 107   *Using a straight edge and spirit level for short distances*

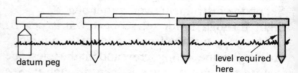

Figure 108   *Using a straight edge and spirit level for long distances*

Note: In order to minimize any small fault in the level or straight edge, and not multiply it, the level and straight edge should be reversed between each peg.

Using a line level

A line level can be used for transferring levels, although it is not considered to be very accurate. It consists of a bricklayer's line with a small spirit level suspended from it. One end of the line is tied to the TBM and the other is stretched out to the required position. Drive a peg in with the line level in the centre of the line, the peg can be driven in until a horizontal level is achieved.

Cowley automatic level

The Cowley automatic level is a very simple levelling instrument which is widely used for general site levelling operations. The instrument consists of three main parts:

The rectangular metal-cased head, which contains a dual system of mirrors. Figure 109 shows the metal-cased head.

Note: Of the two apertures, the one on top is the sighting or viewing aperture, the one on the front is the objective aperture.

The tripod The centre pin of this must point upwards when the tripod is set up. The instrument's metal-cased head is inserted on to this pin, which releases a catch and sets the level ready for use.

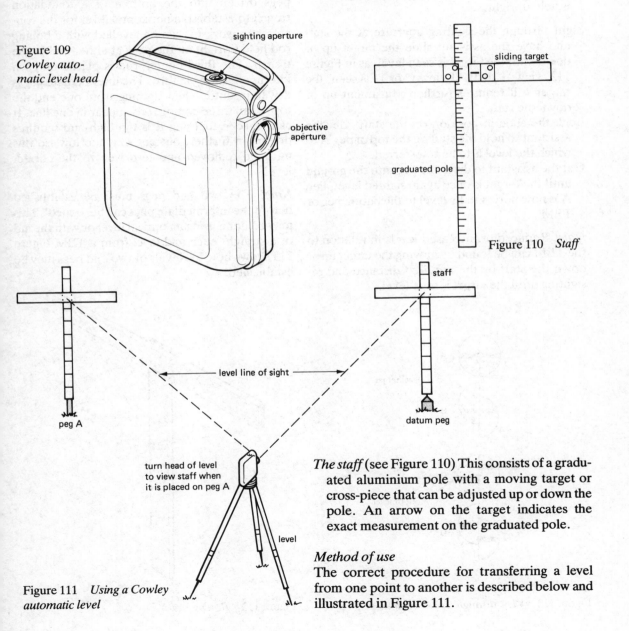

Figure 109
Cowley automatic level head

Figure 110   *Staff*

Figure 111   *Using a Cowley automatic level*

The staff (see Figure 110) This consists of a graduated aluminium pole with a moving target or cross-piece that can be adjusted up or down the pole. An arrow on the target indicates the exact measurement on the graduated pole.

Method of use

The correct procedure for transferring a level from one point to another is described below and illustrated in Figure 111.

Set up the tripod, insert the level on the pin of the tripod, checking that the pin is fully inserted.

Sight through the sighting aperture in the top of the level and adjust the tripod so that the two mirrors are seen to form an approximate circle.

Have an assistant hold the staff on the datum peg, or TBM.

Note: The assistant should ensure that the staff is held upright.

Sight through the sighting aperture at the staff and have the assistant slide the target up or down until the target is seen level, as in Figure 112, view A or B. If view C or D is seen, the target still requires further adjustment up or down the staff.

Lock the slide in position on the staff. Get the assistant to hold the staff on the top of peg A to which the level is to be transferred.

Get the assistant to drive the peg into the ground until the target is once again sighted level. Peg A is now horizontally level to the datum peg or TBM.

Note: Reduced or increased levels in relation to the TBM can be found by moving the target up or down the staff by the required distance and re-sighting until the target is seen level.

Boning rods

The carpenter is often asked to make a set of three boning rods, which are used for establishing a straight line between two known points. This straight line may be either a horizontal level or an even gradient. Figure 113 shows the construction of a typical boning rod. Figure 114 shows how pegs driven into the bottom of a foundation trench to establish a horizontal level for the concreter to work to, can be levelled with a boning rod held upright on the pegs at either end of the trench. The third boning rod is placed on each intermediate peg in turn. The intermediate peg is driven in until, when sighting from one end the tops of all three boning rods appear in one line. It can be seen that peg B is too high and requires driving in further, but peg C is too low, so this must be removed and re-driven to the correct level.

Note: The two end pegs must be established before the intermediate pegs can be 'boned'. This may be done using an optical level or with the aid of a straight edge and level from a TBM Figure 115 shows how the levels of two end pegs may be established.

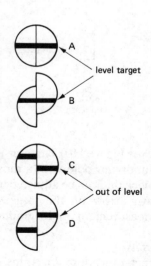

Figure 112   *View through Cowley automatic level*

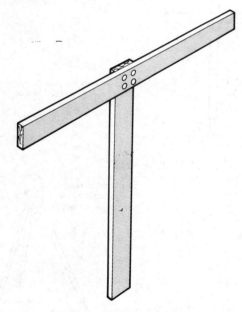

Figure 113   *Boning rod*

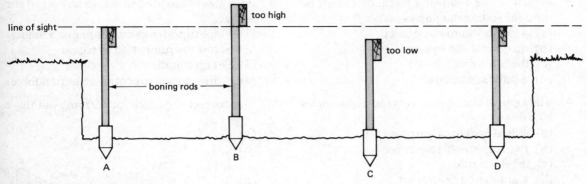

Figure 114   *Using boning rods*

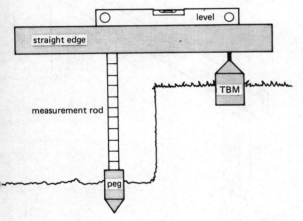

Figure 115   *Establishing a reduced level*

The measurement from the top of the TBM to the top of the foundation concrete will be known. A rod should be cut to this measurement, using the straight edge and level from the TBM. The end peg can be driven in until the measurement rod fits between the straight edge and level. The peg at the other end of the trench is set up in the same way.

As well as levelling, boning rods can be used to establish an even gradient for the bottom of a drainage trench, etc. The method used is the same as before except that the end pegs are first driven to their respective levels.

Note: The middle boning rod is known as the traveller.

Self-assessment questions

1   The illustration in Figure 116 shows:
    (a) a datum peg
    (b) a temporary bench mark
    (c) the ordnance datum
    (d) an ordnance bench mark

2   The ordnance datum refers to:
    (a) the mean sea level nearest the building site
    (b) a point identified by the local authority planning department
    (c) the mean sea level at Newlyn in Cornwall
    (d) an Ordnance Survey map

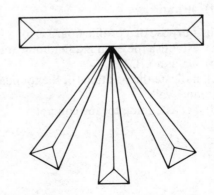

Figure 116

3 Which of the following methods cannot be used for setting out angles on site?
   (a) a Cowley automatic level
   (b) an optical site square
   (c) the 3:4:5 rule
   (d) a builder's square

4 The optical site square sets out right angles by using:
   (a) a dual system of mirrors
   (b) two adjustable telescopes
   (c) the 3:4:5 rule
   (d) a graduated protractor

Figure 117

5 The illustration shown in Figure 117 is of a:
   (a) spot on view through an optical site square
   (b) level target through a Cowley automatic level
   (c) incorrect view through an optical site square
   (d) out of level view through a Cowley automatic level

6 A 3 m straight edge and spirit level is found to give a 5 mm inaccuracy. If this straight edge and spirit level is used correctly to transfer a level between two pegs 12 m apart, the inaccuracy between the two pegs will be:
   (a) 20 mm
   (b) 10 mm
   (c) nil
   (d) 40 mm

7 The purpose of a profile board is to:
   (a) establish the even gradient of a drain
   (b) act as a TBM
   (c) indicate the positions of the foundations and walls
   (d) act as a guide for the concreter

8 Four stages are used to set up an optical site square:
   (1) Place tripod over corner peg of building.
   (2) Screw instrument on to tripod.
   (3) Set up tripod.
   (4) Adjust tripod to centralize spirit bubble.

The correct sequence for carrying out these stages is:
   (a) 1, 2, 3, 4
   (b) 2, 1, 4, 3
   (c) 3, 1, 2, 4
   (d) 3, 1, 4, 2

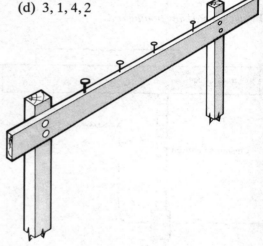

Figure 118

9 The item of equipment shown in Figure 118 is a:
   (a) Cowley level staff
   (b) profile board
   (c) boning rod
   (d) sighting board

10 A building is set out from the:
   (a) building line
   (b) ordnance line
   (c) datum line
   (d) centre of the road

chapter 5

Joinery

After reading this chapter the student should be able to:

1 State the principles involved in making the following items of joinery work:
doors
frames and linings
windows
stairs
fitments
simple wall panelling

2 Identify the component parts of these various items.

3 Produce sketches to show suitable details of these various items.

4 List the sequence of operations for a given job.

5 State any building regulations that are relevant to a given item of joinery work.

6 Select the most suitable item of joinery for a given purpose.

Doors

As stated in *Carpentry and Joinery for Building Craft Students 1,* timber doors may be classified into one of four main groups, these being:

panelled and glazed doors
flush doors
fire-check doors
matchboarded doors

The British Standards, BS 459, Parts 1 to 4, cover these four main groups. It must be pointed out that the design and construction of timber doors is not restricted to this standard, although standard doors are extensively used since they are mass produced, readily available and are normally cheaper than purpose-made doors.

Panelled and glazed doors

The design and construction of panelled and glazed doors are very similar. They consist of a frame which has either a plough groove or rebate run around it to receive the panels or glazing. The framing members for these doors vary with the number and arrangement of the panels. They will consist of horizontal members and vertical members.

All horizontal members are called rails. They are also named according to their position in the door, e.g. top rail, middle rail, bottom rail, intermediate rail.

Note: The middle rail is also known as the lock rail and the upper intermediate rail is sometimes called a frieze rail.

The two outside vertical members are called stiles, while all intermediate vertical members are known as muntins.

Figure 119 shows a typical panelled door, with all its component parts named.

Note: It is normal to leave at least a 50 mm horn on each end of the stiles. This serves two purposes:

It enables the joints to be securely wedged without fear of splitting out.
The horns protect the top and bottom edges of the door before it is hung.

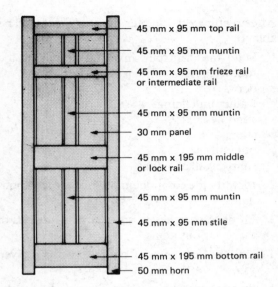

45 mm x 95 mm top rail

45 mm x 95 mm muntin

45 mm x 95 mm frieze rail
or intermediate rail

45 mm x 95 mm muntin

30 mm panel

45 mm x 195 mm middle
or lock rail

45 mm x 95 mm muntin

45 mm x 95 mm stile

45 mm x 195 mm bottom rail

50 mm horn

Figure 119   *A typical panelled door*

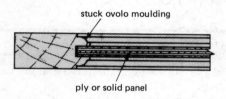

stuck ovolo moulding

ply or solid panel

Figure 120   *Panel detail (plough groove)*

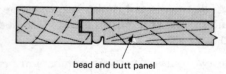

bead and butt panel

Figure 121   *Panel detail (bead butt)*

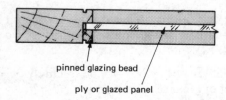

pinned glazing bead

ply or glazed panel

Figure 122   *Panel detail (planted bead)*

Figure 120 shows a ply panel which is held in a plough groove that is run around the inside edge of the framing. Two ovolo mouldings are also worked around the inside edges of the framing for decorative purposes. They are known as stuck mouldings.

Note: The plough groove should be at least 2 mm deeper than the panel. This is to allow for any moisture movement (shrinkage and expansion).

Figure 121 shows a timber panel which is tongued into a plough groove in the framing. This type of panel is known as a bead butt panel because on its vertical edges a bead moulding is worked, while the horizontal edges remain square and butt up to the rails.

Figure 122 shows a thin plywood or glazed panel which is located in a rebate. It is held in position by planted beads, which are pinned into the framing. Where this type of door is used externally, the planted beads should be placed on the inside of the door mainly for security reasons but also because when glazing beads are used externally water tends to get behind them. This makes both the beads and framing susceptible to decay.

Note: For a neat finish, planted beads should not finish flush with the framing.

Figure 123 shows a bevel raised and fielded panel, which is tongued into a plough groove. A bolection moulding is planted around the joint between the framing and the panel for aesthetic reasons. (It looks pleasing.) The bolection mould should be fixed through the panel with screws. The holes through the panel for these screws should be slotted. This allows a certain amount of movement to take place without any possibility of

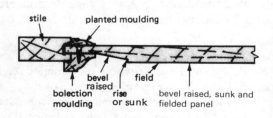

stile

planted moulding

bevel
raised

field

bolection
moulding

rise
or sunk

bevel raised, sunk and
fielded panel

Figure 123   *Bolection mould*

the panel splitting. A planted moulding is used on the other side of the door to cover the screws. This should be pinned to the framing and not the panel.

Joints

Traditionally the mortise and tenon joint was used exclusively in the jointing of panelled and glazed doors. But today the majority of doors are mass produced and in order to reduce costs the dowelled joint is used extensively. The use of the dowelled joint reduces the cost of the door in three ways:

The length of each rail is reduced by at least 200 mm.

The jointing time is reduced as only round holes have to be drilled to accommodate the dowel.

The assembly time is reduced as no wedging, etc. has to be carried out.

Figure 124 shows a six-panel door which has been jointed using dowels. These dowels should be 16 mm × 150 mm and spaced approximately 50 mm centre to centre. The following is the minimum recommended number of dowels to be used for each joint.

Top rail to stile	two dowels
Middle rail to stile	three dowels
Bottom rail to stile	three dowels
Intermediate rail to stile	one dowel
Muntin to rail	two dowels

Figure 125 shows an exploded view of a dowelled joint between a top rail and stile. In addition to the dowel, a haunch is incorporated into the joint. This ensures that the two members finish flush and its use also overcomes any tendency for the rail to twist.

Note: A small groove should be cut along each dowel. This is to let any excess glue and trapped air to escape when the joint it cramped up.

Although the dowel joint is extensively used for mass-produced doors, the mortise and tenon joint is still used widely for purpose-made and high quality door construction.

Figure 126 shows an exploded view of the framework for a typical six-panel door.

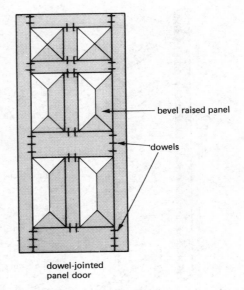

dowel-jointed panel door

Figure 124 *Dowel-jointed panel door*

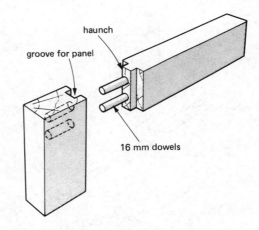

Figure 125 *Exploded view of a dowelled joint*

Haunched mortise and tenons are used for the joints between the rails and stiles.

For the joints between the muntins and rails, stub mortise and tenons are used. As these joints do not go right through the rails, they cannot be wedged in the normal way. Instead fox wedges are used (see Figure 127). These are small wedges which are inserted into the saw cuts in the tenon.

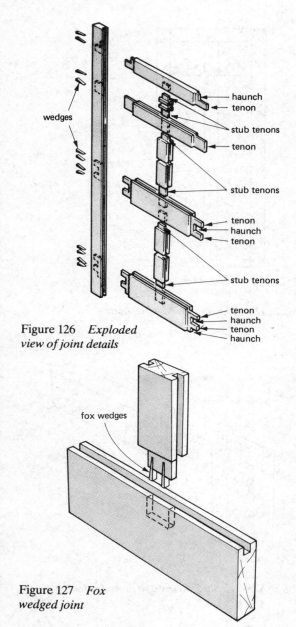

Figure 126 *Exploded view of joint details*

Figure 127 *Fox wedged joint*

When the joint is cramped up the wedge expands the tenon and causes it to grip securely in the mortise.

Note: Mortise and tenon joints should be made in accordance with the following basic rules:

The thickness of the tenon should be approximately ⅓ of the thickness of the timber.

The width of the tenon should not exceed five times its thickness.

Figure 128 is a workshop rod for the six-panel door. The positions of mortises are indicated by crosses.

Note: It must be remembered that as the plough grooves for the panels effectively reduce the width of the timber, the mortises must be positioned accordingly, as shown in the workshop rod.

A traditional half-glazed door is shown in Figure 129. It is constructed with diminishing stiles, in order to provide the maximum area of glass and therefore admit into the building the maximum amount of daylight. This type of door is also known as a gun stock stile door because its stiles are said to resemble the stock of a gun. The mortise and tenon joints used in the construction of this door are indicated in the drawing.

Note: The middle rail has splayed shoulders to overcome the change in the widths of the stiles, above and below the middle rail. An exploded view of this joint is shown in Figure 130.

The top half of the door can either be fully glazed or subdivided with glazing bars as shown in Figure 129. When glazing bars are used they are normally stub tenoned into the stiles and

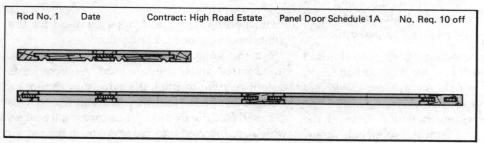

Figure 128
Workshop rod

rails. The joints between the glazing bars themselves could either be stub tenoned or halved and scribed. The halved and scribed method is shown in Figure 131. The bottom half of the door normally consists of a bevel raised and fielded panel with planted bolection mouldings.

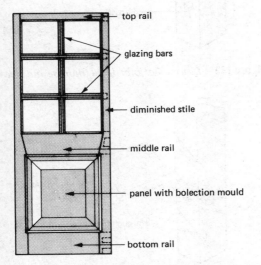

Figure 129   *Half-glazed door with diminishing stiles*

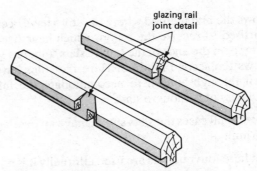

Figure 131   *Glazing rail or bar joint detail*

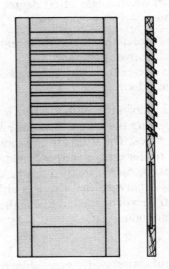

Figure 132   *Louvre door*

Louvred doors

The frame of this type of door is similar in construction to that of a panel door, e.g. mortise and tenons or dowels are used to join the rails to the stiles. Traditionally louvres were only used as a means of ventilation, but now their use is increasing because of their pleasing appearance.

When used externally, the louvre slats are normally set at an angle of 45 degrees. They should also project beyond the face of the framing for weathering purposes. Figure 132 shows an elevation and section of an external half-louvred door.

There are two methods by which the projecting louvre slats can be jointed to the stiles. Figure 133

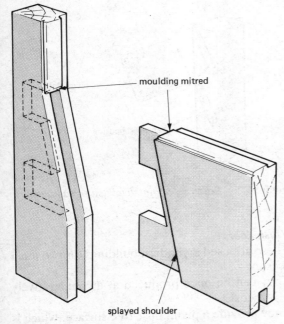

Figure 130   *Diminished stile joint detail*

shows the first method where the stiles have been mortised to receive the tenons which have been formed on the ends of the louvre slats. Figure 134 shows the second method. Here the stiles have been through-housed to accommodate the full thickness of the louvre slats.

Note: In all cases the slats should have an overlap of 6 mm.

Where louvre doors are used internally it is not necessary for the louvre slats to project beyond the face of the framing. The internal slats are normally set at an angle of 60 degrees for two main reasons:

More of the face of the slat is visible and this adds to the decorative appearance.
Fewer slats are required and this gives a more economical door.

Figure 135 shows the method which is normally used for jointing the louvre slats for an internal door to the stiles. The stiles are stop-housed on a high speed router using a purpose-made jig. The housing must be cut to exactly the same size as the louvre slat, otherwise the slat will either be a slack fit or time will be wasted easing the housing to fit each individual slat.

Door sets

Many manufacturers are now able to supply mass-produced door sets. These sets consist of a door frame or lining, door architraves and iron-mongery.

The doors are pre-hung on loose pin or lift-off hinges for easy door removal. The ironmongery, including locks and handles are factory fitted. Architraves are normally fixed on one side of the frame and loose pinned on the other.

Where required the door sets can be supplied completely pre-decorated (painted or polished).

The fixing of door sets is carried out by following a similar procedure to that used when fixing a door lining, although they should not be fixed until at least the second fixing stage. This is to avoid the possibility of any damage during the building process. The main advantage of using door sets is the considerable saving in time and labour on site.

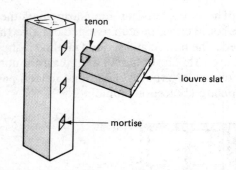

Figure 133   *Louvre slat joint detail (mortise and tenon)*

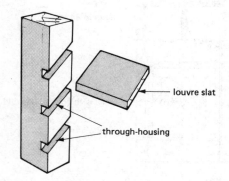

Figure 134   *Louvre slat joint detail (through housing)*

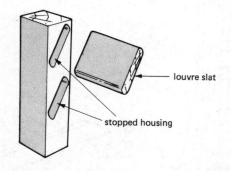

Figure 135   *Louvre slat joint detail (stopped housing)*

Flush doors

These are used in modern buildings for two main reasons.

They can be mass produced at a comparatively low cost.

They provide a plain, dust-free surface, which is easy to clean and decorate.

Flush doors consist of either a hollow or a solid core which is faced with sheets of hardboard or plywood.

Note: An exterior grade (WBP) plywood or oil-tempered hardboard should be used for the facings of external doors.

Flush doors are produced in two thicknesses: 35 mm for internal use; and 44 mm for external use, although some manufacturers are now producing doors which have a thickness of 40 mm.

Hollow core
Hollow core doors are normally the cheapest type of flush door to produce and therefore purchase. There are many ways in which the hollow core can be made. The two main methods are the skeleton core and the lattice core.

Whatever type of hollow core is used, the main disadvantage is the same. This is a tendency for the facing to deflect between the compartments of the core. This produces a ripple effect which is especially noticeable when the facings are finished with a gloss coating such as paint or varnish.

Note: Ventilation holes or grooves must be incorporated between each compartment. This is to prevent air becoming trapped in the compartments when the door is assembled. If this were not done the facings would have a tendency to bulge.

Figure 136 shows a skeleton core door. It consists of 28 mm × 70 mm stiles, top, bottom and middle rails, and 20 mm × 28 mm intermediate rails are used to complete the framework.

Very simple joints can be used in this type of construction, as its main strength is obtained by firmly gluing the facings to the framework. Two main types of joints are used:

The rails are tongued into a groove in the stiles.
The rails are butt jointed and stapled or fixed with corrugated fasteners.

Figure 137 shows a lattice core door. It consists of 28 mm × 30 mm framework which is simply stapled together. The core is made from narrow strips of hardboard which are simply slot jointed

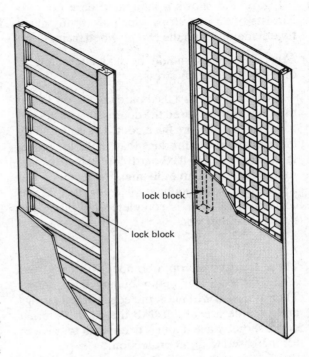

Figure 136   *Skeleton core*   Figure 137   *Lattice core*

to produce the lattice. As with other types of flush door construction the strength of the door is obtained by firmly gluing the facings to both the framework and the core.

Note: A lock block should be provided in all hollow core doors to accommodate a mortise lock or latch. The block also serves to provide a fixing for the lock furniture. The position of the lock block is normally indicated on the edge of the door.

Solid core
Solid core flush doors are considered to be of a better quality than hollow flush doors. There are three main reasons for this view:

Because their facing remains flat and they have no tendency to produce the ripple effect.
Because of their increased rigidity.
Because of their increased sound insulation. Hollow core doors do not appreciably exclude sound.

Figure 138 shows a laminated core door. It consists of 25 mm strips which are firmly glued together along with the two plywood facings.

Note: The strips should be laid alternately in order to balance any stresses.

Figure 139 shows a flaxboard core door. When this type of core is used the door is not considered to be a true solid core flush door. It is only slightly more expensive to produce than the hollow core. It consists of the flaxboard core which is surrounded by a simple 30 mm framework. The framework is normally stapled together at the corners. The door is completed by gluing the facings to either side.

Lippings

These are narrow strips of timber which are fixed along the edges of better quality flush doors. Their purpose is to mask the edges of the facings and provide a neat finish to the door. External doors should have lippings fixed to all four edges for increased weather protection.

Figure 140 shows a plain lipping which is used for internal doors.

Figure 141 shows a lipping which is tongued into the edge of the door. It is used for both internal and external doors. It is more expensive than plain lippings as the door has to be

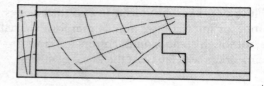

Figure 140   *Flush lipping*

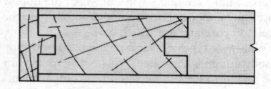

Figure 141   *Tongued lipping*

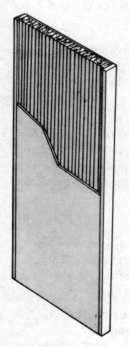

Figure 138
Laminated core

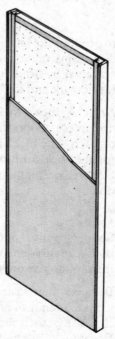

Figure 139
Flaxboard core

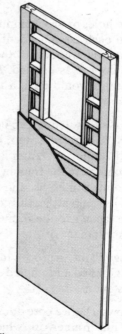

Figure 142
Flush door with vision panel

assembled and then passed through a spindle moulder a number of times to produce the groove for the lipping.

Note: Lipping should be glued in position and not fixed with panel pins.

Vision panels

When vision panels are required in flush doors, the opening should be framed out as shown in Figure 142. This is normally done during the construction of the door, although it is possible to form the opening at a later stage. The glass is held in place by glazing beads.

Figure 143 shows internal glazing beads for an internal door.

Figure 144 shows rebated glazing beads which are suitable for external doors as they provide a more weather-resistant finish.

Figure 145 shows a better method for fixing glazing into external flush doors. It provides far greater security than the previous method.

Note: Glazing beads for doors are normally fixed using countersunk brass screws and recessed cups. This is to enable the glazing beads to be easily removed in the event of the glass needing replacement.

Hinges

Each door must be of a suitable construction to receive hinges in the normal position. Where only one edge of the door is suitable to receive hinges, this must be indicated on the edge of the door.

Locks

Each door must be of a suitable construction to receive a mortise lock in the normal position. Where the lock can only be fitted in a certain position, e.g. in a lock block, this position must be indicated on the edge of the door.

Letter plates

Each door for exterior use must be of a suitable construction to receive a letter plate in the normal position.

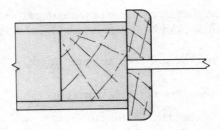
Figure 143   *Internal glazing beads*

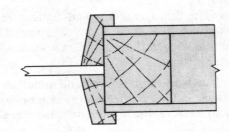
Figure 144   *Internal or external glazing beads*

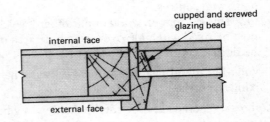
Figure 145   *Alternative external flush door glazing detail*

Fire-resisting doors

These doors, when used in conjunction with the correct type of frame, are able to resist the penetration of fire for a specified length of time. The Building Regulations Part B stipulate the use of fire-resisting/check doors in certain situations, for example the door between a house and an attached garage; the doors of flats which open out onto common areas.

These doors are often constructed in accordance with BS 459: Part 3 which gives details of half-hour and one-hour fire-check doors.

Note: These doors must be marked on their hanging stile with

the manufacturer's name or trade mark;
the British Standard number, e.g. BS 459, Part 3; and
'half hour' or 'one hour' as appropriate.

Half hour construction (Figure 146)

Size The standard widths are 838 mm or 914 mm, with a standard height of 1981 mm. The finished thickness of the door should be not less than 44 mm.

Framing The stiles and top and bottom rails should not be less than 38 mm × 95 mm. The minimum size of the middle rail should be 38 mm × 165 mm.

Note: The stiles, top, bottom and middle rails must have a 10 mm × 25 mm rebate on both sides to receive the protective plasterboard infill.

Protective infill This is 10 mm plasterboard, which must be fixed in the rebate of the framing at 225 mm centres.

Facing This is 3 mm plywood or hardboard which must be fixed with glue over the whole area of the door face.

Note: No metal fasteners must be used when fixing the facings.

Lippings When used they can be fixed with glue to one or both of the stiles or all four edges of the door. They can either be tongued into the framing or fit flush to it.

Note: No metal fasteners must be used when fixing the lippings.

Frame This must have a 25 mm deep rebate to receive the door. Where this is a planted stop it must be fixed with 38 mm no. 8 countersunk screws spaced 75 mm from each end of the stop and at intervals of not more than 600 mm (see Figure 147).

One hour construction (see Figure 148)

Size As for the half hour construction but the finished thickness of the door shall be not less than 54 mm.

Framing As for the half hour construction.

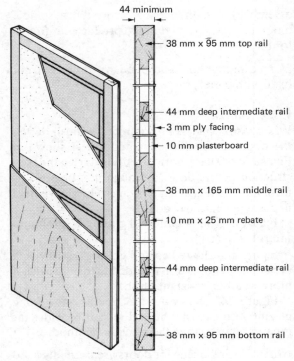

44 minimum

38 mm × 95 mm top rail

44 mm deep intermediate rail
3 mm ply facing
10 mm plasterboard

38 mm × 165 mm middle rail

10 mm × 25 mm rebate

44 mm deep intermediate rail

38 mm × 95 mm bottom rail

Figure 146   *Half hour fire-check door*

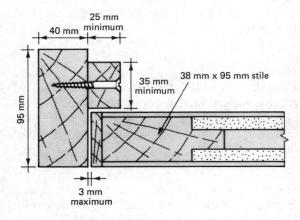

25 mm minimum
40 mm

35 mm minimum

38 mm × 95 mm stile

95 mm

3 mm maximum

Figure 147   *Frame for half hour fire-check door*

Protective infill 10 mm plasterboard as for the half hour construction.

Asbestos layer An asbestos layer must be incorporated under the facing. It must be not less than 4.5 mm thick and must be fixed with glue over the whole area of the door face.

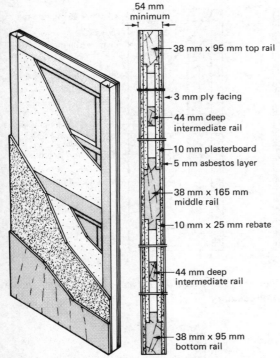

54 mm minimum

- 38 mm x 95 mm top rail
- 3 mm ply facing
- 44 mm deep intermediate rail
- 10 mm plasterboard
- 5 mm asbestos layer
- 38 mm x 165 mm middle rail
- 10 mm x 25 mm rebate
- 44 mm deep intermediate rail
- 38 mm x 95 mm bottom rail

Figure 148   *One hour fire-check door*

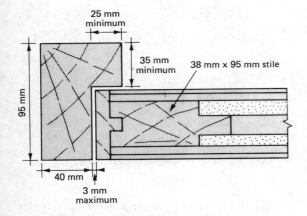

25 mm minimum

35 mm minimum

38 mm x 95 mm stile

95 mm

40 mm

3 mm maximum

Figure 149   *Frame for one hour fire-check door*

Note: No metal fasteners must be used when fixing the asbestos layer.

Facing This is 3 mm hardboard or plywood as for the half hour construction.

Lipping Doors may be used with or without a lipping. Where they are used, they must be tongued to the edges of the door and glued. The lipping must be not more than 9 mm thick.

Note: No metal fixings must be used when fixing the lippings.

Frame As for the half hour construction except that the rebate must be formed from the solid. No planted stops are permitted (see Figure 149).

Impregnation The frame must be pressure impregnated with a 15 – 18 per cent solution of monoammonium phosphate in water. This is a fire inhibiting solution.

Note: For external doors, whether of half hour or one hour construction, the following conditions also apply:

Facing The plywood or hardboard must be of an exterior quality.

Adhesives The construction of the door must be carried out using a synthetic resin adhesive.

Lippings Lippings for external doors must continue around all four edges.

Hanging

When hanging fire-check doors a 3 mm maximum joint should be used between the frame and the door.

One pair of hinges will suffice for the half hour type door, while the one hour type door requires one and a half pairs.

In order to fulfil their function, fire-check doors must be kept closed. Therefore, self-closing springs, or other fittings which ensure that the door is self-closing, must be used.

Although the British Standard specifies two types of timber fire-check doors, any door and its frame, however constructed, which has been proved by tests in accordance with BS 476, Part 1 'Fire tests on building materials and structures', to give a similar performance to that of the half hour or one hour fire-check doors specified in the standard, can be termed and used as a fire-check door for the appropriate period. A door of this type is shown in Figure 150. It is made in a traditional way and consists of stiles, rails, muntins and panels which have a minimum thickness of 44 mm.

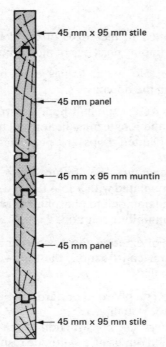

Figure 150   *Solid hardwood fire-check door*

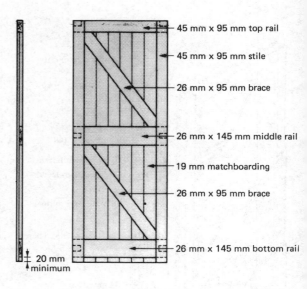

Figure 151   *Framed, ledged, braced and match-boarded door*

Note: Only certain hardwoods are approved for these doors. The main ones being oak, teak, ash, beech and iroko.

Matchboarded doors

These can be divided into two types:

Unframed e.g. ledged, or ledged, braced and matchboarded doors. These were covered in *Carpentry and Joinery for Building Craft Students 1*.

Framed e.g. framed, ledged, braced and match-boarded doors.

Framed, ledged braced and matchboarded doors
This type of door is an improvement on the ledged, braced and matchboarded door, as it includes stiles which are jointed to the top, bottom and middle rails with mortise and tenons.

The use of the framework increases the door's strength, and resists any tendency which the door might have to distort. Braces are optional when the door is framed, but their use further increases the doors strength.

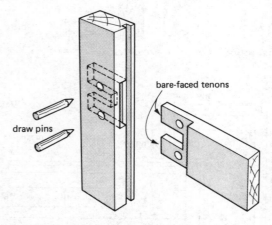

Figure 152   *Bare-faced tenons joint detail*

Figure 151 shows the rear view of a typical framed, ledged, braced and matchboarded door. It can be seen from the section that the stiles and top rail are the same thickness, while the middle and bottom rails are thinner. This is so that the matchboarding can be tongued into the top rail, over the face of the middle and bottom rails, and run to the bottom of the door. As the middle and bottom rails are thinner than the stiles, bare-faced tenons (tenons having only one shoulder) must be used. This joint is shown in Figure 152. These joints are normally wedged, although for extra strength draw pins can be used.

Large garage, warehouse and industrial doors are often made using the framed, ledged, braced and matchboarded principles. This is because this type of door is ideal in situations where strength is more important than appearance. A pair of doors suitable for a garage are shown in Figure 153. The portion of the door, which is normally above the middle rail, is glazed to admit a certain amount of light into the building. The top, middle and glazing rails must be rebated in order to receive the panes of glass. These panes are held in the rebate by glazing spigs and putty.

Note: In this case the middle rail is the same thickness as the stiles. Therefore bare-faced tenons are only used on the bottom rail.

Figure 131 shows the joint which is normally used at the intersections of the glazing rails. The joint is a scribed cross-halving.

Another joint which can be used is a stub tenon, but as the glazing rails are of a small section the joint is not as strong as the halving.

Figure 154 shows a section through the meeting stiles of a pair of garage doors.

Figure 154 also shows how the matchboarding may be jointed to the stiles or rails. An alternative detail is shown in Figure 155.

Note: As with other matchboarded doors, the joints, tongues and grooves, backs of rails and braces and all other concealed surfaces must be treated with a suitable priming paint or preservative before assembly.

Door frames and linings

The main differences between these were defined in *Carpentry and Joinery for Building Craft Students 1*.

In general door frames are delivered onto the building site fully assembled, while it is normal practice to deliver door linings in a knock-down form to be assembled by the carpenter on site.

A number of different types of door frames are considered later in this chapter.

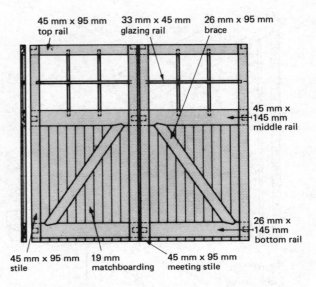

Figure 153 *Part glazed garage doors*

Figure 154 *Rebated meeting stiles*

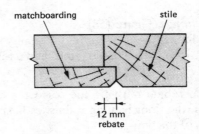

Figure 155 *Alternative matchboarding to stile detail*

Linings

Plain linings (Figure 156)
These consist of two plain jambs and a plain head.

Note: The pinned stop is fixed around the lining after the door has been hung.

The joint used for plain linings is shown in Figure 157.

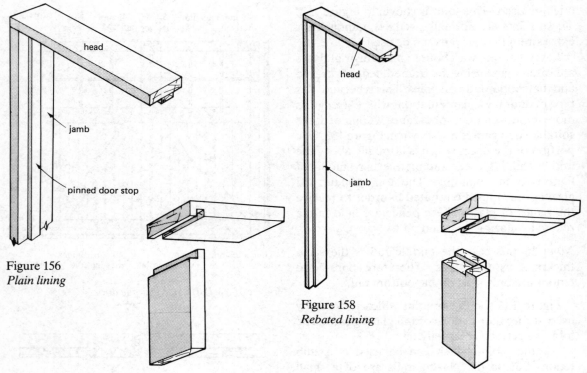

Figure 156
Plain lining

Figure 157   *Joint detail (plain lining)*

Figure 158
Rebated lining

Figure 159   *Joint detail (rebated lining)*

Rebated linings (Figure 158)
Rebated linings are used for better quality work.
They consist of two rebated jambs and a rebated
head.

Note: The rebate must be the correct width so
that when the door is hung it finishes flush with
the edges of the lining.

The joint used for rebated linings is a shoul-
dered housing which is shown in Figure 159.

Skeleton linings (Figure 160)
These are only used for deeper reveals, e.g.
where the brickwork is too thick for a normal
lining to be used.

Skeleton linings consist of a basic framework
which is stub tenoned together. The housing joint
used between the head and the jambs is shown in
Figure 161. A ply or solid timber lining is used to
cover the framework and form the rebate to receive the door.

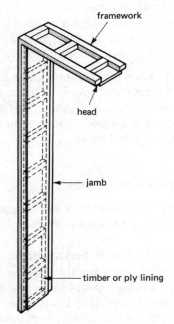

Figure 160   *Skeleton lining*

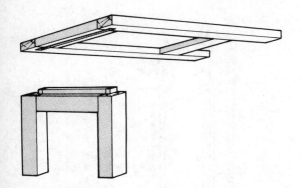

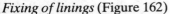

Figure 161 *Joint detail (skeleton lining)*

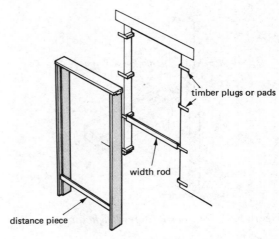

Figure 162 *Fixing a lining*

Fixing of linings (Figure 162)

The opening in the wall to receive the lining is normally formed while the wall is being built and the lining is fixed at a later stage.

Sequence of operations to fix a lining

Assemble lining.

Note: This is normally done by skew nailing through the head into the jambs.

Fix a distance piece near the bottom of the jambs and, when required, diagonal braces at the head.

Rake out brickwork joints and plug. There should be at least four fixing points per jamb.

Note: Omit this stage if the bricklayer has 'built in' wooden pallets or pads into the brickwork.

Offer lining into opening and mark where the plugs need to be trimmed.

Note: The plugs should project equally from both reveals.

Cut the plugs and check the distance with a width, rod.

Note: The ends of the plugs should be in vertical alignment. Check with a straight edge and spirit level.

Fix lining plumb and central in the opening by nailing or screwing through the jambs into the plugs.

Note: Before finally fixing, ensure the lining is out of wind. Check by sighting through the jambs. If their edges appear to be parallel the lining is correct. If not, the lining will be in winding or twisted. This must be corrected or when the door is hung it will not close correctly.

Frames

Storey height door frames (Figure 163)

These are used for door openings in thin non-loadbearing blockwork partitions. The jambs

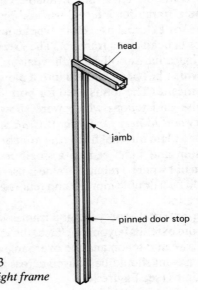

Figure 163
Storey height frame

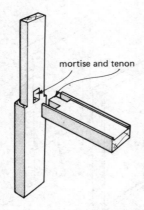

Figure 164   *Joint detail (storey height frame)*

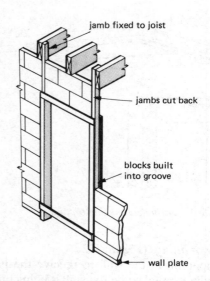

Figure 165   *'Building in' a storey height frame*

and head which make up the frame are grooved out on their back face to receive the building blocks. A mortise and tenon joint is used between the head and the jambs (see Figure 164).

The storey frame should be fixed in position, at the bottom to the wall plate and at the top to the joists, before the blocks are built up (see Figure 165).

Note: The jambs above the head are cut back to finish flush with the blockwork.

Storey height frames with fanlights

Two common types are available. Figure 166 shows a frame for internal use and Figure 167 a frame for external use. Both types consist of two jambs, a head and a transom. The external frame also has a hardwood sill with a galvanized water bar which has been bedded into a plough groove with mastic. The joints used for both frames are mortise and tenons which were shown in *Carpentry and Joinery for Building Craft Students 1*.

For a plain internal frame the joint between the transom and jamb can be a single mortise and tenon but where a rebated frame is used, the joint should be a double mortise and tenon as shown in Figure 168.

On external storey height frames where the transom extends beyond the face, the joint will be a mortise and tenon and the overhanging edge of the transom should be housed across the face of the jambs (see Figure 169).

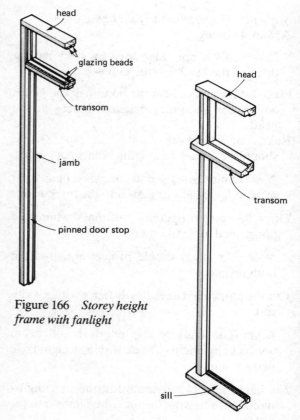

Figure 166   *Storey height frame with fanlight*

Figure 167   *External storey height frame*

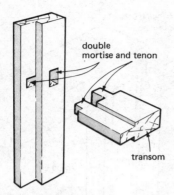

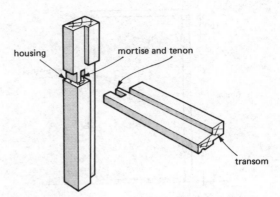

Figure 168 *Transom joint for internal storey height frame with fanlight*

Figure 169 *Transom joint for external storey height with fanlight*

Fixing of frames

Door frames are normally built into the brickwork as the job proceeds. This method is described in *Carpentry and Joinery for Building Craft Students 1.*

In order to protect the door frames from damage, they are sometimes fixed at a later stage in the building process. This mainly applies to expensive hardwood frames. In this case the frames are fixed using a similar method to that used for the fixing of door linings.

Note: The holes for the screws used to fix the hardwood frames should be counter-bored and later filled using cross-grained plugs which have been cut from a matching timber.

Door hanging

Door hanging is normally the first second-fixing operation the carpenter will carry out. The apprentice carpenter will gain speed and confidence in door hanging by following the procedure outlined below:

Locate the top and hanging side of the door.

Note: On flush and fire-check doors these should have been marked by the manufacturer.

Cut off the horns and the bottom of the door if required.

Note: A 6 mm gap under the door is normal, but on uneven floors or where carpet is to be fitted this must be increased.

'Shoot' in hanging stile of door.

'Shoot' door to width. Allow a 2 mm joint all around between door and frame. Many carpenters use a two pence piece to check.

Mark out and cut in hinges.

Screw one leaf of the hinges to the door.

Offer up the door to opening and screw other leaf of the hinges to frame.

Adjust fit if required.

Fix lock.

Fix door stop in the required position.

Fit any other ironmongery, e.g. bolts, letter plates, handles, etc.

Note: It is usual practice to only fit and not fix the other ironmongery, e.g. handles and bolts, etc., at this stage. They should be fixed later during the finishing stage after all painting works are completed.

Figure 170 shows the normal positions for the hinges, and a letter plate where required, on a flush door. If a third hinge is required, this should be placed centrally between the other two hinges.

On glazed doors the hinges are often fixed in line with the rails, as shown in Figure 171. This produces a more balanced effect although it is not as strong as the previous positions.

Figure 172 shows the two methods which can be used to cut in the hinges:

the half-and-half method;
all-in-the-door method.

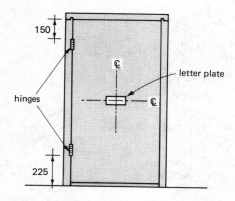

Figure 170   *Position of hinges and letter plate*

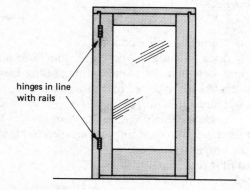

Figure 171   *Position of hinges on glazed doors*

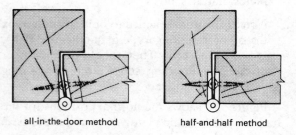

all-in-the-door method   half-and-half method

Figure 172   *Alternative methods of cutting in hinges*

The method used will normally depend on the site foreman or customer's preference, as each method is equally as good.

Where rising butts are used, the top edge of the door must be eased as shown in Figure 173. This is to prevent the top edge fouling the frame as the door closes.

External doors normally have to be rebated

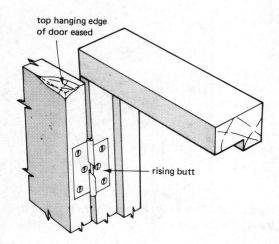

Figure 173   *Easing top of door when rising butts are used*

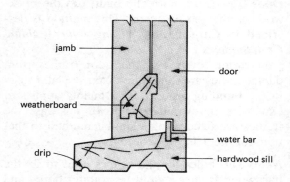

Figure 174   *Threshold detail*

along their bottom edge to fit over the water bar. A weatherboard should also be fitted to the bottom of the door as shown in Figure 174.

Windows

The function and classification of windows was covered in *Carpentry and Joinery for Building Craft Students 1*. In this section the following topics are considered in detail:

casement windows
sliding sash windows
timber sub-frames
bay windows
centre-hung pivot windows
double glazing

Casement windows

Casement windows are comprised of two main parts:

The frame which consists of head, sill and two jambs. Where the frame is sub-divided, the intermediate vertical members are called mullions and the intermediate horizontal member is called a transom.

The opening casements which consist of top rail, bottom rail and two stiles. Where the casement is sub-divided both the intermediate vertical and horizontal members are called glazing bars. Opening casements which are above the transom are known as fanlights.

Figure 175 shows the elevation of a four-light casement window with all the component parts named.

Note: The 'four' refers to the number of glazed openings or lights in the window.

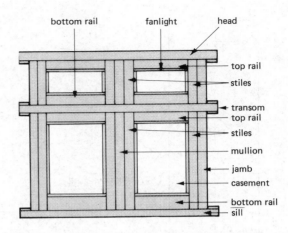

Figure 175   *Four-light casement window*

Traditional casements

Figure 176 shows a vertical section through a traditional casement window. Anti-capillary grooves are incorporated into both the frame and the opening casements. In order to prevent the passage of water into the building, drip grooves are made towards the front edges of the transom and sill to stop the water running back underneath them.

A mortar key groove is run on the outside face of the head, sill and jambs. The sill also has a plough groove for the window sill to tongue into.

Note: The front of the transom and sill is weathered (has a slope for the rain-water to run off).

Figure 177 shows part of a horizontal section through a traditional casement window. It also shows the sizes and positions of the rebates, grooves and moulding in the jambs, mullion and the casement stiles.

All the joints used in traditional casement window construction are mortise and tenons. Haunched mortise and tenons are used for the actual casements. As a matter of good practice the depth of the rebates should be kept the same

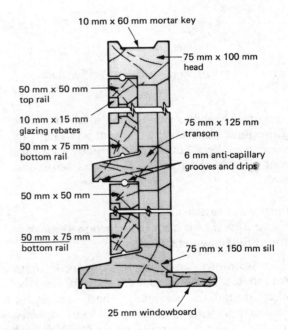

Figure 176   *Traditional casement*

as the depth of the mouldings. This simplifies the jointing as the shoulders of the tenons will be level. All of the joints are fully illustrated in *Carpentry and Joinery for Building Craft Students 1,* except the joint between the transom and the jambs.

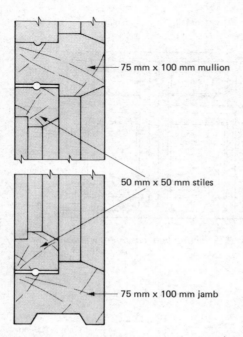

75 mm x 100 mm mullion

50 mm x 50 mm stiles

75 mm x 100 mm jamb

Figure 177   *Part horizontal section of traditional casement*

Figure 178 shows an exploded isometric view of the joint between the transom and jamb. In order to make a better weatherproof joint, the front edge of the transom is housed across the jamb.

Stormproof casements
Figure 179 shows a vertical section through a stormproof casement window.

Note: Stormproof casement windows incorporate two rebates. One around the main frame and the other around the casement. These rebates, in conjunction with the drip and anti-capillary grooves, make this type far more weatherproof than the traditional casements.

Figure 180 shows an alternative sill which must be used in conjunction with a stone, concrete or tiled sub-sill.

Note: This type is normally only used where the window is set well back from the brickwork face.

Figure 181 shows part of a horizontal section

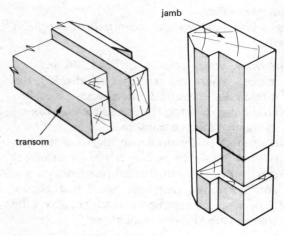

jamb

transom

Figure 178   *Transom joint detail*

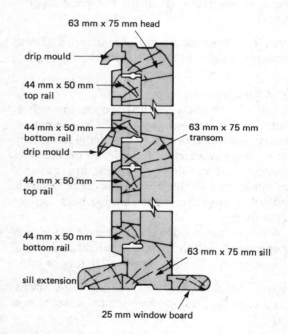

63 mm x 75 mm head

drip mould

44 mm x 50 mm top rail

44 mm x 50 mm bottom rail

drip mould

44 mm x 50 mm top rail

44 mm x 50 mm bottom rail

sill extension

63 mm x 75 mm transom

63 mm x 75 mm sill

25 mm window board

Figure 179   *Stormproof casement*

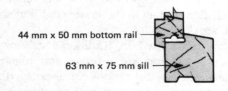

44 mm x 50 mm bottom rail

63 mm x 75 mm sill

Figure 180   *Alternative sill*

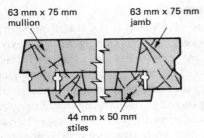

Figure 181 *Part horizontal section of stormproof casement*

of a stormproof casement. It shows the jambs, mullion and casement stiles.

The jointing of the main frame of the stormproof casement window is the same as that of the traditional casement except for the transom which is not housed across the face of the jambs because it is usually of the same width.

Comb joints fixed with metal star dowels are normally used for jointing the actual casements, although mortise and tenon joints can be used.

French casements
Figure 182 shows a french casement window with double opening casements. This type of window is often referred to as french doors. The construction of the frame is similar to that of the traditional casement frame. The opening casements and the fixed side lights are constructed in a similar way to external glazed doors.

Figure 183 shows how the meeting stiles are rebated together.

Note: If a mortise lock is required, a rebate pattern must be used.

Inward-opening casements
Inward-opening casements are rarely used as they are very difficult to weatherproof. They also present problems for the occupier of the building, because they obstruct the curtains.

Figure 184 shows a typical vertical section through an inward-opening casement.

Note: The bottom rail is rebated over a galvanized water bar which is set in the sill. This prevents the passage of water into the building between the bottom rail and the sill.

Figure 182 *French casement window*

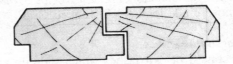

Figure 183 *Rebated meeting stiles*

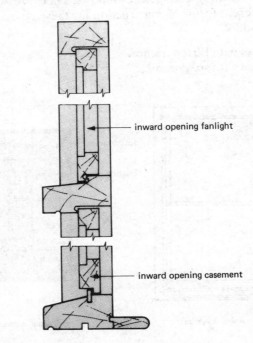

Figure 184 *Inward-opening casement*

Fixing casement windows

All types of casement window are normally fixed by 'building in' using galvanized frame cramps as covered in *Carpentry and Joinery for Building Craft Students 1.*

The face of the frame is normally set back up to 50 mm from the face of the brickwork. This gives only a limited amount of weather protection, so therefore the joint between the frame and brickwork should be sealed with mastic pointing.

Sliding sash windows

These may be classified into two groups according to their direction of opening:

vertical sliding sash;
horizontal sliding sash.

Only vertical sliding sashes are considered in this section, horizontal sliding sashes being covered in purpose-made joinery: Advanced Craft.

Vertical sliding sashes

These consist of two sashes which slide up and down in a main frame. They are also known as double-hung sliding sash windows. There are two different forms of construction for these types of window:

those with boxed frames;
those with solid frames.

Boxed frames

This type of window is the traditional pattern of sliding sashes and for many years has been superceded by casements and solid frame sash windows. This was mainly due to the high manufacturing and assembly costs of the large number of component parts. An understanding of their construction and operation is essential as they will be met with frequency in renovation and maintenance work.

The double-hung boxed window consists of two sliding sashes suspended on cords which run over pulleys and are attached to counterbalanced weights inside the boxed frame.

Figure 185 shows an elevation, horizontal and vertical section of a boxed frame sliding sash window. It shows the make up of this type of window and names the component parts.

Figure 186 shows an alternative sill detail, with a draughtboard tongued into the sill. This allows the bottom sash to be partly opened to provide ventilation without causing a draught.

Figure 187 shows how the pulley stiles are jointed to the head and sill.

Note: The inside and outside linings are tongued and nailed to the stiles and head.

Figure 188 illustrates how the outside lining and parting bead should be cut away in order to prevent water and dirt being trapped at this

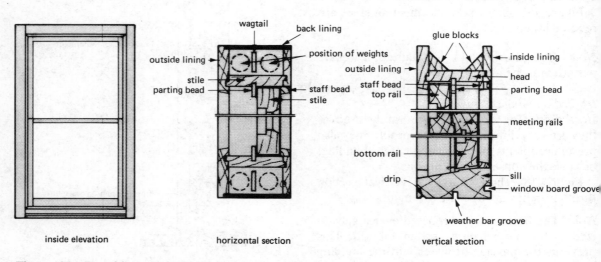

inside elevation   horizontal section   vertical section

Figure 185   *Boxed frame sliding sash window*

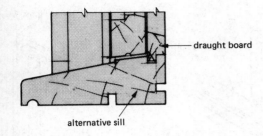

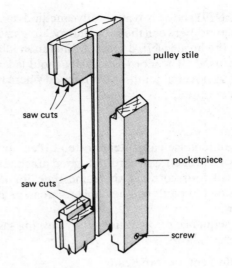

Figure 186   *Alternative sill detail*

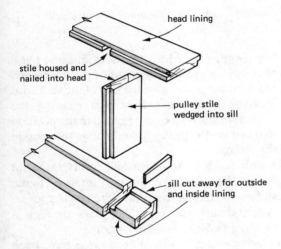

Figure 189   *Pocket piece*

Figure 187   *Boxed frame joint details*

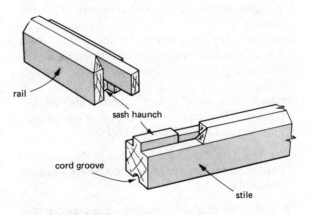

Figure 190   *Joint detail (sash haunch)*

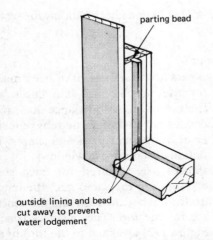

point. A pocketpiece is cut in the pulley stiles to provide access to the weights. It is cut out by making saw cuts as shown in Figure 189 and firmly tapping out from the back of the stile.

Figure 190 shows the mortise and tenon joint which is used between the sash stile and rail.

Note: The sash haunch or reverse franking is used instead of a normal haunch. If this was not done the joint would be seriously weakened by the sash cord groove which is run into the edge of the stile.

Figure 188   *Cutting away of outside lining and parting bead*

Figure 191 shows two alternative methods used for the joints between the stiles and meeting rails. Where the horn is left, a mortise and tenon joint can be used. The horn is usually moulded as shown. A dovetail joint should be used where no horn is required.

Re-cording sashes

The maintenance carpenter is often called upon to renew a broken sash cord. It is good practice to renew all four cords at the same time for the remaining old cords will be liable to break in the near future.

The sequence of operations for renewing sash cords is as follows:

Carefully remove staff beads.

Carefully remove pockets.

Take out bottom sash. The sash cords should be wedged at the pulley and removed from the groove in the sash.

Carefully remove parting beads. Break paint joints first and carefully prise out with a chisel.

Take out top sash in a similar manner to bottom sash.

Remove the weights and cords through the pockets. The wagtail will move to one side to give access to the outside weights.

Note: The weights may not all be the same, so ensure they are returned to their original positions.

Thread new cords over pulleys and down to the pockets. A 'mouse' can be used to thread the cords easily. A 'mouse' is a small lead weight which is attached to a 2 m length of string which in turn is tied to the cord. The mouse is inserted over the pulley and drops to the bottom of the frame. The sash cord can now be pulled through. Many carpenters use a length of small chain instead of a mouse.

Fasten sash cords to weights. To obtain the length of cord for the top sash, rest the sash on the sill and mark on the pulley stile the end of the sash cord groove. Pull the weight up to almost the top and cut cord to the position marked on the pulley stile. Wedge the cord in the pulley to prevent the weight from dropping. To obtain

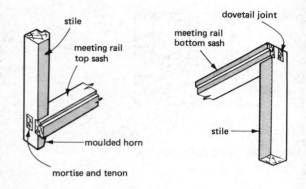

Figure 191   *Alternative meeting rail joint details*

the length of cord for the bottom sash, place the sash up against the head of the frame and mark on the pulley stile the end of the sash cord groove. With the weight just clearing the bottom of the frame cut the cord to the position marked on the pulley stile. Wedge the cord in the pulley.

Fix sash cords to top sash and insert sash into frame. The cords are normally attached to the sashes by nailing them into the cord grooves. Alternatively the cord can pass through a closed groove and end in a knot.

Replace parting beads. Where these have been damaged new ones should be used.

Fix sash cords to bottom sash and insert sash into frame.

Replace staff beads and check window for ease of operation.

Solid frames

For many years now balances have been manufactured for use in place of sash cords and weights. The use of the sash balance does away with the need for boxed frames, thereby reducing the number of component parts and simplifying the construction of sliding sash windows.

Two balances are required for each sash. Where the sashes are the same size, the longer balances are for the bottom sash and the shorter balances are for the top. The balances (one is shown in Figure 192) are fixed to the tops of the jambs with a screw. The plate on the other end is attached to the bottom rail of the sash. As each

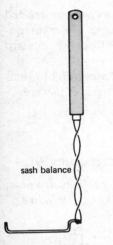

Figure 192   *Balance*

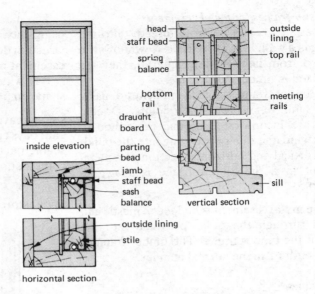

inside elevation

horizontal section

Figure 193   *Solid frame sliding sash window*

sash is raised or lowered, the spring is tensioned. The sash is then supported or balanced by the tension of the springs. If the sash is not balanced both springs on the sash should be adjusted. The tension of the springs may be adjusted by un-screwing the sash plate and twisting it one turn in a clockwise or anticlockwise direction. The plate should then be re-screwed to the sash and the operation of the sash checked to see if it is correct.

Note: Springs should not be adjusted for balance until the sashes have been glazed.

Figure 193 illustrates the elevation, horizontal and vertical section of a solid frame sliding sash window. It can be seen from this that apart from the solid jambs, the arrangement of the com-ponent parts is similar to that of the boxed frame sash window. The frame and sashes can be jointed using mortise and tenon joints, although modern mass-produced windows are now exclu-sively manufactured using comb joints with metal star dowels.

Note: for lightweight domestic sashes, the spring balances are accommodated in grooves run in the

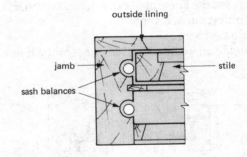

Figure 194   *Part horizontal section*

back of the sash stiles. The spring balances for heavyweight industrial sashes are accommodated in grooves which are run in the actual jamb of the frame as shown in Figure 194.

Fixing of sash windows
Solid frame sash windows are usually 'built in' in the normal manner using galvanized frame cramps.

Boxed frame sash windows are normally fixed into a prepared opening in the wall by driving wedges in behind the jambs.

Timber sub-frames for metal casements

Metal casements can be fixed directly into the opening in a wall. However, as these windows are produced from light section material, they are better fixed in timber sub-frames.

The timber frames are manufactured using mortise and tenons or comb joints. Double rebates are incorporated around the frame to prevent wind and rain penetrating into the building. A vertical and horizontal section of a metal casement in a timber sub-frame is shown in Figure 195.

Note: the metal casement is bedded in mastic and screwed through the holes provided into the rebate of the timber frame. The timber frame is usually 'built in' in the normal manner.

Bay windows

A bay window is normally incorporated into a building for one or a combination of three reasons:

to increase the amount of daylight and ventilation admitted into a room;
to increase room size;
to provide an architectural feature for the house.

The majority of bay windows are constructed using outward opening casements. The main construction details vary very little from the standard casement windows covered previously.

Bay windows are classified according to their shape on plan. The four main types of bay are:

square bays (Figure 196)
cant bays (Figure 197)
segmental bays (Figure 198)
combination of square and cant (Figure 199)

Note: A bay window which projects from an upper storey only is known as an oriel window.

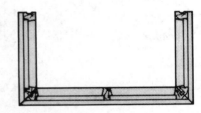

Figure 196   *Square bay*

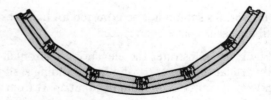

Figure 197   *Cant bay*

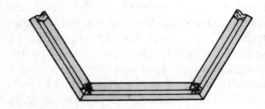

Figure 198   *Segmental bay*

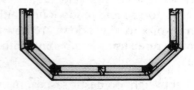

Figure 199   *Combination bay*

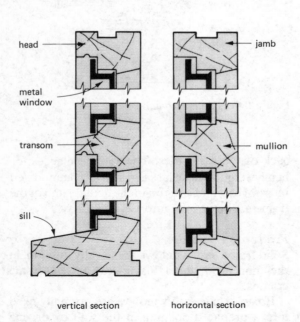

vertical section   horizontal section

Figure 195   *Metal casement in a timber sub-frame*

The angled intersections of the head and sill are normally mitred. These mitres are drawn up tight using hand rail bolts. Two hardwood dowels are also used for each joint to overcome any tendency which the joint has to twist (see Figure 200).

The mullions or angle posts can be made from solid timber, although for ease of manufacture these are often made in two sections (see Figure 201).

Figure 202 shows the best method of 'building in' the bay. The wall jambs should be cut square and the brickwork cut or angled in order to meet the frame.

Figure 203 shows an alternative 'building in' method which entails splaying the back of the jambs to fit the brickwork.

The carpenter is often asked to make a template of the bay shape to help the bricklayer build his wall. Two different kinds of template can be used, one cut from a sheet of hardboard and the other made up from a number of pieces of timber in a similar manner to that used for making the ribs of a made-up centre. The method used will depend on the material available and the window size.

Note: The template should be made to the required brickwork sizes and not those of the actual window.

Centre-hung pivot windows

This type of window is often used for high-rise buildings. This enables both sides of the glass to be cleaned from the inside of the building with ease. The main disadvantage of this type is the fact that when opened the top of the sash interferes with the curtains.

Figure 204 shows an elevation and width section of a stormproof centre-hung pivot window.

The construction and the joints used in the frame and sash are similar to the joints used for casement windows, e.g. mortise and tenon and comb joints.

The moulded stop which is mitred around the frame and cut on the pivot line is glued and pinned to the top half of the frame and the bottom half of the sash.

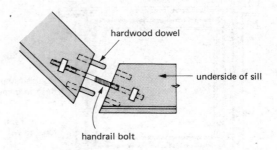

Figure 200 *Joining head and sill*

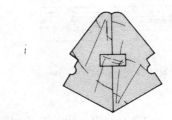

Figure 201 *Two piece mullion*

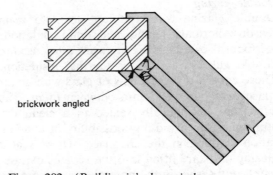

Figure 202 *'Building in' a bay window*

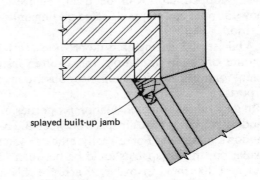

Figure 203 *'Building in' a bay window*

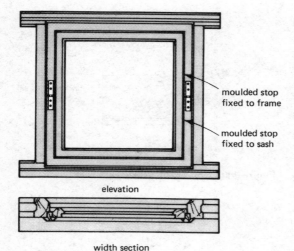

elevation

width section

Figure 204   *Centre-hung pivot window*

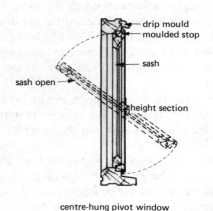

centre-hung pivot window

Figure 205   *Centre-hung pivot window*

The partially opened sash is shown as a broken line on the height section in Figure 205.

Double glazing

Double glazing is carried out for two main reasons: thermal insulation and sound insulation.

Modern sealed glazing units are often used to double glaze windows for thermal insulation. These consist of two panels of glass with an air space of 4 mm to 12 mm between them. The edges are hermetically sealed in a clean dry atmosphere to avoid any possibility of condensation forming in the air space. These sealed glazing units are fitted into the rebates of casements and sashes in the normal way. Where the rebate is too small to take the extra thickness of glass, stepped units can be used. Figure 206 shows normal and stepped sealed glazing units in position.

While sealed glazing units do provide a certain amount of sound insulation, this is often insufficient for noisy locations, e.g. near busy roads or airports.

In general the sound insulation properties of a window increase as the air space between the two windows increases. For a really efficient sound insulation, the air space should be between 100 mm and 200 mm. In order to achieve this air space, a second window can be built on the inside

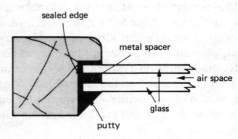

standard sealed glazing unit

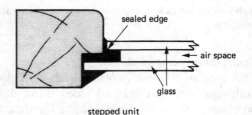

stepped unit

Figure 206   *Sealed glazing units*

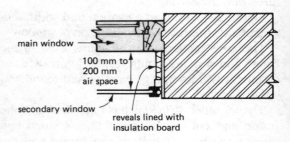

Figure 207   *Secondary double glazing*

of the reveal behind the existing window. This type of double glazing is known as secondary double glazing.

Figure 207 shows a secondary double glazing detail. As a further improvement, the reveals between the two frames can be lined with a sound absorbent material, such as strips of insulation board.

Stairs

The construction of stairs is controlled by the Building Regulations, Part K. These divide stairs into a number of categories depending on their use. Stairways for common use by more than one dwelling are known as common stairways. A stairway for use exclusively by one dwelling is known as a private stairway. Other categories are for stairways in public buildings, etc.

Note: These requirements do not apply to stairways outside the building; ladders; or stairways with a rise of less than 600 mm, except where the drop at the side is more than 600 mm.

Terminology (Figures 208, 209 and 210)

Apron lining The boards used to finish the edge of a trimmed opening in a floor.

Balustrade The handrail and the in-filling between it and the string, landing or floor. This can be termed either an open or closed balustrade, depending on the in-filling.

Baluster The short vertical in-filling members of an open balustrade.

Bull-nose step The rounded step at the bottom of a flight of stairs.

Carriage This is a raking timber fixed under wide stairs to support the cente of the treads and risers. Brackets are fixed to the side of the carriage to provide further support across the width of the treads (see Figure 211).

Newel The large sectioned vertical member at each end of the string. Where an upper newel does not continue down to the floor level it is known as a pendant or drop newel.

Nosing The front edge of a tread or the finish to the floor boards around a stairwell opening.

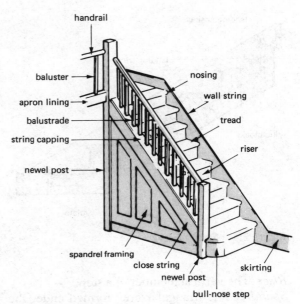

Figure 208　*Stairway terminology*

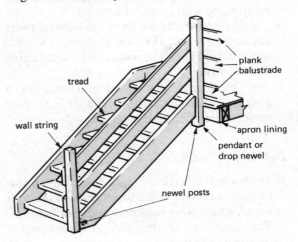

Figure 209　*Open plan stairs*

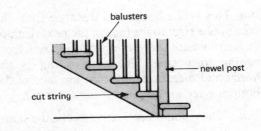

Figure 210　*Cut string*

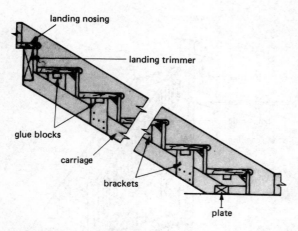

Figure 211   *Stair carriage*

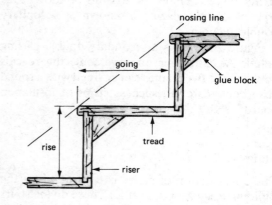

Figure 212   *Stairway definitions*

Riser The vertical member of a step.

Spandrel The triangular area formed under the stairs. This can be left open or closed in to form a cupboard with spandrel framing.

String The board into which the treads and risers are housed or cut. They are also named according to their type, e.g. wall string, outer string and cut string.

Tread The horizontal member of a step. It can also be called a parallel tread or a tapered tread, depending on its shape.

Definitions (Figures 212 and 213)

Rise This is the vertical height from the top surface of one tread to the top surface of the next tread, which is immediately above or below it. The total rise is the vertical measurement between the finished floor levels.

Note: The rise of each step in a flight must be equal.

Going This is the horizontal distance from the face of one riser to the face of the next riser, or in stairs where there are not any risers from nosing to nosing. The total going is the horizontal measurement from the face of the bottom riser to the face of the top riser.

Note: The going of each step must be the same.

Nosing line This is also known as the 'pitch line'.

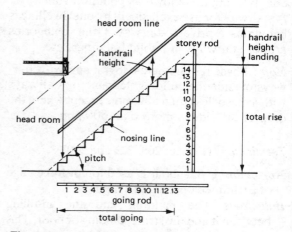

Figure 213   *Stairway definitions*

It is an imaginary line drawn down the stairs to connect the nosings.

Pitch This is the angle of the flight stairs between the pitch line and the floor.

Headroom line This is a line representing the maximum available headroom parallel to the nosing line.

Headroom This is the vertical distance between the nosing line and the floor above.

Regulation requirements

The chart shown in Table 5 shows the main requirements of common and private stairs with regard to the regulations.

Table 5

Regulation	Common Stairs	Private Stairs
Pitch (degrees)	38 max.	42 max.
Headroom	2 m min.	2 m min.
Rise	190 mm max.	220 mm max.
Going	240 mm min.	220 mm min.
Twice rise plus going (2R+G) must fall between	550 mm min., 700 mm max.	550 mm min., 700 mm max.
Width (unobstructed)	900 mm min.	800 mm min.
Handrail height (wall)	840 mm min., 1 m max.	840 mm min., 1 m max.
Balustrade height (flight)	900 mm min.	840 mm min.
Balustrade height (landing)	1 m min.	900 mm min.

Note: The unobstructed width of stairs is measured from the face of the handrail to the face of the wall or face of handrail to face of handrail as appropriate, minor projections such as skirting, strings and newels are ignored.

Construction

Before constructing a flight of stairs a visit should be made to the site to obtain the relevant measurements. These should take the form of a going rod and a storey rod, and also the width of the opening in the floor. A note should also be made of any doorways at either end of the stairs. The rods are divided up into the required number of goings and risers.

Note: There will always be one more rise than going.

Once the rise and going of the stairs has been decided, they can be set out. In order to do this a number of templates can be made. These are shown in Figure 214. The pitchboard and margin template is used to mark out the face of the treads and risers. The housing for the tread and risers is marked out with the tread and riser templates. These templates are equal to the shape of the tread and riser plus an allowance for wedging. The use of the templates to mark out the strings is shown in Figure 215. The housing in the string can be cut out using a portable router and a stair housing template. Where this is not available the sequence of operations shown in Figure 216 can be used.

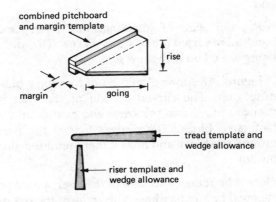

Figure 214 *Setting out templates*

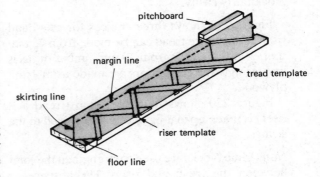

Figure 215 *Templates in use*

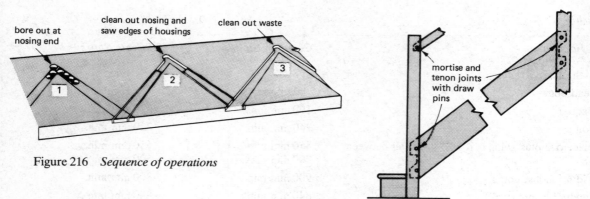

Figure 216   *Sequence of operations*

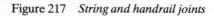

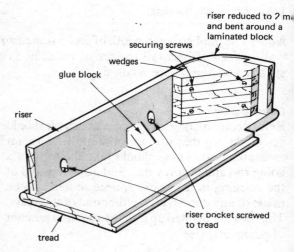

Figure 217   *String and handrail joints*

Sequence

Bore out at nosing end with brace and bit.
Clean out nosing and cut edges of housing with a
tenon saw.
Clean out waste with chisel and hand router.

Figure 217 shows that the outer string and
handrail are mortised into the newels at either
end.

Note: For ease of handling, the newels and
handrail are fixed to the stairs on site. The joints
being closed up with draw pins.

Figure 218 shows a method of forming a bull-
nose step. The curved section of the riser is
reduced to a 2 mm thickness and bent around a
laminated block. The wedges tighten the riser
around the block and hold it there until the glue
has set.

Note: The reduced section of the riser should be
steamed before bending. This reduces the risk of
it breaking and enables it to bend around the
block fairly easily.

Figure 219 shows three choices for tread and
riser details. The tread can be made from 25 mm
timber and the riser from 19 mm timber or, as is
increasingly the case, risers are made from 9 mm
plywood.

Figure 220 shows how each step (tread and
riser) is made up in a jig before being fixed to the
strings.

Note: Glue blocks are used to strengthen the joint
between the tread and riser. The absence or
loosening of these often results in squeaky stairs.

Figure 218   *Forming a bull-nose step*

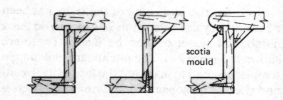

Figure 219   *Tread and riser details*

Figure 221 gives a part view of the steps fixed
into a string.

Note: Both the treads and risers are securely
wedged in position.

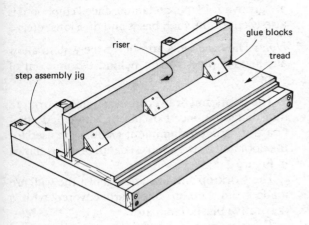

Figure 220   *Step assembly jig*

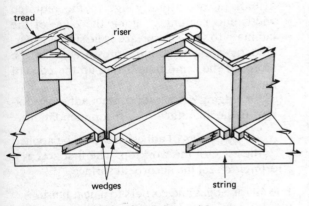

Figure 221   *Fixing of steps into string*

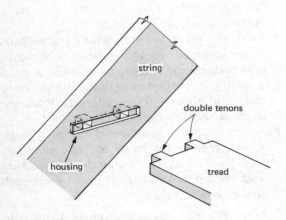

Figure 222   *Open plan stairs*

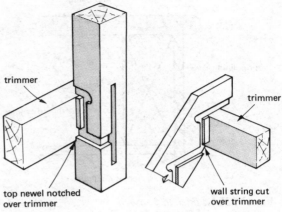

Figure 223   *Positioning top of stairs*

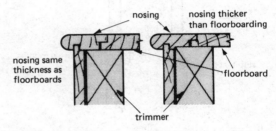

Figure 224   *Alternative nosing details*

Shown in Figure 222 is a method used to join the treads to the strings in a riserless flight of stairs (open plan).

Note: Where open plan stairs are used, the edges of the treads must overlap by at least 15 mm.

The top of the stairs are held in position by notching the newel over the trimmer and this is often bolted to it. The wall string is also cut over the trimmer and nailed or screwed back to the wall from underneath (see Figure 223).

Shown in Figure 224 are two alternative finishes between the nosing and the floor or landing.

Figure 225 shows the finish of the apron lining and nosing around the stairwell opening.

The balusters may be either stub tenoned into the string or fitted into a groove run into the string capping (see Figure 226). The same joints can be used where the balusters meet the handrail,

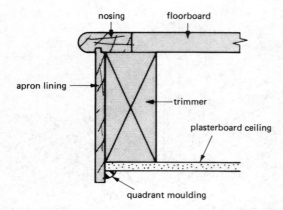

Figure 225   *Finish to stairwell*

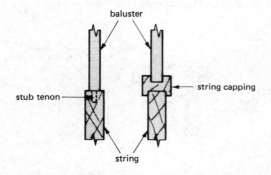

Figure 226   *Alternative balustrade joints*

except that when they fit into the groove, this will be run on the underside of the handrail itself.

Note: Openings in balustrades and between treads must not permit the passage of 100 mm diameter sphere (prevents children's heads from becoming stuck in gap); balustrade design should prevent children readily climbing up it.

Fitments

Fitments can be either 'built in' or free standing. Using modern methods of construction, both types utilize sheet materials to a large extent.

Kitchen units

Figure 227 shows the plan, elevation and section of a kitchen base unit and wall unit. Both units consist of two frames made from 25 mm x 50 mm hardwood, mortised and tenoned together, into which 12 mm melamine-faced chipboard sides

are grooved. 12 mm melamine-faced chipboard is also used for the shelf bases and divisions, etc.

Note: The base units are set off the wall to allow any service pipes to run behind the unit out of sight.

The doors and drawer fronts are made from 18 mm melamine-faced or plastic laminated chipboard. Extruded aluminium sections are used for the door and drawer pull. A detail of this is shown in Figure 228.

The worktop and upstand against the wall are made from 18 mm chipboard covered with a decorative plastic laminate.

The procedure for covering a worktop with a plastic laminate is as follows:

Cut edging strips. This can best be done by setting a marking or cutting gauge to the required width and running it along the edge of the laminate to score its surface. The strip is separated by applying thumb pressure along the score, at the same time lifting up the edge of the strip.

Stick on edging strips with contact adhesive, following the manufacturer's recommendations.

Note: Two coats of adhesive should be applied to the edge of the worktop. The first acts as a primer to seal the absorbent surface.

File all the edges and corners to a neat finish.

Cut top laminate slightly over the required size. This can be done by scoring the sheet with a laminate cutter and breaking the sheet upwards along the scored line.

Thoroughly dust off the work surface and the back of the laminate. Apply a contact adhesive to both surfaces and allow to become touch dry.

Lay small prepared strips of timber on the work surface at about 150 mm intervals. Place the laminate sheet on top of the strips.

Ensuring that the laminate is correctly positioned, remove the strips one at a time and press the laminate down onto the top, working from the centre to the edge of the sheet each time to avoid air traps.

Note: The purpose of the timber strips is to separate the two surfaces until they are cor-

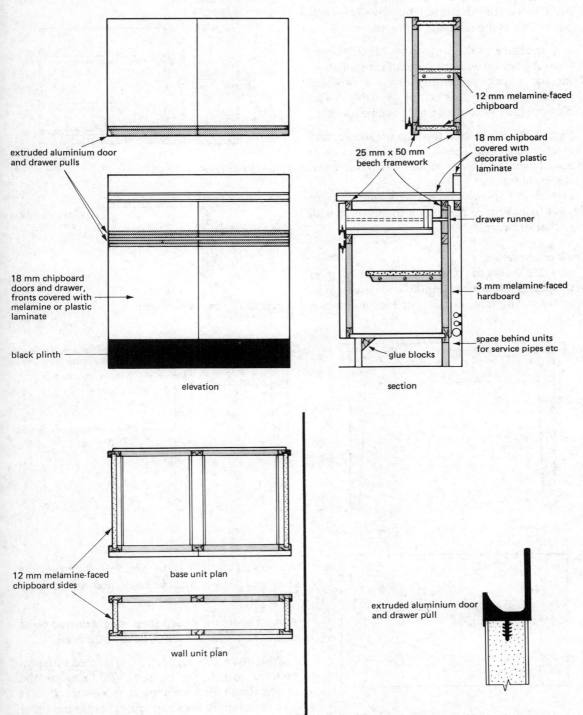

extruded aluminium door
and drawer pulls

18 mm chipboard
doors and drawer,
fronts covered with
melamine or plastic
laminate

black plinth

elevation

12 mm melamine-faced
chipboard

18 mm chipboard
covered with
decorative plastic
laminate

25 mm x 50 mm
beech framework

drawer runner

3 mm melamine-faced
hardboard

space behind units
for service pipes etc

glue blocks

section

12 mm melamine-faced
chipboard sides

base unit plan

wall unit plan

extruded aluminium door
and drawer pull

Figure 227   *Kitchen units*

Figure 228   *Extruded aluminium section*

rectly located. A sheet of building paper can be used instead of the strips. This is progressively pulled out as the laminate is pressed down.

Apply pressure to the surface by rubbing down from the centre with the palm of the hand.

Trim the edges, preferably using a powered router, or where this is not available a file, block plane or cabinet scraper can be used.

Figure 229 is a section through the drawer and drawer runner. It shows that the drawer is grooved over the drawer runner which is screwed to the main frame.

Figure 230 shows that on sink units a false drawer front is fixed to the unit to match up with the other drawers.

Table construction

Figure 231 shows the plan, elevation and section of a typical table which is suitable for use in most situations. The table consists of four legs which

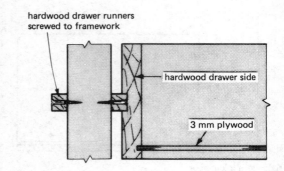

Figure 229   *Drawer details*

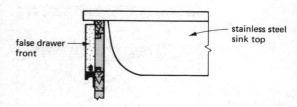

Figure 230   *False drawer front*

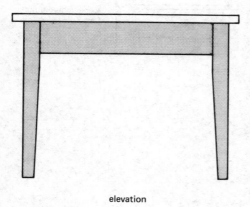

elevation

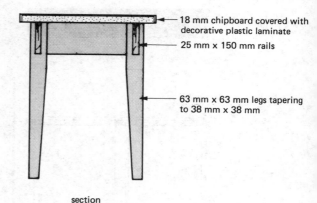

section

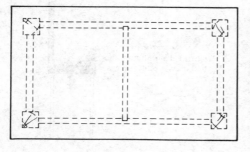

plan

Figure 231   *Typical table*

are joined by four rails. The joint between the rails and legs is a table haunched mortise and tenon. This is shown in Figure 232.

Note: The tenon is bare-faced and is mitred on its end to allow for the tenon of the other rail.

Also shown in Figure 232 are three different methods which can be used for fixing on the plastic laminated chipboard table-top. Pocket screwing rigidly fixes the top, whereas the other two methods allow for some moisture movement.

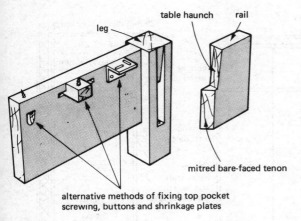

alternative methods of fixing top pocket
screwing, buttons and shrinkage plates

Figure 232   *Table details*

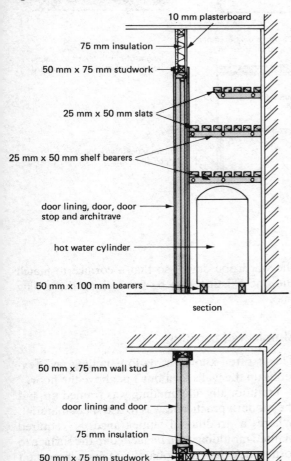

Figure 233   *Airing cupboard*

This would be particularly important if a solid timber table-top were to be used.

'Built-in' fitments

The plan and section of an airing cupboard is shown in Figure 233. It consists of a standard door lining and a solid core flush door. The studwork forming the side of the cupboard and over the door is made from 50 mm × 75 mm timber covered on both sides with plasterboard. To avoid heat loss, the space between the studs is filled with 75 mm glass-fibre insulation. 25 mm × 50 mm softwood slats fixed 25 mm apart on bearers are used for the shelves. The spaces between the slats allow the warm air to circulate within the cupboard.

Figure 234 shows the plan, elevation and section of a cupboard that is built into a reveal at the side of a fireplace. It has been framed up using 38 mm × 75 mm framing. The skirting is continued across the front of the frame to match in with the existing timber work. The doors which have rebated meeting stiles are also framed up and 9 mm plywood is used for the panels. The top, base, shelf and front framework are fixed to 25 mm × 50 mm battens that have been plugged and screwed to the walls. A 75 mm skirting upstand is used to mask the joint between the top

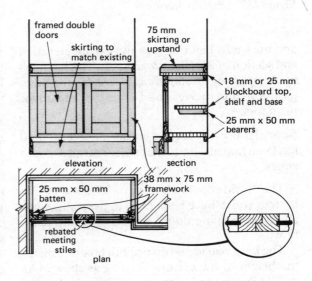

Figure 234   *Reveal cupboard*

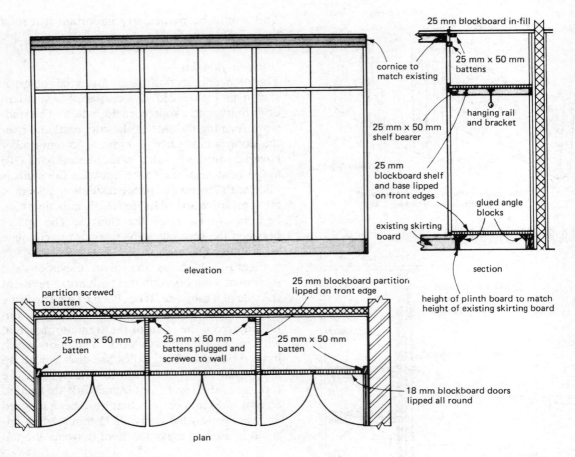

25 mm blockboard in-fill

25 mm × 50 mm battens

cornice to match existing

hanging rail and bracket

25 mm × 50 mm shelf bearer

25 mm blockboard shelf and base lipped on front edges

glued angle blocks

existing skirting board

section

elevation

partition screwed to batten

25 mm blockboard partition lipped on front edge

height of plinth board to match height of existing skirting board

25 mm × 50 mm batten

25 mm × 50 mm battens plugged and screwed to wall

25 mm × 50 mm batten

18 mm blockboard doors lipped all round

plan

Figure 235   *'Built-in' wardrobe*

and the walls. Figure 235 shows a plan, elevation and section of a 'built in' wardrobe. This has been made up using 25 mm blockboard for the base, partitions and shelves and 18 mm blockboard for the doors.

Note: To provide a good finish, the blockboard has been lipped with 10 mm timber on all exposed edges.

The outside doors are hung on 25 mm × 50 mm battens which have been fixed to the walls, while all the remaining doors are hung on the partitions.

The base is made up on a plinth board to match the height of the existing skirting as shown. An in-fill piece is used at the top to drop the head of

the wardrobe down, so that a cornice to match the one existing, can be fixed along the ceiling line.

Simple wall panelling

This is often known as dado panelling, as it extends up the walls to about 1 m above the floor.

Traditionally all panelling was framed up, but the modern practice now is to use sheet material. Where a traditional appearance is required planted mouldings can be tacked to the surface to form mock panels. Probably the most important thing to remember with panelling is to have a straight and level surface on which to fix it. This can be provided by battening out the wall with

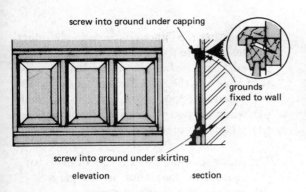

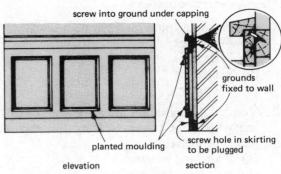

Figure 236   *Traditional dado panelling*

Figure 237   *Modern dado panelling*

grounds. These can be packed out from the brickwork as required.

Figure 236 shows the elevation and section of a simple traditional panel. It consists of a framework which is mortised and tenoned together. The raised and fielded panels are held in the grooves run around this framework. The panelling is screwed to the grounds at intervals as shown. The screw holes are concealed by the capping and the skirting which is pinned along the top and bottom of the panelling.

Figure 237 shows the elevation and section of a modern dado panelling. This has been made using blockboard. Planted moulding has been used to give a mock traditional panel effect. The screws that fix the top of the panelling to the grounds have been concealed under the capping. The bottom of the panelling is fixed by screwing the skirting into the grounds. This hole can be plugged.

Figure 238 shows two methods by which the panelling may be secured using concealed fixing methods. They both involve fixing prepared rebated or splayed grounds to the back of the panelling and the wall. The panelling can then be 'hooked' in position on the grounds.

Note: The splayed or rebated grounds can be used at both the top and bottom of the panelling.

Figure 239 shows alternative details that can be used where panelling turns around external and internal corners.

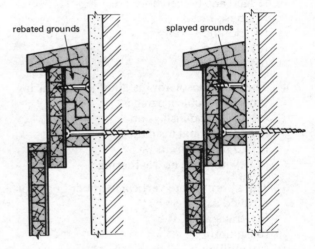

Figure 238   *Concealed fixing methods*

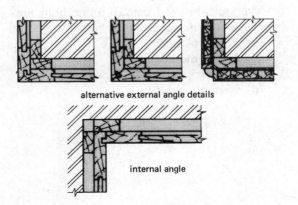

Figure 239   *Alternative angle details*

Self-assessment questions

1 The maximum pitch for a private stairway is:
   (a) 44 degrees
   (b) 38 degrees
   (c) 36 degrees
   (d) 42 degrees

2 Vertical sliding sashes are to slide in a solid frame. The best way to hang the sashes would be to use:
   (a) chains and weights
   (b) sash cords and weights
   (c) spring balances
   (d) a sliding track

3 The tenons on the middle rail of a framed ledged and braced door are:
   (a) bare-faced.
   (b) double
   (c) twin
   (d) stubbed

4 The main reason for installing sealed glazing units for double glazing is:
   (a) for sound insulation
   (b) for thermal insulation
   (c) to reduce drafts
   (d) to improve its weathering

5 The intermediate vertical member in a door is called a:
   (a) transom
   (b) muntin
   (c) mullion
   (d) jamb

6 The stops in the frame of a one hour fire-check door must be:
   (a) 12 mm planted
   (b) 12 mm moulded
   (c) 25 mm planted
   (d) 25 mm moulded

7 When using a contact adhesive for bonding plastic laminate to a chipboard worktop, the two surfaces can be joined together:
   (a) as soon as the adhesive has been applied
   (b) when it no longer gives off a spirit smell
   (c) when the two surfaces are touch dry
   (d) when the colour changes

8 The purpose of diminished stile doors is to:
   (a) provide the maximum area of glass
   (b) improve the door's appearance
   (c) strengthen the door's stability
   (d) increase the width of the stile for the panel groove

9 Pockets in vertical sliding sash windows are removed to:
   (a) remove the cords
   (b) take out the sashes
   (c) allow access to the weights
   (d) enable the frame to be fixed to the wall

10 Only two of the following statements are correct.
   (1) The outside vertical member of a door is called a jamb.
   (2) The triangular area under a flight of stars is called the spandrel.
   (3) Solid core flush doors are normally considered to be of a better quality than hollow core flush doors.
   (4) Ground floor bay windows are known as oriel windows.

   Which are they?
   (a) 1 and 3
   (b) 2 and 3
   (c) 2 and 4
   (d) 1 and 4

chapter 6

Construction work

After reading this chapter the student should be able to:

1   State the principles involved in the following items of construction work:
    suspended floors
    flat roofs
    pitched roofs
    studwork
    prefabricated timber-framed buildings

2   Identify the component parts of these various items

3   Produce sketches to show suitable details of these various items

4   List the sequence of operations for a given job

5   State any building regulations that are relevant to a given item of construction work.

6   Select the most suitable method of construction for a given situation

Timber upper floor construction

The joists used for upper floors must be of a deeper section than those used for ground floors. This is because no intermediate support in the form of sleeper walls is available.

The depth of the joist depends on its span – as the span increases so must its depth. Therefore in order to use an economic depth of joist, the maximum span for simple floors is normally restricted to 4.8 m. For spans in excess of this, a more complex form of construction is required.

Upper floors may be classified into three groups, according to their method of construction: single floors; double floors; and triple or framed floors.

Single floors (Figure 240)
These are the most common type of upper floors for domestic house construction. They are used for spans up to 4.8 m where common or bridging joists span from wall to wall.

Double floors (Figure 241)
These are used where the shortest span of the room is over 4.8 m and up to about 6 m. The room

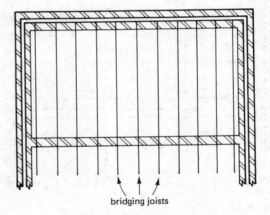

Figure 240   *Single floor*

is divided up into a number of bays, each of which is not more than 4.8 m long, by binders which provide intermediate support for the bridging joists. These binders may be of steel, commonly known as a universal beam (UB) or timber usually either a solid, laminated or a plywood box beam.

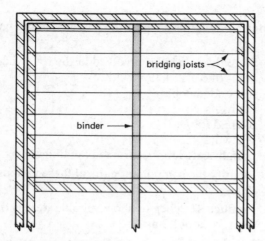

Figure 241   *Double floor*

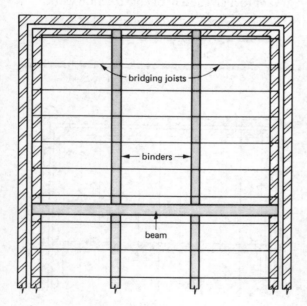

Figure 242   *Triple floor*

Triple or framed floors (Figure 242)

These are now almost obselete, as floors where the span is over 6 m reinforced concrete or other forms of floor construction are used, although when engaged in maintenance or renovation work, triple floors may be encountered. The room is divided up into bays by very heavy, large-sectioned steel universal beams. These beams provide support for the steel or timber binders,

which in turn provide support for the bridging joists.

Joist terminology

Bridging joist A joist spanning from support to support, also known as a common joist.

Trimmed joist A bridging joist that has been cut short (trimmed) to form an opening in the floor.

Trimmer joist A joist placed at right angles to the bridging joist, in order to support the cut ends of the trimmed joists.

Trimming joist A joist with a span the same as the bridging joist, but supporting the end of a trimmer joist.

Note: As both the trimmer and the trimming joists take a greater load, they are usually 25 mm thicker than the bridging joists.

Layout of floor joists

The positioning of floor joists is a fairly simple operation, the outside bridging joists being placed in position first, leaving a 50 mm gap between them and the wall. The other joists are then spaced out evenly in the remaining space.

However, when openings for fireplaces and stairwells, etc. are required in the floor, the layout of the floor joists is governed by these openings. This is because the bridging must be cut short in order to form the opening. This necessitates the use of a trimmer and trimming joists. The trimming and outside bridging joists are the first to be positioned, once again leaving a 50 mm gap between the joist and the wall. The other joists are then spaced out in the remaining space.

Note: Before positioning joists, it is worth checking the finished floor-to-ceiling height to ensure the walls are at the correct level.

Figure 243 shows the layout of joists for a single floor with a fireplace opening.

The dovetail strips shown in Figure 243 are bedded into the top of the concrete hearth to provide a fixing for the ends of the floorboards.

Note: The dovetail strips and the ends of floorboards must be at least 150 mm away from the edge of the opening.

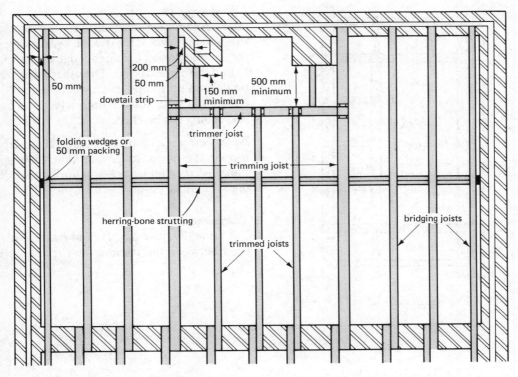

Figure 243 *Layout of floor around fireplace*

Figure 244 shows a section through the fire hearth. The 6 mm asbestos, which is supported on the brickwork, and the batten fixed to the trimmer acts as permanent framework for the concrete.

The Building Regulations 1985 Part J restrict the use of combustible materials in the vicinity of a fireplace. These restrictions are interpreted as:

No timber is to be built into the flue, or be within 200 mm of the flue lining, or be nearer than 40 mm to the outer surface of a chimney or fireplace recess (a 50 mm air space between any joist and wall is standard practice). Floorboarding, skirting, architrave, mantle-shelf and other trim are exceptions to this requirement.

There must be a 125 mm minimum thickness solid non-combustible hearth which extends at least 500 mm in front of the fireplace recess and 150 mm on either side.

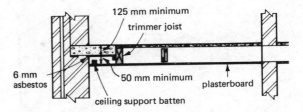

Figure 244 *Section through fire hearth*

Combustible material used underneath the hearth is to be separated from the hearth by an air space of at least 50 mm or be at least 250 mm from the hearth's top surface. Combustible material supporting the edge of the hearth is permitted.

Figure 245 shows the layout of joists around a stairwell. It can be seen that this is a similar arrangement to the trimming around the fireplace.

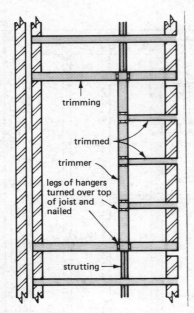

Figure 245   *Trimming to stairwell*

Levelling joists

After positioning, the joists should be checked for line and level. This is done by working round the building using a straight edge and spirit level to find the highest point. The other joists can then be packed up to this level, where required, thus ensuring a level surface onto which the flooring and ceiling can be fixed.

Note: Temporary battens can be nailed across the top of the joists to ensure that their spacing remains constant before and during their 'building in'.

Trimming joints

Traditionally, tusk mortise and tenon joints were used between the trimmer and trimming joists,

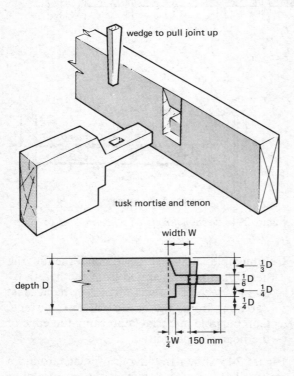

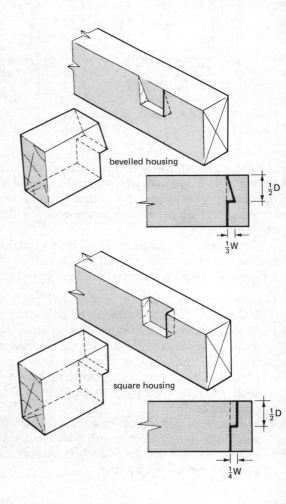

Figure 246   *Traditional trimming joists*

while housing joints were used between the trimmed joists and the trimmer. The joints along with their proportions are shown in Figure 246. All of these joints are based on the fact that there are neutral stress areas in joists. Therefore, if the joint is mainly cut out in these areas the reduction in the joists strength will be minimal.

Figure 247 shows the end section of a joist on which the neutral stress areas have been shaded.

Joist hangers are a quicker, modern alternative to the traditional joints (see Figure 248). As these hangers are made from thin material, they do not require notching in, but they must be securely nailed to both joists with 32 mm galvanized plasterboard nails.

Notches and Holes in Joist
These are controlled by the Building Regulations Part A. See pages 38-39 and Figure 37 for further details.

Joist sizes and spacing
The joists for all forms of construction must be large enough to safely carry the loads which are imposed upon them. The size of the joists depends on three factors:

the span of the joists
the spacing of the joists
the load per m^2 on the floor

The Building Regulations, Part A Tables B, gives the required size of joists for various spans, spacing and loads.

The approximate depth of 50 mm thick joists spaced at 400 mm centres can be found by using the following rule of thumb method.

$$\frac{\text{span of joists in millimetres}}{20} + 20 = \text{depth of joist}$$

Example
For joists with a span of 4 m.

$$\frac{4000}{20} + 20 = 220 \text{ mm (rounded up to the nearest standard size, 225 mm)}$$

Note: The depth of joist found by using this method is suitable for use in all normal domestic housing.

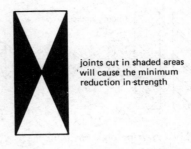

joints cut in shaded areas will cause the minimum reduction in strength

Figure 247   *Neutral stress areas*

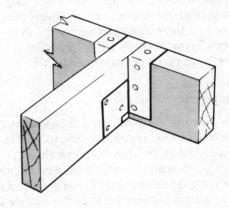

Figure 248   *Trimming using a joist hanger*

Span of flooring
The chart shown in Table 6 gives the spacing for joists in relation to the type of boarding used.

Table 6

Material	Finished thickness (mm)	Maximum spacing of joists (mm)
Softwood T & G boarding	16	450
Softwood T & G boarding	19	600
Flooring-grade chipboard	18	400–500
Flooring-grade chipboard	22	600

Note: The spacing of joists is measured from the centre of one joist to the centre of the next.

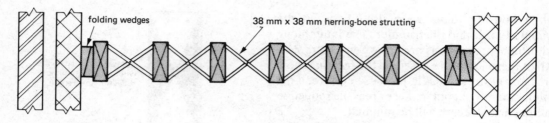

Figure 249   *Herring-bone strutting*

Strutting

In order to stiffen the floor joists and stop their sideways (lateral) movement, the joists should be strutted in their mid-span or where their span exceeds 3.6 m, at about 1.8 m intervals.

There are two types of strutting:

solid strutting;
herring-bone strutting.

Solid strutting is considered to be inferior. This is because solid strutting tends to loosen and become ineffective when the joists shrink.

Figure 249 is a section through a floor showing the herring-bone strutting. Folding wedges or 50 mm packing is inserted between the outside joists and the wall.

Note: The struts should finish about 5 mm short of the top and bottom of the joists so that they do not interfere with the floor or ceiling line.

The method used to mark out the struts is shown in Figure 250.

Mark across the joists the centre line of the strutting.
Mark a second line across the joist so that the distance between the lines is 10 mm less than the depth of the joist.
Place the length of strutting on top of the joists as shown and mark underneath against the joists at A and B.
Cut two struts to these marks.

Note: If these joists are spaced evenly, all the strutting will be the same size and can be cut using the first ones as a template. If not, each set of struts will have to be marked individually.

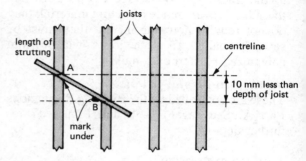

Figure 250   *Marking out strutting*

Fix struts on either side of the centre line using wire nails, one in the top and bottom of each strut and one through the centre.

Joist supports

The ends of the joists may be supported in a number of different ways. The two most common are described here.

'Built-in' (Figure 251)

The ends of the joist are treated with a preservative and built into the inner leaf of the brickwork. An improvement of this method is to incorporate a steel-bearing bar under the joists.

Note: Ends of joists are splayed off to prevent them from penetrating into the cavity and possibly catching mortar droppings. Also as a fire precaution, this method cannot be used for supporting joists in a party wall (a dividing wall between two dwellings).

Hangers (Figure 252)

The ends of the joist are supported by galvanized

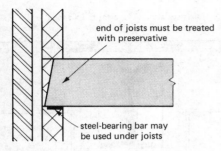

Figure 251 *Joist 'built-in'*

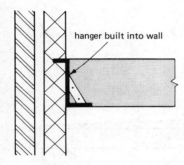

Figure 252 *Joist on hanger*

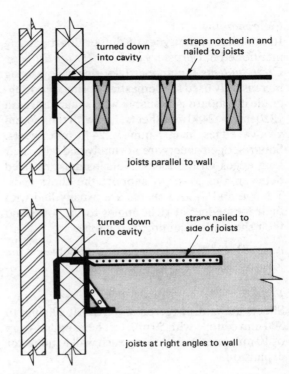

Figure 253 *Restraint straps*

joist hangers which are built into the brickwork. An advantage of this method is that the joists can be fixed after the wall is completely built, unlike the previous method where the bricklayers have to wait for the carpenters to position the joists before they can continue with the brickwork.

Restraint straps

With modern lightweight materials now being used for wall construction, floors require positive ties between the joists and the walls at intervals of not more than 2 m. This is in order to prevent lateral movement.

Figure 253 shows joists tied into the wall using restraint straps.

Sound insulation

The need for sound insulation in domestic floors is fairly limited. But where required the detail shown in Figure 254 A will reduce the passage of sound through the floor. For a more efficient sound insulation a floating floor should be incorporated, as shown in Figure 254 B.

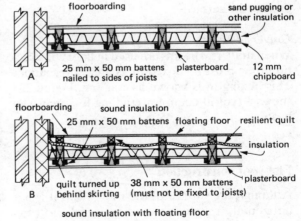

Figure 254 *Sound insulation of floors*

Note: The passage of sound will find the point of least resistance, therefore do not forget to insulate the 50 mm gap between the outside joists and the brickwork.

Floorboarding

In addition to the types of timber floorboarding mentioned in *Carpentry and Joinery for Building Craft Students 1,* chipboard flooring is now being increasingly used for domestic flooring. Flooring-grade chipboard is available with square edges in 1220 mm × 2440 mm sheets, and with tongue and groove edges in 600 mm × 2440 mm sheets. Square-edged sheets are normally laid with their long edges on the joists. Noggins must be fixed between the joists to support the short ends. Tounge and groove sheets are usually laid with their long edges at right angles to the joists and their short edges joining over a joist.

Note: Both types require noggins between the joists where the sheet abuts a wall.

Fixing

Sheets are laid staggered and fixed at 200 mm to 300 mm centres with 50 mm lost head nails. A gap of 10 mm must be left along each wall to allow for expansion.

Note: It is recommended that the floor is covered with building paper after laying and that this is left in position until occupation in order to protect the surface.

Universal beams

When universal beams are used in floor construction they must be boxed in as a fire precaution. This boxing in is known as cradling. Figure 255 shows a typical detail for cradling to a universal beam.

Flat roof construction

Although the surface of the roof is flat, it is not horizontal. It should have a slope or fall on its top surface of about 25 mm for every metre run of the joist (1 in 40). This ensures that rain-water will be quickly cleared and will not accumulate on the roof. There are three ways of forming the slope, described below.

Level joists (Figure 256)

The joists are laid level and the slope is formed by

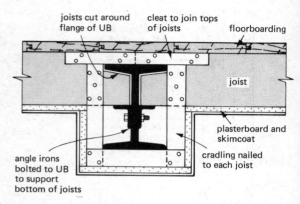

Figure 255   *Cradling to a universal beam*

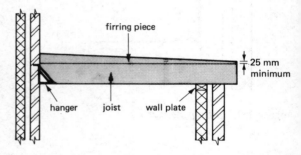

Figure 256   *Level joist*

nailing long tapering pieces of timber (firring pieces) to their top edges. This is the most common method as it forms a level ceiling.

Note: The thinnest end of the firring pieces should be at least 25 mm thick.

Sloping joists (Figure 257)

The joists themselves are laid to the required slope and therefore no firrings are required. The disadvantage is that this forms a sloping ceiling.

Diminishing firrings (Figure 258)

The joists are laid level at right angles to the slope. This method is rarely seen, but it is a useful method when timber boards are used for the roof decking, as these should be fixed parallel to the roof slope. This is because the boards are prone to become slightly 'cupped' and if they were fixed at right angles to the fall, the cupping would

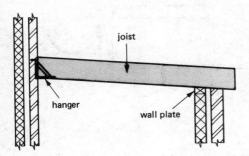

Figure 257   *Sloping joist*

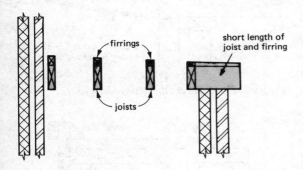

Figure 258   *Diminishing firrings*

restrict the flow of rain-water off the roof and tend to form puddles.

Note: This problem can be overcome to some extent where timber boards are used for the first two forms of flat roof construction, by fixing the boarding diagonally across the roof.

Joint size and spacing

The size of flat roof joists can be found in the same way as floor joists, e.g. The Building Regulations, Part A or by the following rule:

$$\frac{\text{span in mm}}{20} + 20 = \text{depth}$$

The spacing of the joists depends on the type of material used for the decking. The chart shown in Table 7 can be used as a guide.

Table 7

Decking material	Finished thickness (mm)	Maximum spacing of joists (mm)
Softwood T & G boarding	19	600
Chipboard	18	450
Chipboard	22	600
Plywood	12	400
Plywood	18	600
Wood wool	50	600

Layout of joists

The positioning and levelling of flat roof joists is similar to the positioning and levelling of floor joists, except that flat roofs only occasionally have to be trimmed around openings, e.g. roof lights, chimney stacks, etc.

Note: Flat roofs, like floors, also require some form of strutting at their mid-span or at 1.8 m centres.

Eaves details

The ends of the joists which run at right angles to the wall can be finished at the eaves in one of two ways:

flush eaves (Figure 259);
overhanging eaves (Figure 260).

Both of these methods involve the use of a deep fascia board. An alternative to this is to reduce the depth of the joists at the eaves.

Figure 261 shows that this may be done with a splay or square cut to the ends of the joists.

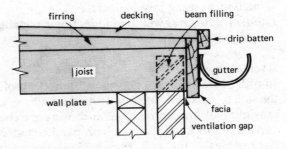

Figure 259   *Flush eaves*

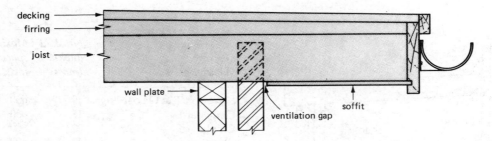

Figure 260   *Overhanging eaves*

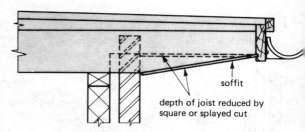

Figure 261   *Reducing the depth of the joist*

Note: The brickwork is normally continued partially up between the joists. This stiffens the joists at their ends and is called beam filling. The cavity should also be closed, for example with a damp proof course cavity closer.

Rain-water is discharged from the roof surface into the gutter at the lowest eaves. An angle fillet should be used around the other edges of the roof as shown in Figure 262. This prevents the rain-water from dripping or being blown over the edges of the roof.

Note: An angle fillet should also be fixed along the edges of the roof which abut the brickwork, to enable the roof covering (bitumin roofing felt, etc.) to be turned up into the brickwork joint.

In order to finish the eaves which are parallel to the main joists, short joists must be fixed to these at right angles. Figures 263 and 264 show two alternative details that may be used:

Returned eaves where short joists are fixed to the main joists using joist hangers.
Ladder frame eaves where a ladder frame is made up and fixed to the last joist.

Anchoring joists

In order to prevent strong winds lifting the roof, the joists must be anchored to the walls at a maximum of 2 m centres. This anchoring must be carried out to joists that run both parallel and at right angles to the wall. Figure 265 shows a flat roof joist anchored to the wall using an anchoring

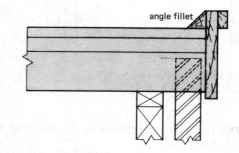

Figure 262   *Eaves detail*

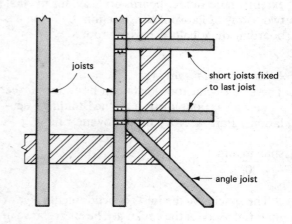

Figure 263   *Returned eaves*

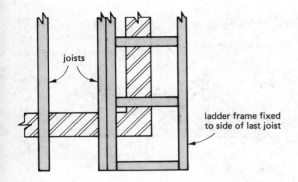

Figure 264   *Ladder frame eaves*

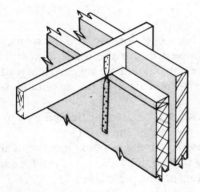

Figure 265   *Anchoring flat roof joist*

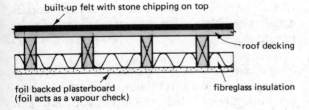

Figure 266   *Insulation in roof space*

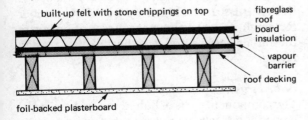

Figure 267   *Insulation above roof space*

strap. The strap is nailed to the side of the joist and fixed to the wall by either nailing or plugging and screwing.

Thermal insulation

In order to prevent heat loss or absorption through the roof, e.g. to stop the building being too cold in the winter and too hot in the summer, thermal insulation should be incorporated into the roof design.

Note: Thermal insulation is a requirement of The Building Regulations, Part L.

There are two methods by which a flat roof can be insulated:

Insulation in the roof space (Figure 266)
This has thermal insulation and a vapour check at ceiling level. The roof space itself is cold and must be vented to the outside air.
Insulation above the roof space (Figure 267)
This has its thermal insulation and vapour barrier placed over the roof decking. The roof space is kept warmer than the outside air temperature.

Note: Vapour checks and barriers are used to restrict or prevent the passage of water vapour from penetrating into the insulation which, when damp, becomes ineffective. As there is a risk of condensation within the roof space, it is advisable that all timber used in flat roofs should be pressure-impregnated with a preservative.

Pitched roof construction

Terminology

Pitched roofs may be constructed as single or double roofs depending on their span. Figure 268 shows a double roof which has a gable end, hipped-end and a valley. The component parts of this roof are as follows:

Common rafter The main loadbearing timbers in a roof, which are cut to fit the ridge and bird's-mouthed over the wall plate.
Ridge The backbone of the roof which provides a fixing point for the tops of the rafters.

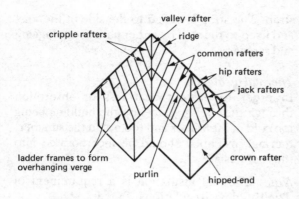

Figure 268   *Terminology*

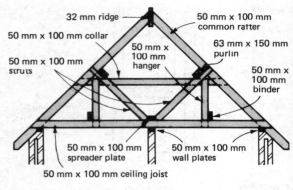

Figure 269   *Double roof for spans up to 7.2 m*

Jack rafters Span from the wall plate to the hip rafter, like common rafters that have had their top shortened.

Hip rafter Used where two sloping roof surfaces meet at an external angle. They provide a fixing point for the jack rafters and transfer their loads to the wall.

Cripple rafters Span from the ridge to the valley, like common rafters that have had their feet shortened (the reverse of jack rafters).

Valley rafter Like the hip rafter but forming an internal angle.

Purlin A beam that provides support for the rafters in their mid-span.

Ladder frame This is also known as a gable ladder and is fixed to the last common rafter to form the overhanging verge on a gable roof. It consists of two rafters with noggins nailed between them.

Double roofs

Single roofs (see *Carpentry and Joinery for Building Craft Students 1*) are not economically viable when the span of a roof exceeds about 5.5 m. This is because very large-sectioned timber would have to be used. In double roofs, purlins are incorporated to support the rafters in their mid-span.

Figure 269 shows a section through a double roof which is suitable for spans up to 7.2 m.

Common rafters These are cut to the ridge and bird's-mouthed over the wall plate as usual.

Purlin This is best notched into the struts.

Struts These transfer the loads imposed by the purlins onto a loadbearing partition wall.

Spreader plate This provides a suitable bearing for the struts.

Collar This acts as a collar tie and also provides some support for the purlins.

Ceiling joists As well as being joists on which the ceiling is fixed, they also act as ties for each pair of rafters at wall plate level.

Binders and hangers These stiffen and support the ceiling joists in their mid-span, to prevent them from sagging and distorting the ceiling.

Note: The struts, collars and hangers are spaced evenly along the roof at every third or fourth pair of rafters.

Roof trusses and trussed rafters

The partition walls in modern domestic houses are normally of a lightweight construction and are not suitable for supporting loads from the purlin. This has given rise to the need for roof designs that do not require intermediate support. Bolted trusses developed by TRADA (Timber Research and Development Association) were the earlier designs, followed by nail plate trussed rafters.

Bolted trusses

The component parts of bolted trusses have overlapped joints which are connected up using bolts and toothed plates. They are normally prefabri-

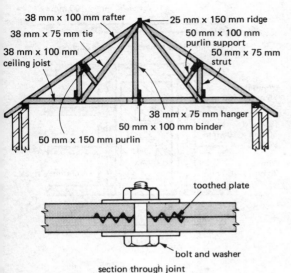

38 mm × 100 mm rafter
38 mm × 75 mm tie
38 mm × 100 mm ceiling joist
25 mm × 150 mm ridge
50 mm × 100 mm purlin support
50 mm × 75 mm strut
38 mm × 75 mm hanger
50 mm × 100 mm binder
50 mm × 150 mm purlin

toothed plate

bolt and washer

section through joint

Figure 270   *Bolted truss*

cated in a shop and arrive on site in two easily managed halves, which must be bolted together once the truss has been positioned.

Figure 270 shows a typical bolted truss with an enlarged joint detail. The trusses are spaced along the roof at about 1.8 m centres, to support the roof components. The purlins and ceiling binders are then fixed to these. The spaces between the trusses are in-filled with normal common rafters and ceiling joists. Half trusses are used in place of the crown rafter for hipped-end roofs, normal hip and jack rafters being inserted as required.

Nail plate trussed rafters

These are prefabricated by a number of specialist manufacturers in a wide range of shapes and sizes. They consist of prepared timber laid out in one plane, with their butt joints fastened with nail plates.

Figure 271 shows a typical design for a trussed rafter.

Note: The trussed rafter sits on the wall plate and is not bird's-mouthed over it.

In use they are spaced along the roof at between 400 mm to 600 mm centres and fixed to the wall plate preferably using truss clips.

In order to provide lateral stability, the roof requires binders at both ceiling and apex level and diagonal rafter bracing fixed to the underside of the rafters. These must be in accordance with the individual manufacturer's recommendations.

Ladder frames are available for the overhanging verges of gable roofs, as are special trussed rafters for forming hipped ends and valleys.

Trimming

Where openings occur in roofs, in either the rafters, ceiling joists or both, these have to be trimmed, framing anchors or housing joints being used to join the trimmers, trimmings and trimmed components together.

Figure 272 is a section through a ceiling showing the trimmed opening and hatch lining.

Figure 273 is a part plan and section through a

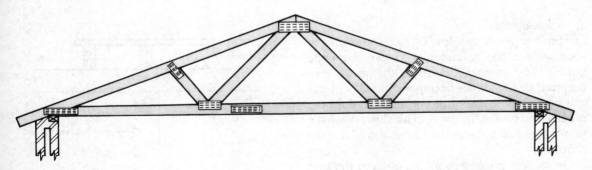

Figure 271   *Trussed rafter*

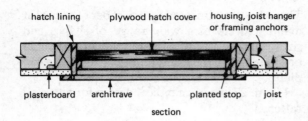

Figure 272 *Trimming to loft hatch*

roof showing the trimming around a chimney stack and the back gutter detail.

Note: To comply with The Building Regulations, no combustible material, including timber, is to be placed within 200 mm of the inside of the flue lining, or where the thickness of the chimney surrounding the flue is less than 200 mm, no combustible material must be placed within 40 mm of the chimney.

Whenever possible, openings for loft hatches and chimneys in roofs made up of trussed rafters should be accommodated within the trussed rafter spacing. If a larger opening is required for the chimney stack, a trussed rafter is placed on either side of the stack and the space between is in-filled using normal rafters and ceiling joists.

Water tank platforms
These are ideally situated centrally over a load-bearing wall. The platform should consist of boarding supported by joists laid on top of the ceiling joists and at right angles to them. Figure 274 shows a typical water tank platform.

Sprocketed eaves
On pitched roofs the flow of rain-water off the roof surface has a tendency to overshoot the gutter. The steeper the roof, the more pro-nounced this tendency becomes. Sprocket pieces can be nailed on top of the rafters to reduce the pitch of the roof at the eaves. This slows down the rain-water and reduces the likelihood of it over-shooting.

On steeply pitched roofs the pitch of the roof can be reduced near the eaves by fixing large

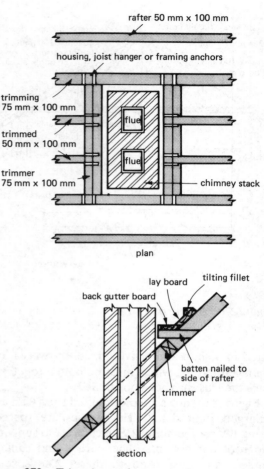

Figure 273 *Trimming to chimney stack*

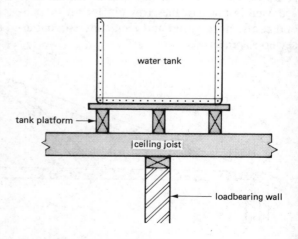

Figure 274 *Water tank platform*

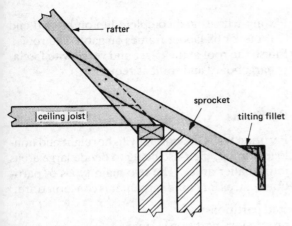

Figure 275   *Sprocketed eaves*

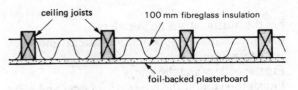

Figure 276   *Pitched roof insulation*

sprockets on to the sides of each rafter, as shown in Figure 275.

As well as slowing down the flow of rain-water, sprocketed eaves enhance the appearance of a roof.

Anchoring roofs

Rafters can be skew-nailed to the wall plates or, in areas noted for their high winds, framing anchors or truss clips where appropriate can be used.

Wall plates must be secured down to the wall with straps at 2 m centres. The rafters adjacent to the gable end should also be tied into the wall with straps at 2 m centres.

Note: These are tied in using a similar method to that used for joists that run parallel to a wall.

Thermal insulation in pitched roofs

This is a requirement of the Building Regulations Part L. Normally this is achieved by placing insulation between the ceiling joists taking care not to block the eaves. See Figure 276.

Ventilation

In order to limit the risk of condensation in roof spaces above insulated ceilings, the Building Regulations Part F states that roof spaces should have ventilation openings in opposite eaves or at eaves and opposite high level in the case of a lean-to roof. The area of the opening along each side should be equivalent to a continuous gap of 10 mm for pitched roofs, or

25 mm for flat roofs and those of less than 15 degrees pitch.

Roof erection

The procedure for roof erection is similar for most untrussed types of roof.

The procedure of erection for a hipped-end roof would be as follows:

The wall plate having been bedded and levelled by the bricklayer, must be tied down.

Mark out the position of the rafters on the wall plate.

Make up two temporary 'A' frames. These consist of two common rafters with a temporary tie joining them at the top, leaving a space for the ridge, and a temporary tie nailed to them in the position of the ceiling joists.

Fix ceiling joists in position.

Stand up the 'A' frames at either end of the roof in the position of the last common rafter and skew nail to the wall plate.

Fix temporary braces to hold the 'A' frames upright

Mark out the spacing of the rafters on the ridge and fix in position (see Figure 277).

Fix the crown and hip rafters.

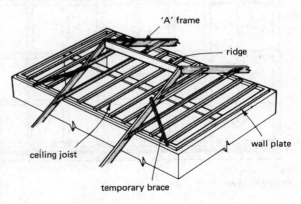

Figure 277   *Roof erection*

Fix the purlin, struts and binders.

Fix the remaining common rafters and jack rafters.

Fix the collars and the hangers.

Finish the roof at the eaves with fascia and soffit as required.

The erection procedure for roofs containing trusses is similar except that two trusses are substituted for the 'A' frames and the remaining trusses are fixed in position before the purlins and common rafters.

Trussed rafters

The main problem encountered with the erection of trussed rafters is their handling. In order not to strain the joints of the trussed rafters they should, wherever possible, be lifted from the eaves keeping the rafter in a vertical plane with its apex uppermost. The procedure is as follows:

Once up on the roof, the first trussed rafter can be placed in position, fixed, plumbed and temporarily braced.

Fix the remaining trussed rafters in position one at a time. Each rafter is temporarily tied to the preceeding one with a batten.

Fix diagonal bracing and binders.

Fix hip trusses and complete hip on hipped-end roofs, or fix ladder frames on gable-end roofs.

Finish the roof at the eaves and verge with fascia, bargeboard and soffit as required.

Partitions

Partition walls are normally lightweight and non-loadbearing, their use being to divide large areas into smaller areas. The two main types of partition wall, as far as the carpenter is concerned are:

stud partitions;
proprietary partition systems.

Stud partitions

These consist of vertical timbers called studs (hence their name stud partitions) which are fixed to two horizontal timbers, one at the ceiling level called a head plate and the other at floor level called a sole plate. Short horizontal timbers called noggins are fixed in between the studs to stiffen them and provide additional fixing points for the covering material.

The actual covering material can vary, e.g. plasterboard, plywood, insulation board, hardboard and matchboarding, etc.

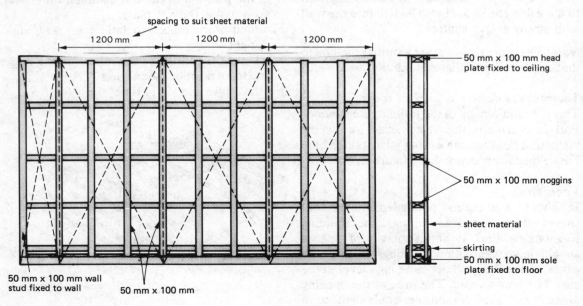

Figure 278   *Stud partitions*

It is important that the material to be used is known before the stud is erected as the studs must be spaced accordingly. Most sheet materials require a stud on either edge and two intermediate studs. This makes the stud spacing approximately 400 mm. The positions for the noggins also vary with the covering material but in general noggins are fixed at skirting height, knee height (600 mm), waist height (1.2 m) and shoulder height (1.8 m) (these being the most vulnerable points). Additional noggins are fixed where horizontal joints occur between sheet material.

Figure 278 shows a typical stud partition. The position of the sheet material covering is indicated in the elevation by the diagonal broken lines.

Figure 279 shows the joints used between the studs and the head and sole plates. These joints must be fixed with nails. The noggins are butt jointed and skew nailed. On cheaper work the studs are also butt jointed and skew nailed. An alternative to both methods would be to use framing anchors.

The correct sequence of operations for the erection of stud partition is as follows:

House out and fix head plate.
Plumb down from the head plate and fix the sole plate.
Cut and fix the wall studs.
Cut and fix intermediate studs.
Cut and fix the noggins.

Note: If services are to be accommodated in the partition, they should be installed at this stage.

Cut and fix the plasterboard or other covering.

Note: Most sheet materials require fixing at between 150 mm and 200 mm centres. The fixing should commence at the centre of the sheet, working out to the edges. This is in order to avoid any bulging of the sheet.

Figure 280 shows the arrangement of studs where two partitions join at right angles.

Note: Using this method, one partition must be erected and sheeted on one side before the other partition is erected. Alternatively, additional studs can be inserted to take the plasterboard.

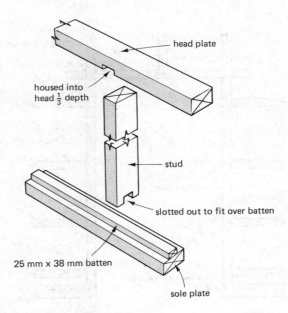

Figure 279   *Joint details*

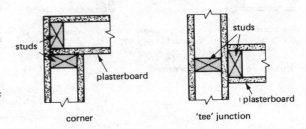

Figure 280   *Corner details*

Where openings are required in the studwork for doors, hatches and borrowed lights, etc., the studs and noggins must be positioned accordingly.

Note: A borrowed light is a window in an internal wall.

Figure 281 shows the detail around a door opening. On the section the door lining, plasterboard and architrave have been included.

Figure 282 shows the joint used between the door stud and the door head and also between the door stud and the sole plate. Once again, on cheaper work, these are often housed or butt jointed.

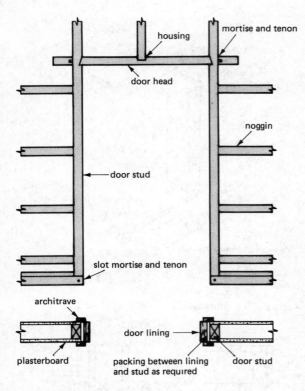

Figure 281   *Door opening*

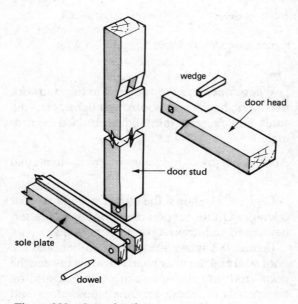

Figure 282   *Joint details*

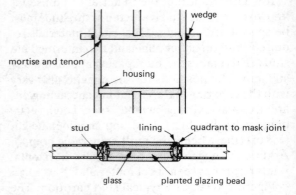

Figure 283   *Borrowed light*

A borrowed light detail is shown in Figure 283. The same detail could be used for a hatch opening, except that the glass and glazing beads would be replaced by a pair of small hinged doors. An alternative finish around the opening would be to reduce the width of the lining and fix architraves to cover the joint.

Insulation

Stud partitions can be given a reasonable amount of sound and thermal insulation for most domestic purposes by filling the spaces between the studs and noggins with fibreglass insulation.

For a greater degree of insulation, alternative methods must be used. Figure 284 shows a detail of a partition that is extremely effective in resisting the passage of sound and heat. It consists of normal studwork filled with fibreglass insulation and covered with 12 mm insulation board on both sides. When this has been done, vertical battens are nailed over the stud partitions and a layer of plasterboard fixed to these.

The standard of insulation will be improved even further if, before fixing the head plate, sole plate and wall studs, strips of insulation board are cut and fixed to the back of them. This isolates the partition from any vibrations in the surrounding structure. The door lining in insulated partitions should also be isolated by nailing strips of insulation board between the stud and the back of the lining. The weak link is usually the door and its joint. This is improved by using a purpose-made

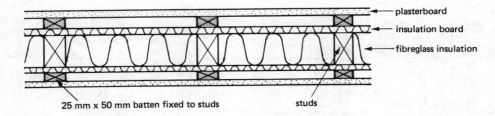

Figure 284   *Insulation of stud partition*

door capable of resisting the passage of sound and heat. The joint between the door and the lining can be sealed with a sealing strip. Sealing strips are normally made from felt or rubber and are available for fixing all around the opening, including the bottom of the door. If borrowed lights are used in the partition these should be double glazed.

Proprietory partitions

Various proprietory partition systems are available from a number of manufacturers, but probably the most popular for domestic work is Paramount dry partitions. They are constructed using prefabricated panels which consist of two sheets of plasterboard separated by a cellular core (see Figure 285). The panel rests on a timber sole plate and fits over timber battens which are fixed to the wall and ceiling. Battens are also inserted between the panels where they join.

Prefabricated timber-framed buidings

Timber-framed construction can be divided into two main groups:

'Knock down' buildings These are buildings which remain in one position for a relatively short amount of time, and are 'knocked down' (dismantled) and re-erected elsewhere. Site huts, sheds, stores, offices and canteens all fall within this group.

Permanent buildings For domestic, office and industrial accommodation.

'Knock down' buildings

The use of each building will determine its size

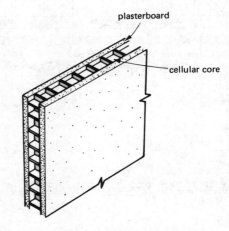

Figure 285   *Paramount dry partition board*

and the standard of facilities required. In general, site accommodation needs to be well ventilated, waterproof, thermally insulated and have some provision for lighting and heating.

Figure 286 shows details of a typical site hut. The framing sections for the walls, roof and floors which bolt together are all made up in standard sizes, thereby making the panels fully interchangeable and enabling larger or smaller huts to be erected as required. In order to facilitate this, all bolt holes should be drilled using a template. Where sheet material is being used the ideal panel width is 1.220 m. The larger window or door panels should be made up in multiples of the panel size, e.g. 2.440 m for sheet material.

The wall covering material (cladding) may consist of either shiplap boarding, matchboarding or WBP plywood. Where plywood is used for the cladding, the diagonal braces can be omitted, as the sheets themselves will provide

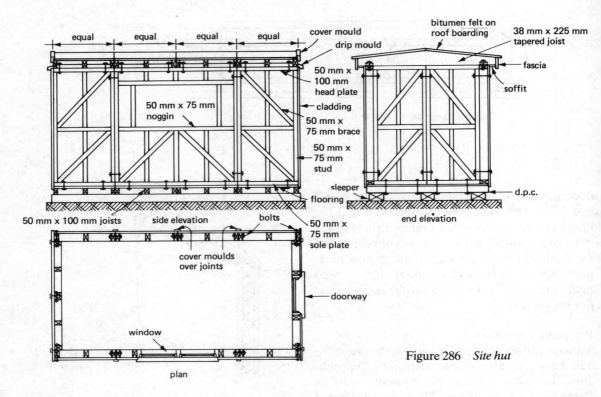

Figure 286   *Site hut*

sufficient rigidity. Where shiplap or matchboarding is to be used for the cladding, a moisture barrier can be fixed between the cladding and the studs to prevent the penetration of wind-driven rain. Plywood or tongue and groove boarding can be used for the floor and roof coverings.

Note: The hut is erected on sleepers which have been levelled and to prevent dampness and decay a damp proof course is inserted between the sleepers and the joists.

Figure 287 is a section through the wall panel showing the opening casement. Fixed glazing could be used as an alternative if required, but provision must be made for ventilation. This could take the form of a timber louvred ventilator placed over the door or in a wall panel (see Figure 288).

The inside of some site huts are lined with insulation board. This not only improves their thermal insulation but also their internal appearance. Additional insulation can be provided by

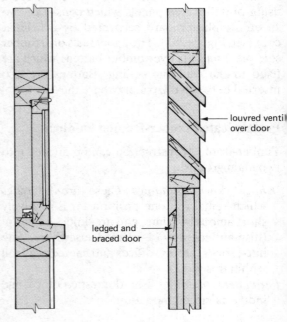

Figure 287
Window detail

Figure 288
Ventilator detail

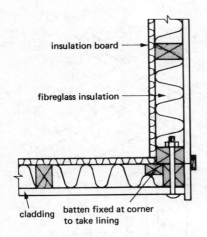

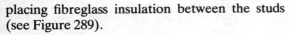

Figure 289 *Lining and insulation*

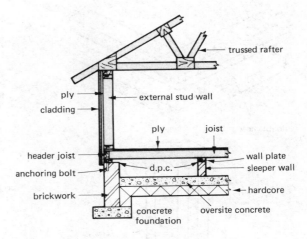

Figure 290 *Platform frame method*

placing fibreglass insulation between the studs (see Figure 289).

Note: Where the hut is lined, a batten must be fixed to the corner panel to take the lining and pockets must be left for the bolts.

Permanent timber-framed buildings

These are normally prefabricated under factory conditions and transported to the site for erection on prepared foundations, although they are equally suitable for on-site manufacture. In timber-framed buildings, all the structural parts above the damp proof course level, e.g. the walls, floor and roof are constructed from timber and plywood. The external cladding provides a weatherproof finish and may range from bricks and stone, which give the building a traditional appearance, to various types of timber boarding.

There are two main types of timber frame construction and these are described below.

The platform frame method

Using this method the walls are built in single storey height sections. Once the first wall sections have been erected on the ground floor, the first floor joists and sheeting are fixed on top of them. This creates a platform (hence platform frame) on which the second storey walls can be erected. Further floors are formed by continuing this process.

Balloon frame method

This method uses timber frames that are the full height of the building. The studs are continuous from the damp proof course level up to the eaves with intermediate floor joists being supported on ribbons. These are timbers that are notched into the studs.

The platform frame is normally preferred because of its smaller, more easily managed components and the fact that a working platform is created at each stage. Generally, for single storey buildings, which are considered in this chapter, there is little difference between them. As well as providing complete buildings, timber frame methods can also be used when constructing extensions to existing buildings, or for curtain walling (a non-loadbearing external wall between loadbearing cross walls).

Figure 290 shows a sectional detail of a timber-framed building, using the platform method. The floor is constructed as a hollow ground floor with honeycomb sleeper walls, supporting the joists at about 1.8 m intervals. The floor sheeting is 12 mm plywood and it extends right to the edges of the building. A header joist (a joist fixed at right angles to the main joists) should be fixed at the ends of the main joists to support the plywood. The wall frames can then be made and erected. These consist of prepared 50 mm × 100 mm studwork with studs spaced at about 400 mm

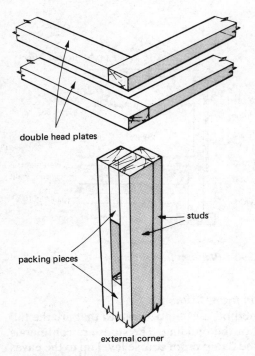

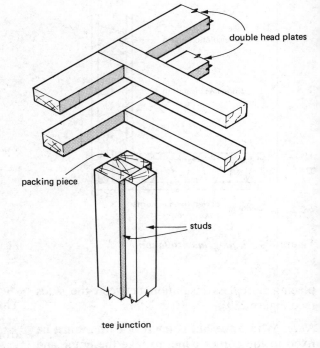

Figure 291   *Corner details*

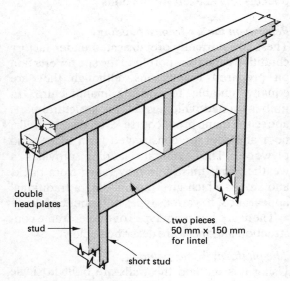

Figure 292   *Opening detail*

centres for two-storey buildings, to suit the sheet sizes. But this may be increased to 600 mm centres for single storey buildings. No noggins or diagonal braces are required as the 9 mm plywood sheathing, which is nailed to the studs, provides the required rigidity.

Double head plates are used for additional strength so that joist and trussed rafter spacing are not dependent on the stud positions. Where walls intersect, additional studs should be used to provide a fixing for the internal sheeting. Figure 291 shows details of these intersections.

Lintels must be provided over openings, where these occur in external walls. This is normally two pieces of 50 mm × 150 mm timber fixed together and stood on edge. This is supported on either side of the opening by double studs, one stud being cut shorter to provide a bearing for the lintel (see Figure 292). Trussed rafters spaced at 600 mm centres are normally used for the roof, although flat roofs are also suitable.

Figure 293 shows a trussed rafter which can be made up on site using 50 mm × 100 mm timbers which are jointed by nailing 9 mm ply gusset plates on either side of the joint. For maximum strength the roof must be sheathed on top of the trussed rafters with 9 mm plywood.

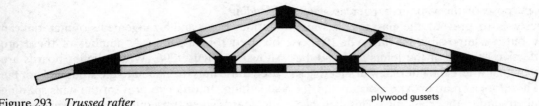

Figure 293   *Trussed rafter*

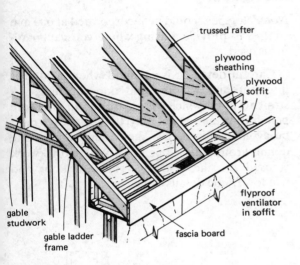

Figure 294   *Eaves and gable detail*

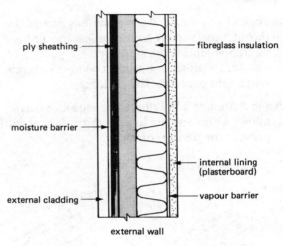

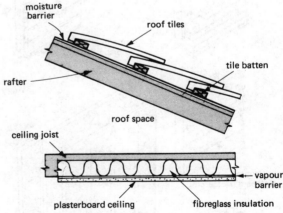

Figure 295   *Insulation*

Roofs can be finished with either hipped or gable ends. Where hipped ends are used, they can be formed by using normal hip and jack rafters. Gable ends require a triangular gable studwork and for overhanging verges a gable ladder can be used (see Figure 294).

The eaves are normally closed and have flyproof ventilators cut in them to ventilate the roof space.

Insulation

All new buildings and additions must now, in accordance with The Building Regulations, be insulated to a high standard. This is easily achieved in timber-framed buildings by installing insulation in the spaces between the studs of the external walls and between the ceiling joists in the roof space. It is most important that a vapour barrier is used on the warm side of the insulation and a moisture barrier used on the cold side in between the sheeting and the cladding or, in the case of roofs, the tiling. This is to stop condensation and prevent the insulation from becoming damp. Figure 295 shows a typical wall and roof space with insulation details.

The purpose of the vapour barrier as stated previously is to prevent the passage of water vapour, but it is impossible for this to be 100 per cent effective because of the joints in it and the nails through it where the internal wall sheeting is fixed. Therefore a breather-type moisture barrier is installed under the cladding. This has two functions:

It enables any water vapour that has penetrated through the vapour barrier to escape and not be trapped inside the studwork.

It provides a protection against wind-driven rain that might penetrate the cladding.

Note: Although a breather-type moisture barrier allows water vapour to pass through it, it will prevent the passage of water.

Cladding

Various types and arrangements of material can be used for cladding. A number of these are shown in Figure 296. When timber boards are used these must be nailed to the studs and not the sheathing. In order to prevent the nails splitting the boards when subsequent moisture movement takes place, they must be carefully positioned (see Figure 297).

Note: Noggins should be incorporated at 600 mm centres to provide a fixing where vertical boarding is used.

Careful detailing is required where claddings finish around window and door openings. A straight joint which would result in moisture penetration and eventually timber decay, must be avoided. Figure 298 shows suitable finishing details around these openings. Where brickwork is used for the cladding, standard door and window frame details can be used.

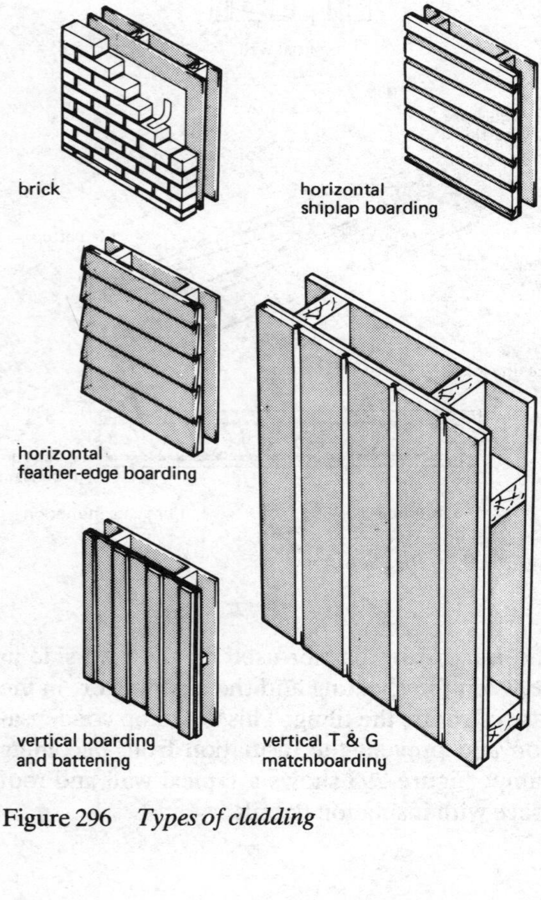

brick

horizontal
shiplap boarding

horizontal
feather-edge boarding

vertical boarding
and battening

vertical T & G
matchboarding

Figure 296　*Types of cladding*

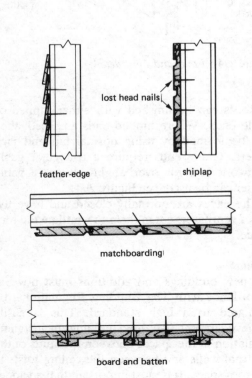

lost head nails

feather-edge

shiplap

matchboarding

board and batten

Figure 297　*Nailing timber cladding*

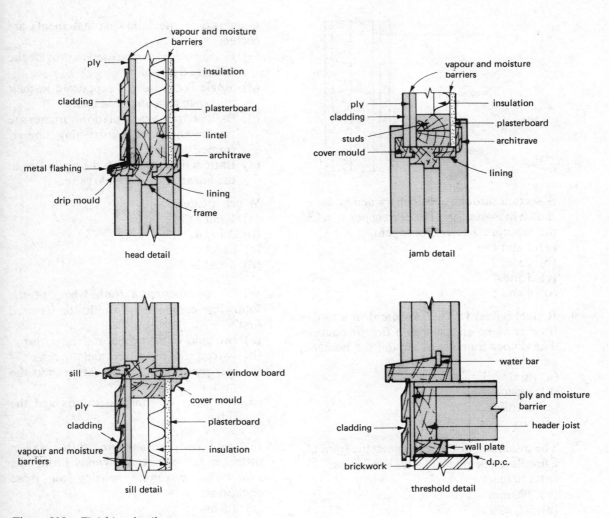

Figure 298 *Finishing details*

Self-assessment questions

1 'Trimming' is a term used in floor and roof construction to describe:
   (a) cutting joists and rafters to length
   (b) fixing herring-bone strutting
   (c) the framing of joists and rafters around openings
   (d) the laying of boarding to floors and roofs

2 The purpose of a gable ladder is to provide a:
   (a) quick, safe access to the gable end
   (b) fixing for the bargeboard and soffit of an overhanging verge
   (c) fixing for the fascia board and soffit of overhanging eaves
   (d) working platform for fixing the gable

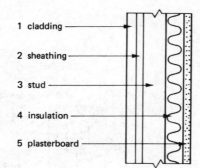

1 cladding

2 sheathing

3 stud

4 insulation

5 plasterboard

Figure 299

3   A section through a timber-framed house is shown in Figure 299. The correct position for the moisture barrier is between:
(a) 1 and 2
(b) 2 and 3
(c) 3 and 4
(d) 4 and 5

4   R steel binder (universal beam) in a timber floor is to be encased as a fire precaution. The timber framework around the binder is known as:
(a) studwork
(b) grounds
(c) cradling
(d) boxing

5   The minimum distance between the front of a fireplace opening and a timber joist is:
(a) 150 mm
(b) 300 mm
(c) 500 mm
(d) 750 mm

6   Which of the following methods of roof construction would be most suitable for a 6 m span where no intermediate loadbearing walls are available?
(a) trussed rafters
(b) double roof
(c) hipped-end roof
(d) single roof

7   Only two of the following statements are correct.
(1) Firring pieces can be used to provide the fall on a flat roof.
(2) Single floors can be supported in their mid-span by a universal beam.
(3) Balloon frames and platform frames are two methods of constructing timber-framed buildings.
(4) Rafters that span from the wall plate to the hip are called cripple rafters.

Which are they?
(a) 1 and 3·
(b) 2 and 4
(c) 1 and 4
(d) 3 and 2

8   When constructing a roof, which of the following components would be erected first?
(a) two pairs of hip rafters and the purlin
(b) two pairs of hip rafters and the ridge
(c) two pairs of common rafters and the purlin
(d) two pairs of common rafters and the ridge

9   Flat roof joists are anchored to the wall in order to prevent strong winds lifting the roof. The maximum spacing for these anchors is:
(a) 2.5 m
(b) 1 m
(c) 2 m
(d) 1.5 m

10   The intermediate uprights in a timber partition wall are known as:
(a) noggins
(b) plates
(c) firrings
(d) studs

chapter 7

Temporary construction and site works

After reading this chapter the student should be able to:

1 State the principles involved in the following items of temporary construction and site works:
   shoring
   hoarding
   fences
   centres for arches
   formwork for concrete
2 Identify the component parts of these various items.
3 Produce sketches to show suitable details of these various items.
4 List the sequence of operations for a given job.
5 Select the most suitable method of construction for a given situation.

Shoring

It is sometimes necessary to give temporary support to the walls and floors of a building, e.g. during alteration work or when the building is considered to be structurally unsound. This temporary support is called shoring. At this stage of the course two types are considered:

vertical or dead shores;
raking shores.

Vertical shores

The purpose of vertical shores is to support the superimposed or dead loads of a section of a building during alteration or repair work. A typical situation where vertical shores are used would be where an opening is to be made in a loadbearing wall. The wall above the opening must be supported while a lintel is inserted and the wall made good around the lintel.

Figure 300 shows a typical detail for vertical shores.

Sequence of operations

Strut all window openings. This is done by placing lengths of 50 mm × 75 mm timber in the window reveals and driving struts tightly between them.

Prop floors using 75 mm × 225 mm head and sole plates and adjustable steel props.

Note: On hollow ground floors, some boards should be removed so that the prop can extend down to the oversite concrete.

Cut holes in the wall for the needles. These should be spaced at 1.2 m centres, under solid brickwork and not placed under windows, etc.

Place the sole plates on firm ground both inside and outside the building, as these are going to spread the load.

Note: It is a good idea to place the lintel in position on the floor before the shoring is erected, as access may be restricted afterwards.

Insert the needles through the wall and support them on dead shores. Drive hardwood folding wedges between the vertical shores and the sole plates, to bring the needles tight up under the brickwork. Packings may be needed between the needles and the brickwork.

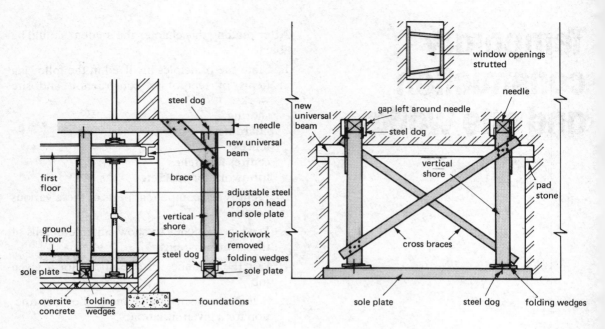

Figure 300 *Vertical shores*

Note: Where cement mortar is used for the packings it must be allowed to harden before any load is placed upon it.

Securely fix all joints between the sole plates, vertical shores and the needles with steel dogs.

Cross-brace the vertical shores, to prevent any possibility of them overturning.

Check all of the shoring for tightness, e.g. props, wedges, struts and bracing, etc., and adjust if required.

Remove wall and build piers and padstones to support the lintel.

Insert the lintel. This is usually either a universal beam or a concrete lintel.

Make good the brickwork around the lintel and allow at least seven days for this to thoroughly set.

Ease and remove the shoring and make good the holes in the wall through which the needles passed.

Note: The easing entails partially slackening the wedges. After about one hour these should be checked. If they are still loose then all of the shoring can be removed using the reverse order to that in which it was erected. But if the wedges have tightened, some form of settlement has occurred. The new brickwork around the lintel should be checked for any signs of cracking. If this is satisfactory then only some initial settlement has taken place and the easing procedure can be repeated.

The size of timbers used for vertical shores will depend on the building to be supported, but an approximate method of determining a suitable section of timber for a two-storey building is to divide the shores height by twenty.

For example: To find the section required for vertical shores which are 3 m high
$3000 \div 20 = 150 \, mm$
Therefore the section required is 150 mm × 150 mm.

Where the building exceeds two storeys, 50 mm should be added to the section for each additional storey.
e.g. 3 m shores for a three-storey building = 150 mm + 50 mm
Therefore the section required = 200 mm × 200 mm

In order to save on costs, second-hand timber can be used providing it is sound and free from defects. Where large-section timber is not available, this can be built up or laminated from smaller sections, e.g. three lengths of 50 mm × 150 mm, bolted together will give a 150 mm × 150 mm section.

Raking shores

These are shores that are inclined to the face of a building. Their purpose is to provide support to a building that is in danger of collapsing or they may be used in conjunction with vertical shores for support during alteration or repair work.

In order to provide maximum support to the floors and to prevent 'pushing in' defective brickwork, the tops of the rakers must be positioned in relation to the floors (see Figure 301). When the joists are at right angles to the wall the centre line of the raker should, when extended, intersect with the centre of the joist's bearing. For joists that are parallel to the wall, the centre line of the floor, wall and raker should intersect. Figure 302 shows the front and side elevation of a single raking shore. These should be positioned at each end of the building and over intermediate cross walls at between 2.5 m and 5 m apart, depending on the building's condition.

Note: The term single raking shore does not refer to the number of shores used but to the number of rakers in each shore, single, double, triple, etc.

Figure 303 shows the jointing arrangement at the top of the raker. The raker is cut to fit the wallpiece and notched around the needle. This locates it and prevents lateral movement. A

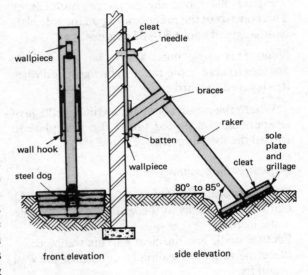

Figure 302   *Single raking shore*

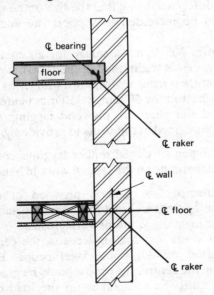

Figure 301   *Positioning rakers*

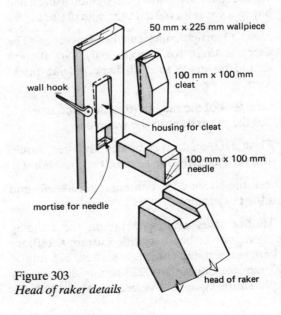

Figure 303
Head of raker details

straight-grained hardwood must be used for the needle which is mortised through the wallpiece and allowed to project into the brickwork by about 100 mm. The function of the wallpiece is to spread the thrust of the raker evenly over a large area of the wall. In order to do this effectively, it must be securely fixed back to the wall using wall hooks. The cleat which is housed into the wall-piece stiffens the needle.

Figure 304 shows the detail at ground level. This consists of the raker bearing on the sole plate at an angle of about 80–85 degrees.

Note: This angle must always be less than 90 degrees to enable the raker to be tightened when it is levered forward.

Where the ground is weak, a grid or grillage of sleepers can be placed under the sole plate to spread the load over a larger area.

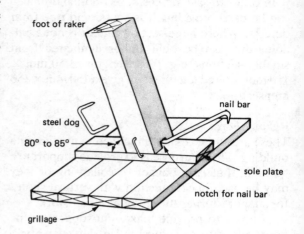

Figure 304　*Foot of raker details*

Sequence of operations

Strut windows as before.
Cut out half bricks in the wall to accommodate the needles.
Fix the needle and the cleat into the wallpiece.
Place the prepared wallpiece up against the wall and fix.
Prepare the sole plate and grillage.
Place the raker in position and tighten using a nail bar to lever it forward on the sole plate.

Note: Overtightening can be dangerous. The shore is there for support only. No attempt should be made to push back bulging brick-work.

Fix the foot of the raker with a cleat and dogs.
Brace the raker back to the wallpiece.

Note: Diagonal cross-braces and ties should also be used between adjacent raking shores.

Check the shoring for tightness periodically and adjust as required.

Timber sizes again depend on the building being supported but as a guide 150 mm × 150 mm rakers are suitable for single shores, 175 mm × 175 mm for double and 225 mm × 225 mm for triple shore systems. As before, these sections can be laminated by bolting a number of smaller sections together.

Centres for arches

Turning pieces and centres for arches up to 1 m span were covered in *Carpentry and Joinery for Building Craft Students 1*. Centres for larger spans can be made using the same methods, the only difference being that the size of the timbers should be increased to support the additional load.

Figure 305 shows a centre for an equilateral arch which is traditionally called a Gothic arch. The centre is made up from two whole ribs joined at the bottom by 50 mm × 150 mm bearers and around the curve by plywood lagging. Cross-braces are fixed to the struts to provide rigidity.

Note: Open or closed timber laggings could be used depending on the type of work in hand.

Remember, in general plywood or closed timber laggings are used for brickwork and open timber laggings for stonework. Instead of using timber posts and folding wedges, the centre is supported by adjustable steel props. Before striking the centre, the props should be gradually eased until the arch takes up the load of the structure.

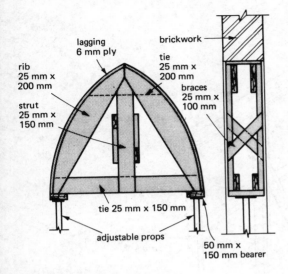

Figure 305   *Equilateral arch centre*

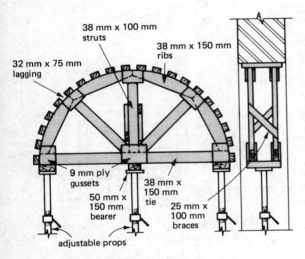

Figure 306   *Semicircular arch centre*

Figure 306 shows a modern arch centre which is suitable for spans up to 3 m. The method of making up this centre is very similar to a trussed rafter. The components are butt jointed together and secured by nailing plywood gussets or nail plates on either side. Before assembly the timber used should be prepared and individual ribs pre-cut to a template. The ribs should be assembled over an outline of the centre which has been marked out on the workshop floor. This ensures that the ribs are made up to the required shape.

Note: When setting out the ribs, an allowance must be made for the thickness of the laggings.

Once the ribs have been assembled, the laggings, bearers and braces can be nailed in position.

Note: Large span centres require an additional intermediate prop in order to support the increased load.

The setting out of variously shaped arch outlines is covered in Chapter 8 of this book. A centre for all of these shapes can be made up using the gusset plate method.

Hoardings

These are, in effect, screens which shield from public view for various reasons, e.g. protection, safety, security and aesthetics, areas such as wastelands, allotments, demolition sites and building sites.

Figure 307 shows the rear view of a typical hoarding. It is constructed using panels which are framed up in sections from 50 mm × 100 mm timbers, and sheeted with 18 mm WBP plywood. These panels are secured at their base by 50 mm × 50 mm stakes, which are driven approximately 600 mm into the ground. Braces are fixed to the tops of the panels to hold them plumb. These braces are also fixed at their bottom end, to 50 mm × 50 mm stakes. Where the hoarding is adjacent to a scaffold, the stakes and braces can be omitted and the panels fixed back to the scaffold using hooks and bolts. Viewing screens are sometimes incorporated in the hoarding to give the public a view of the building works that are going on behind it. Where there is the possibility of a large amount of public interest in the building, which could result in congestion on the pavement, a short set-back in the hoarding could be formed to create a viewing area. If access is required through the hoarding, this can be provided by including a wicket gate in the panel as shown. For vehicular access, several panels could be hinged to form a large pair of gates.

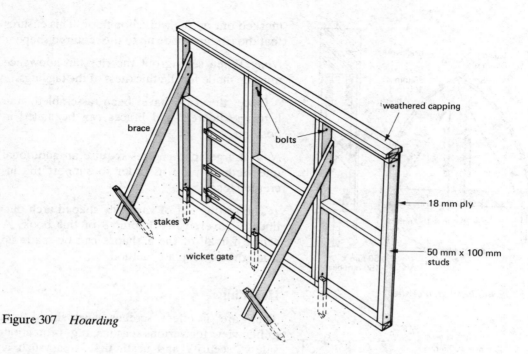

Figure 307   *Hoarding*

Figure 308 shows a temporary footpath which must be used in conjunction with the hoarding when the pavement is partially blocked.

Figure 309 shows a slip-proof ramp that should be formed at either end of the footpath to give pedestrians easy access. The provision, sizes and details of hoardings for particular situations is at the discretion of the highways officer from the local authority, from whom a permit to erect a hoarding must be obtained.

Boundary fences

Timber fences can be classified into two main types. These are:

Open-boarded fences. These define the boundary by providing a visual barrier.
Close-boarded fences. These, as well as defining the boundary, also provide a certain amount of privacy and security.

Preserving fences

All timber which is used for fencing must be preservative-treated. This is done by steeping the fencing material in creosote. Where the fence is

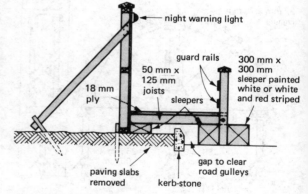

Figure 308   *Hoarding with a temporary footpath*

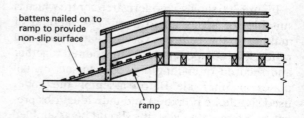

Figure 309   *Ramp to temporary footpath*

to have a painted finish, e.g. small picket or ranch-type fences, the timber should be treated with a preservative that is capable of receiving a paint finish. The preservative treatment of the posts is particularly important, as untreated or ineffectively treated timber that is in contact with the ground will rot in a very short space of time. It is often for this reason that oak posts are used, but even so these must still be treated. This can be done by coating the bottom part of the post with bitumen, thereby forming a weatherproof skin. In order to keep the timber posts clear of the ground, or where the posts of existing fences have rotted through at ground level, they may be repaired by bolting to a short concrete spur post, that has been concreted behind the timber post (see Figure 310).

Different fences

Figure 311 shows a modern ranch stile fence which consists of 25 mm × 150 mm boards screwed to the face of the 75 mm × 75 mm posts. The matching gate is made in a similar way, using two stiles and a brace.

Figure 312 shows a simple picket fence which consists of 75 mm × 75 mm posts, 50 mm × 75 mm weathered edge rails and 25 mm × 75 mm shaped top pickets or paling.

Note: The rails are mortised and pinned into the posts.

Figure 313 shows a close-boarded fence. This is made up from 100 mm × 100 mm or 100 mm × 125 mm posts, 75 mm triangular arris rails and 19 mm × 100 mm feather-edge boarding. Fences up to 1.2 m in height require two arris rails and for fences above this and up to 1.8 m, three are required. The capping and gravel board are often omitted on cheaper work, but this is a false economy as their purpose is to prevent moisture absorption into the end grain of the feather-edge boarding, which if allowed to take place would quickly result in decay.

Note: The boarding should overlap by about 20 mm and be fixed by one nail in each rail. Care must be taken to ensure the nails do not go through two boards where they overlap.

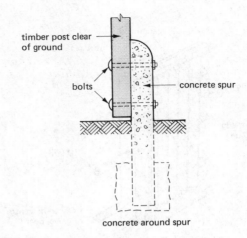

Figure 310   *Concrete spur*

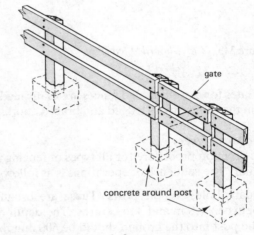

Figure 311   *Ranch stile fence*

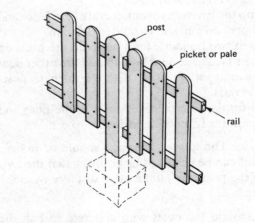

Figure 312   *Picket fence*

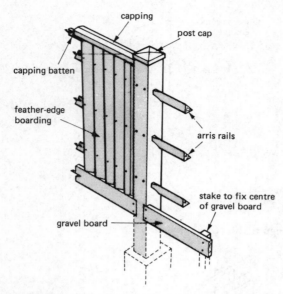

Figure 313   *Close-boarded fence*

Gates for close-boarded fences are usally made up in the same way as ledged and braced doors.

Erection of fences

The erection procedure for all types of fencing is similar. The sequence of operations is as follows:

Prepare holes for the posts. These are usually between 1.8 m and 3 m centres. The depth of the post into the ground should be 600 mm for fences up to 1.2 m in height and 750 mm for fences up to 1.8 m.

Plumb the two posts at either end of the fence and temporarily brace, to hold in position.

Stretch two builder's lines between the posts on their face, one near the top and the other near the bottom. Position the intermediate posts and rails.

Line up the intermediate posts to the lines and temporarily brace in position.

Note: The tops of the posts should be in line. This can be achieved by ensuring that the tops of the posts are all the same distance from the top line.

Fill around the posts with concrete to half the depth of the hole and allow to cure. Fill the

remainder of the hole with earth, ramming as the filling proceeds.

Fix gravel board, boarding and capping, using 50 mm galvanized nails.

Note: The last two steps are often reversed, but it is preferable, especially on close-boarded fences, to allow the concrete to cure first. This is because, once boarded, the fence can be subject to wind loads which could loosen the posts before the concrete has cured.

Formwork for concrete

As stated in *Carpentry and Joinery for Building Craft Students 1,* formwork is a temporary structure which is designed to shape and support wet concrete until it cures sufficiently to become self-supporting. This can be done using one of two methods:

Pre-cast Where the product is cast out of location on site or in a factory and later placed in its final location.

In-situ cast Where the product is cast in the actual location or position where it is required.

Pre-cast moulds

Illustrated in Figure 314 is a concrete sill which has been pre-cast. The easiest way to cast this sill is upside down in a rectangular mould box. In-fill pieces are used to form the required shape. A section through the mould box is shown in Figure

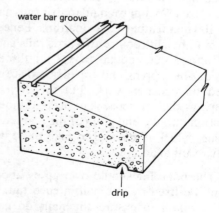

Figure 314   *Pre-cast concrete sill*

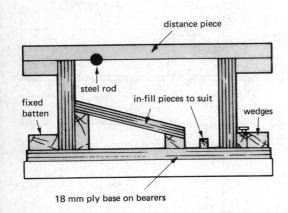

Figure 315   *Section through a mould box*

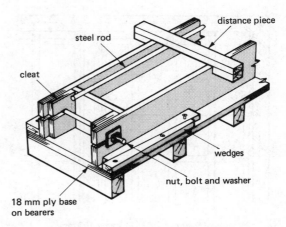

Figure 316   *Mould box for pre-cast concrete*

315. The weathering and the water bar groove are formed with ply and timber in-fill pieces and the drip groove is made by pressing a length of steel re-inforcing rod into the freshly poured concrete.

Note: In order to avoid a distorted sill, the base must be levelled before the mould is assembled.

Figure 316 is an isometric view of part of the sill mould box showing the method of construction. Bolts are used to hold the sides of the mould together and for easy removal the hole for these bolts can be slotted. Cleats are screwed to the sides to locate the plywood ends. The sides are prevented from spreading by the batten which is fixed to the base along one side, and long folding wedges fixed to the other. Distance pieces are used to prevent spreading on the top edge. Where a large number of identical items are required, mould boxes can be made to cast more than one item at a time. These moulds are called gang moulds. Figure 317 is an isometric view of a part of a gang mould which is used for casting two concrete lintels at a time. The concrete must be poured steadily into both sides of the mould to avoid deflecting the centre division.

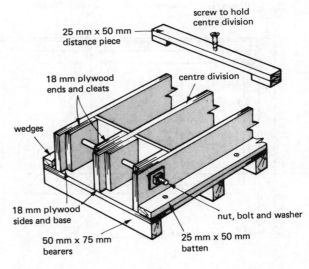

Figure 317   *Gang mould*

In-situ formwork

When floors or roof slabs are cast, they require a temporary decking. This usually consists of either plywood, joists and ledgers supported on adjustable steel props, or various proprietary steel formwork systems which have been developed by a number of companies. In this chapter the first method is considered. The steel formwork systems being covered in CGLI Part 3: Advanced Craft.

Figure 318 shows a part plan and a vertical section of a floor decking. It consists of 75 mm × 150 mm ledgers spaced at 1.5 m centres and supported by adjustable steel props.

Note: Timber props, headtrees and folding wedges which were at one time used to support

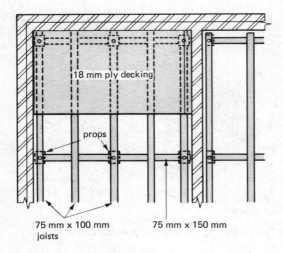

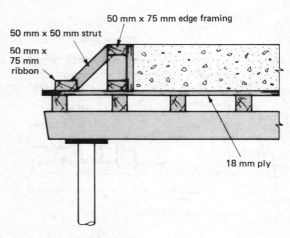

Figure 319   *Edge detail*

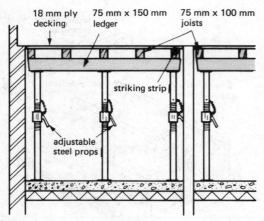

Figure 318   *Formwork for decking*

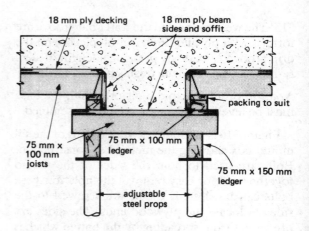

Figure 320   *Drop beam detail*

decking have now been almost exclusively replaced.

The 75 mm × 100 mm joists are laid out on the ledgers at 400 mm centres to carry the 18 mm plywood decking. Where sheets fit between brickwork it is usual to include a narrow striking piece along the wall. This aids striking and prevents the sheet being trapped between the walls.

The props used to support large areas of decking may need to be tied and braced to prevent lateral movement. This can be done using scaffold tubes and clips.

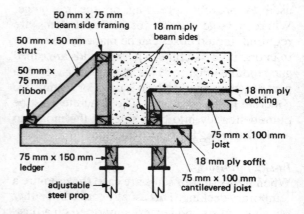

Figure 321   *Edge beam detail*

Note: The spacing of the props, ledgers and joists will vary depending on the loads and pressures to be placed on the formwork.

Figure 319 shows how a slab may be finished at an open edge. The edge, which sits on top of the decking is framed up from 50 mm × 75 mm timbers and strutted in position off the 50 mm × 75 mm ribbon with 50 mm × 50 mm struts. The ends of the struts are shown bird's-mouthed over the edge framing and ribbon, but in practice these are often cut square.

Figures 320 and 321 show details of the formwork required where beams are incorporated in the slab.

Figure 320 shows a drop beam which is in the centre of a slab. The beam soffit is made up of 18 mm plywood, 75 mm × 100 mm joists and 75 mm × 100 mm ledgers and supported by adjustable steel props. The ends of the main joists are supported by the beam soffit. These are packed off a 75 mm × 100 mm ledger to the required height.

Note: The ends of the joists are splayed so that one end can be dropped when striking without binding.

Figure 321 shows the detail of an edge beam. The joists which support the beam soffit have been cantilevered out so that the beam side may be strutted. The cantilevered joists are often necessary at upper floor levels where no bearing is available for the base of the adjustable steel props.

Sequence of operations
The sequence of operations for the erection of the decking for a floor slab is as follows:

Erect and level the beam ledgers, beam joist and beam soffits.
Erect and level other ledgers, joists and decking.
Fix and strut the beam sides and edges.

Sweep out the forms and coat all surfaces that will be in contact with the concrete with a mould oil or another suitable release agent.

The procedure for striking is normally the reverse of the erection, but care must be taken to avoid collapse. Before striking, adjustable props can be put directly under each decking sheet to hold it in position while the ledgers and joists are removed.

Figure 322 shows a column box form. This is made up in four separate sections using 50 mm × 100 mm timbers and 18 mm plywood. These sections are held together with steel column clamps and the whole column is plumbed up and held in position by an adjustable steel prop on each side. A small pocket is often cut in the bottom of one form to enable the box to be cleaned out before the concrete is poured.

Note: The column clamps are closer together at the bottom because of the increased pressure of

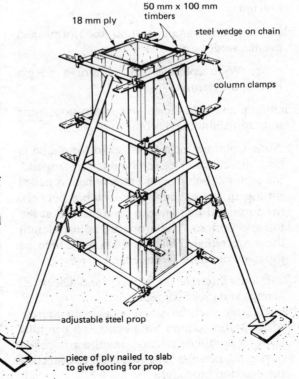

Figure 322   *Column formwork*

the concrete on the forms. The clamps should also alternate to avoid twisting the column.

Before a column box can be erected a kicker must be cast at its base. This is a small upstand of concrete, the same size as the finished column. Its purpose is to locate the bottom of the form and prevent any concrete grout escaping.

Figure 323 shows a typical kicker box for a column. When it is being cast it can be held in the required position by notching battens around the reinforcement starter bars and nailing the battens to the edge of the box (see Figure 324). The sequence of operations for the erection of a column box is as follows:

Make up and cast the kicker. This should be at least twenty-four hours before casting the column.

Make up, coat contact surfaces with a mould oil and stand up the column forms around the kicker.

Note: The steel reinforcement cage must be fixed in position before the column forms are erected.

Place column cramps around the forms and evenly 'wedge up'.

Note: Wide columns will require a noggin behind the clamps.

Plumb up and hold the column in position, using four adjustable steel props.

Note: Columns must be checked for plumb in both directions. This can be done by suspending a plumb bob from a batten which is nailed on top of the column. The distance between the form and the line can be measured at the top and bottom. The props are adjusted until these are equal. This plumbing must then be repeated on the adjacent edge.

Clean out through the pocket and check all clamps and props for tightness.

Immediately after the concrete has been poured, recheck the column for plumb and carefully adjust if required, as it may have been knocked during the pouring. The striking is a reversal of the erection procedure.

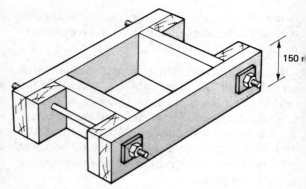

Figure 323   *Kicker box for column*

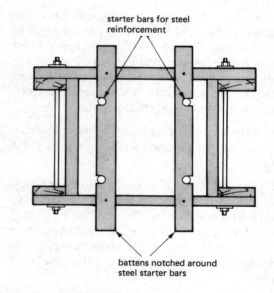

starter bars for steel reinforcement

battens notched around steel starter bars

Figure 324   *Locating a kicker box*

Figure 325 shows the section through the formwork to a concrete wall. This consists of panels which are made from 50 mm × 100 mm timber and 18 mm plywood. The panels are joined and held in line by 50 mm × 100 mm walings that run the complete length of the wall. The two wall forms are kept a constant distance apart by the use of bolts, wall ties and hardwood cones.

Note: When the formwork is removed the tie will remain in the concrete. The hole left where the cone is removed should be filled with grout.

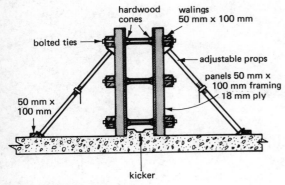

Figure 325 *Wall formwork*

Adjustable steel props are used to plumb up and hold the forms in position.

Note: As with columns, walls also require a kicker to be cast before the panels are erected. Large or high walls can be cast in a number of lifts usually about 2 m in height at a time. The forms for the second lift are bolted to the top ties left in the wall from the first lift. When this method is used it is known as climbing forms.

Striking of formwork

The time between the pouring of the concrete and the striking of the formwork varies widely. This depends on the following:

the type of formwork, e.g. wall, column, slab or beam;
the concrete used and the type of surface finish required;
the weather conditions and exposure of the site.

No formwork must be removed until the concrete has cured sufficiently for it to be self-supporting and capable of carrying any loads imposed upon it.

Vertical surfaces such as walls, columns and beam sides, etc., can in very good weather be struck as little as nine hours after pouring. Horizontal surfaces normally require a much longer time and this can be up to twenty-eight days in poor winter weather. It is usual after striking horizontal formwork to re-prop the concrete in strategic positions for up to a further fourteen days.

Note: After striking it is good practice for economic as well as safety reasons, to clean, de-nail, repair and store under cover, ready for re-use, all formwork material. In addition all props, clamps and bolts, etc., should be cleaned, lubricated and coated with a rust inhibitor.

Self-assessment questions

1 A gravel board is used on a close-boarded fence to:
  (a) line up the posts
  (b) ensure that the posts are correctly spaced
  (c) keep the fence boards clear of the ground
  (d) provide a fixing for the board

2 A large opening for a shop front is to be made in the front wall of a structurally sound building. To provide support to the structure during the alteration work, it will be necessary to:
  (a) erect a hoarding
  (b) erect a flying shore
  (c) block off the opening
  (d) erect a vertical shore

3 What is the purpose of a kicker in concrete construction work?
  (a) It locates and provides a bearing for the column clamps.
  (b) It locates the form and prevents the escape of grout.
  (c) It enables a column to be levelled and plumbed.
  (d) It joins the starter bars and steel reinforcement cage.

4 The purpose of a sole plate which is used in shoring work is to:
  (a) distribute the load evenly over a large area
  (b) provide a fixing point for the various components
  (c) allow the shores to be easily levelled
  (d) keep the bottom of the shores in line

5 In shoring, the component that penetrates into the wall and locates the top of the raker is a:
   (a) cleat
   (b) needle
   (c) wall hook
   (d) wallpiece

6 Mould oil is used on formwork as a:
   (a) lubrication oil
   (b) waterproofing
   (c) rust inhibitor
   (d) release agent

7 A fence is to be erected around the boundary of a property to provide privacy and an amount of security. The most suitable type to use would be a:
   (a) close-boarded fence
   (b) tall ranch stile fence
   (c) chain-link fence and barbed wire
   (d) picket fence

8 The term 'in-situ' concrete refers to concrete that has been cast:
   (a) at a factory
   (b) in a mould box
   (c) in its location
   (d) in large units

9 The following operations have to be carried out when erecting a column box.
   (1) plumb up
   (2) cast kicker
   (3) fix clamps
   (4) apply mould oil
   (5) stand up forms

   The correct sequence for carrying out these operations is
   (a) 5, 4, 3, 2, 1
   (b) 2, 4, 5, 3, 1
   (c) 2, 5, 4, 3, 1
   (d) 2, 4, 5, 1, 3

10 The angle between the raker and the sole plate of a raking shore should be:
   (a) 90 – 95 degrees
   (b) 80 – 85 degrees
   (c) 95 – 100 degrees
   (d) 75 – 80 degrees

Drawing practice and geometry

After reading this chapter the student should be able to:

1 Prepare drawings to show various geometrical constructions, including plans, elevations, sections and developments, involving polygons, prisms, pyramids, cylinders and cones.

2 Set out a true and an approximate ellipse using different methods.

3 Determine the centres for, and draw the outlines of, common arches.

4 Determine the lengths and angles for hipped, double and valley roof members using geometrical methods and the roofing square.

5 Identify and draw various Roman and Grecian mouldings.

6 Determine from a given section required, enlarged or reduced mouldings.

7 Determine the true shapes and angles required for splayed work.

8 Apply geometric principles to solve practical problems.

Polygons

A polygon is a plane figure which is bounded by more than four straight lines. Polygons may be classified as either:

Regular These have sides of the same length and equal angles.
Irregular These have sides of differing lengths and unequal angles.

Both regular and irregular polygons are further classified by the number of sides which they consist of. The main ones which the carpenter and joiner may encounter are shown in Figure 326.

A shows a pentagon which consists of five sides.
B shows a hexagon which consists of six sides.
C shows a heptagon which consists of seven sides.
D shows an octagon which consists of eight sides.

Some other polygons not illustrated are the:

nonagon which consists of nine sides.

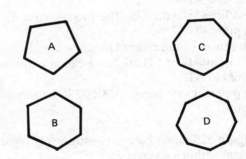

Figure 326   *Polygons*

decagon which consists of ten sides.
undecagon which consists of eleven sides.
duodecagon which consists of twelve sides.

Construction
Figure 327 shows how to construct any regular polygon, given the length of one side.

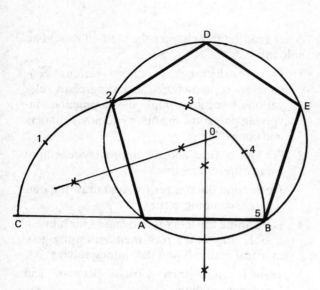

Figure 327   *Constructing a regular polygon*

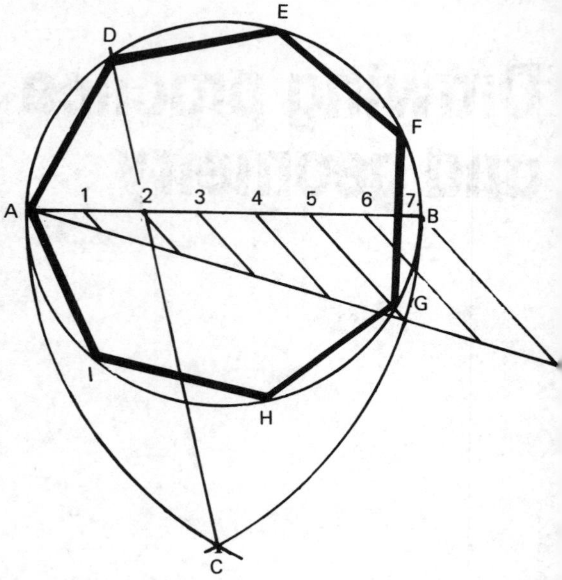

Figure 328   *Constructing a regular polygon within a circle*

Draw line AB to given length.

With centre A and radius AB, draw semicircle CB.

Divide semicircle CB into a number of parts equal to the number of sides required in the polygon (in this example five).

Draw side A2

Bisect lines A2 and AB. The two bisectors cross at point O.

With centre O and radius OA draw a circle.

Mark points D and E on the circle, at a distance equal to AB.

Join points up as shown. ABED2 is the required figure.

Figure 328 shows how to construct any regular polygon within a given circle.

Draw the given circle and mark diameter AB.

Divide AB into a number of parts equal to the number of sides required in the polygon (in this example seven).

With centres A and B and radius AB, draw two arcs to cross at C.

Draw a line from C through 2 to touch circle at D.

Mark points E, F, G, H and I on the circle at a distance apart equal to AD.

Join points up as shown. ADEFGHI is the required figure.

Figure 329 shows how to circumscribe a given circle with any regular polygon.

Draw the given circle with centre O.

Draw radius O1.

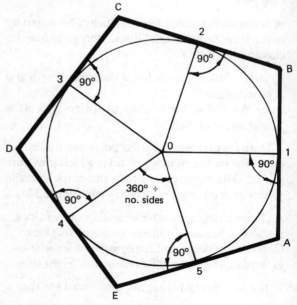

Figure 329   *Circumscribing a given circle*

Divide 360 degrees by the number of sides of the polygon, to obtain the internal angle. (In this example the circle is to be circumscribed with a pentagon. The internal angle is therefore, 360 degrees ÷ 5 = 72 degrees.)

Using a protractor. mark angles of 72 degrees around the circle. (Angles 102, 203, 304, 405 and 501.)

Draw lines to touch the circumference at right angles (tangential) to O1, O2, O3, O4, O5. ABCDE is the required figure.

Note: The angles of hexagons, octagons and duo-decagons may be marked out with the use of 60, 45 or 30 degree set squares respectively.

Figure 330 shows how to construct a regular octagon within a given square.

Draw the given square, ABCD.

Draw the diagonals. (Diagonals cross at centre point O.)

With centres A, B, C and D, with radius AO, draw four arcs cutting the square.

Join up the points of intersection between the arcs and the square as shown, to give the required octagon.

The ellipse

An ellipse is a plane figure bounded by a continuous curved line described about two points called foci. An ellipse is derived from a section of cylinder or cone made by a cutting plane inclined to the axis of the solid.

The major axis of an ellipse is its longest diameter. The minor axis is its shortest diameter and it bisects the major axis at right angles.

There are many methods by which an ellipse may be drawn, a number of which are covered in the following figures.

Figure 331 shows an ellipse drawn using the trammel method.

Draw major and minor axes AB and CD.

Make trammel from a strip of card. Mark points so that 1 – 3 is equal to ½ major axis and 2 – 3 is equal to ½ minor axis.

Move trammel so that point 1 travels on the

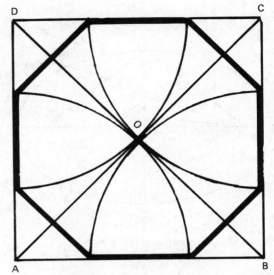

Figure 330 *Constructing a regular octagon within a square*

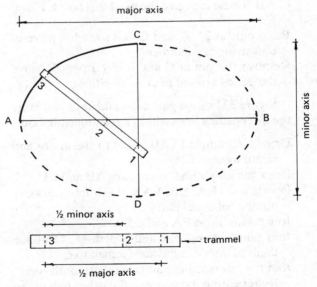

Figure 331 *Trammel method of drawing an ellipse*

minor axis and point 2 travels on the major axis. Mark off at suitable intervals point 3.

Join the point 3 marks to draw an ellipse.

Figure 332 shows an ellipse drawn using the foci pins and string method.

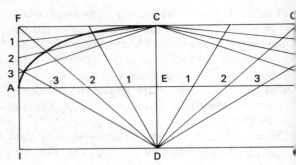

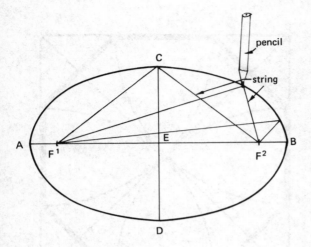

Figure 332   *Foci pins and string method*

Figure 333   *Intersecting lines method*

Draw major and minor axes AB and CD.

With centre C and radius AE, mark two arcs on AB. These arcs give the two focal points F^1 and F^2.

Place pins at F^1, F^2 and C and stretch a piece of taut string around them.

Remove the pin at C and insert a pencil. Move the pencil around to draw an ellipse.

Figure 333 shows part of an ellipse drawn using the intersecting lines within a rectangle method.

Draw a rectangle FGHI equal to the major and minor axes.

Draw the major and minor axes AB and CD.

Divide lines EA, EB, FA and GB into the same number of equal parts.

Join points along FA and GB to C.

Join points along EA and EB to D. Continue them to intersect the lines joined to C.

Join the intersecting points with a smooth curve. By repeating the process, the other half of the ellipse can be drawn.

Figure 334 shows an ellipse drawn with the aid of two circles.

Draw two concentric circles with diameters equal to the major and minor axes.

Divide the circumference of the larger circle into twelve equal parts. Join these points to the centre of the circle.

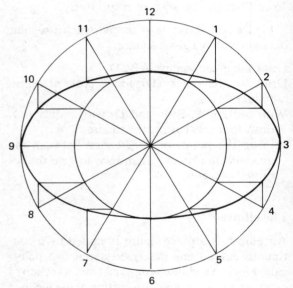

Figure 334   *Concentric circles method*

Note: The circle can be divided into twelve parts with the aid of a 30, 60 degree set square.

Draw vertical lines from the points on the outer circle and draw horizontal lines from the points on the inner circle.

A smooth curve can be drawn through the intersection of the vertical and horizontal lines to form the required ellipse.

Figure 335 shows part of an ellipse drawn using another method of intersecting lines within a rectangle.

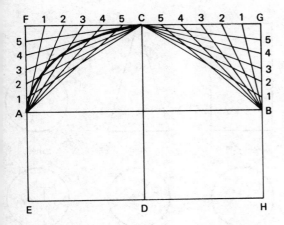

Figure 335 *Alternative intersecting lines method*

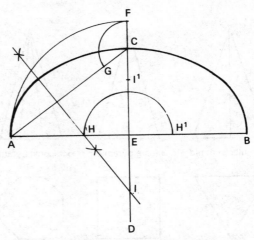

Figure 336 *False ellipse drawn using compasses*

Draw rectangle EFGH with sides equal to the major and minor axes.

Draw the major and minor axes AB and CD.

Divide lines AF, FC, GC and BG in to the same number of equal parts.

Join the points on FC to A, points on GC to B and points on AF and BG to C.

Join the points where the same numbered lines intersect with a smooth curve. By repeating the process, the other half of the ellipse can be drawn.

Figure 336 shows part of a figure which resembles an ellipse drawn using compasses. This shape is also known as a false ellipse.

Draw the major and minor axes AB and CD.

Draw line AC.

With centre E and radius AE, draw arc AF.

With centre C and radius CF, draw arc FG.

Bisect line AG to give points H and I.

With centre E and radius EH, draw an arc to give H^1.

With centres H, H^1 and I, draw arcs to give the semi-ellipse. The other half of the ellipse can be completed by drawing arcs with centres H, H^1 and I^1.

Geometric solids

Solid geometry deals with three-dimensional objects having length, width and thickness.

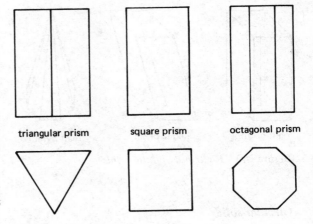

Figure 337 *Prisms*

Prisms

A prism is a solid figure contained by plane surfaces which are parallel to each other. All prisms are named according to the shape of their bases. Figure 337 shows the plan and elevation of a number of prisms.

Pyramids

A pyramid is a solid figure contained by a base and triangular sloping sides. These sides meet at a point called the apex. All pyramids are also named according to their bases. Figure 338 shows the plan and elevation of a number of pyramids.

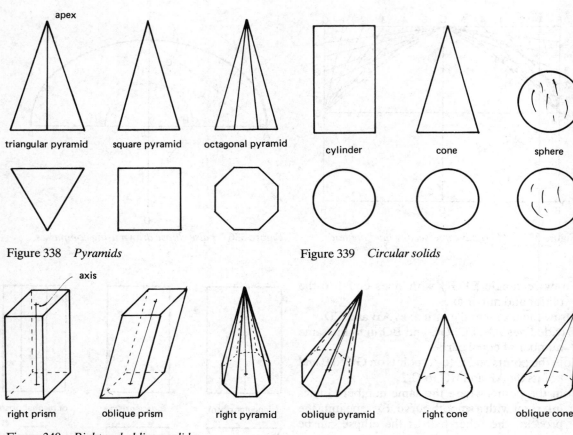

Figure 338   *Pyramids*

Figure 339   *Circular solids*

Figure 340   *Right and oblique solids*

Circular solids

Cylinder

A cylinder is a solid figure described by the revolution of a rectangle about one of its sides which remains fixed and is called its axis. The bases or ends of a cylinder are circular in shape.

Cone

A cone is a solid figure described by the revolution of a right-angled triangle about one of its sides, which remains fixed and is called its axis. The base of a cone is circular in shape.

Sphere

A sphere is a solid figure described by the revolution of a semicircle about its diameter which remains fixed and is called its axis.

Note: All sections of a sphere will be circular in shape.

Figure 339 shows the plan and elevation of a cylinder, cone and sphere.

Figure 340 shows a number of right and oblique solids. Right solids have their central axis vertical, while the central axis in oblique solids is inclined.

Sections

When a solid is cut through, the cut surface is called a section. A solid that has had its top cut off is called a truncated solid. The remaining portion is called the frustum of the solid.

The following figures deal with the true shape of the section of the frustum of a solid.

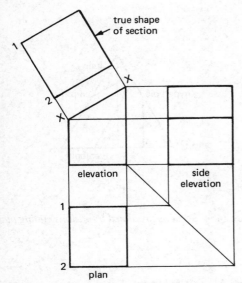

Figure 341   *True section of the frustum of a rectangular prism*

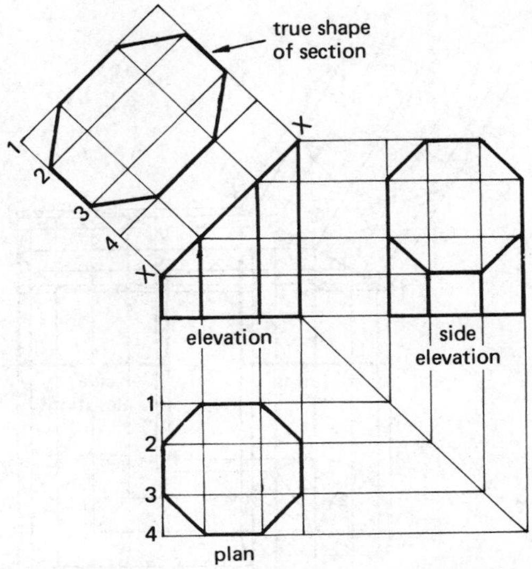

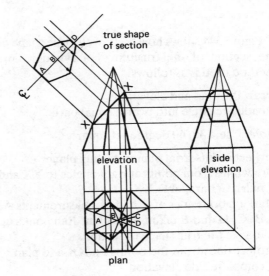

Figure 342   *True section of the frustum of an octagonal prism*

Figure 341 shows how to draw the true shape of the section of the frustum of a rectangular prism. The method used is as follows:

Draw the plan and elevation as shown.
Draw lines at right angles from the cutting plane XX
Mark width of section 1–2 taken from plan. This gives the true shape of section.

Figure 342 shows how to draw the true shape of the section of the frustum of an octagonal prism. The method used is the same as that used for the frustum of a rectangular prism, except that in the third step points 1, 2, 3 and 4 have to be transferred from the plan to the section.

Figure 343 shows how to draw the true shape of the section of the frustum of an octangonal pyramid. The method used is as follows:

Draw the plan and elevations of the complete pyramid.
Draw the cutting plane XX and project vertical lines from the edges on the cut section down to the same edge on the plan. This gives the points to draw the plan of the section.
Draw lines from points at right angles to XX and mark ₵ parallel to XX.

Figure 343   *True section of the frustum of an octagonal pyramid*

Mark on both sides of ₵ half of measurements A, B, C and D taken from section on plan. Join points up to give the true shape of section.
Project lines from the points on XX and section on plan to complete side elevation.

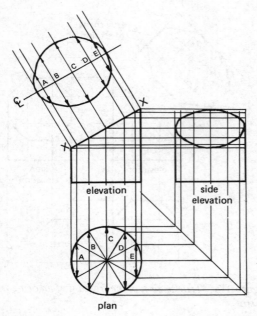

Figure 344 *True section of the frustum of a cylinder*

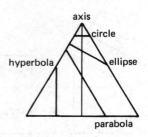

Figure 345 *Sections produced by various cutting planes*

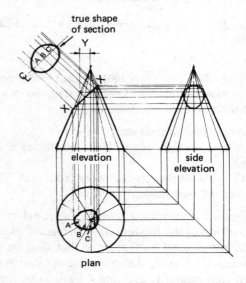

Figure 346 *True section of the frustum of a cone*

Figure 344 shows how to draw the true shape of the section of the frustum of a cylinder. The method used is as follows:

Draw the plan and elevations.
Divide the circle into twelve equal parts.

Note: Use a 30, 60 degree set square.

Project points from plan to cutting plane.
Draw lines from points at right angles to XX and mark ₵ parallel to XX.
Mark on both sides of ₵ half of measurements A, B, C, D and E taken from plan. Join points up to give the true shape of section.
Project lines from the points on XX and plan to complete side elevation.

Sections of cones
Figure 345 shows a cone with four cutting planes marked on it. The true shapes of the sections on these cutting planes are shown in Table 8.

Figure 346 shows how to draw the true shape of the section of the frustum of a cone. The method is as follows:

Table 8

Section	Produced by a cutting plane
Circle	at right angles to the axis
Ellipse	inclined to the axis and touching both slanting sides
Parabola	parallel to one slanting side
Hyperbola	parallel to the axis

Draw the plan and elevations of the complete cone.

Divide the circle into twelve equal parts and project lines up to the base of cone.

Join each of the points on the base to the apex (top of the cone) with radiating lines.

Mark the cutting plane XX and project vertical lines down from the points on XX where the radiating lines cut it, onto the corresponding lines on the plan. Join the points to give the plan of section.

Note: The width of the centre line is found by taking twice the length of line Y on the elevation. Line Y is the radius for the axis on the cutting plane to the edge of the cone.

Draw lines from points at right angles to XX and mark ₵ parallel to XX.

Mark on both sides of ₵ half of measurements A, B, C, etc., taken from section on plan. Join points up to give the true shape of section.

Project lines from the points on XX and plan to complete side elevation.

Figure 347 shows how to draw the true shape of section when the cutting plane is parallel to one of its sides. The method used is the same as that used for the previous example of the frustum of a cone.

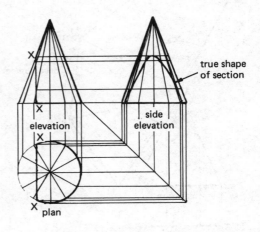

Figure 348   *True shape of a vertical section of a cone*

Figure 348 shows how to draw the true shape of the vertical section of a cone. The method used is as follows:

Draw the plan and elevations showing the cutting plane XX.

Divide the circle into twelve equal parts and project lines up to the base of both elevations of the cone.

Join each of the points on the bases with radiating lines to the apexes.

At the points where radiating lines cut XX on the elevation, project horizontal lines to touch the corresponding radiating lines on the side elevation. Join the points to give the true shape of the section.

Developments

The development of a solid is a drawing of the shape of all the faces of the solid laid out flat in one plane.

Figure 349 shows how to develop the frustum of a square pyramid. The method is as follows:

Draw the plan and elevation of the complete pyramid.

Mark the cutting plane XX and project its edges down onto the plan. Draw section on plan.

With centre O and radius O 1, draw arc to give point 1^1. Project vertically to give point 1^{11}.

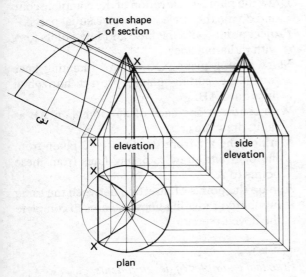

Figure 347   *True section of a cone*

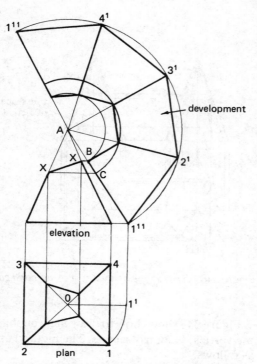

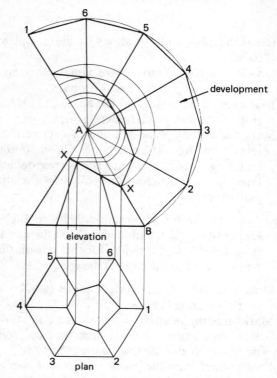

Figure 349 *Development of the frustum of a square pyramid*

Figure 350 *Development of the frustum of a hexagonal pyramid*

Draw line A 1^{11}. This is the true length of the edge.

With centre A and radius A 1^{11}, draw arc. Mark on arc the lengths $1^{11}-2^1$, 2^1-3^1, 3^1-4^1, 4^1-1^{11}.

Note: Lengths of sides are taken from the plan.

Join points on arc to each other and point A. This gives the development of the whole pyramid.

Project horizontally the ends of the cutting plane XX to give points B and C on line A 1^{11}.

With centre A and radii A B and A C, draw arcs to touch the developed edges of the sides.

Join the points of intersection as shown. This gives the required development.

Figure 350 shows how to develop the frustum of a hexagonal pyramid. The method used is similar to that used to develop the frustum of a square pyramid.

Note: Line AB in the elevation is the true length of the edge, so this does not have to be found as it did in the previous example.

Figure 351 shows how to develop the frustum of a cone. The method used is as follows:

Draw the plan and elevation of the complete cone and divide the circle into twelve equal parts.

Project points onto the base and join points to A with radiating lines.

Mark cutting plane XX. Where radiating lines touch the cutting plane, project horizontal lines onto AB.

With centre A and each of the points on AB as radii, draw the arcs.

Mark on the arc from B points 1–12 taken from the plan and draw radiating lines from these points to A.

Join up the points of insertion between the same numbered radiating lines and arcs to complete the development.

Practical examples of developments

Figure 352 shows a part elevation and plan of a

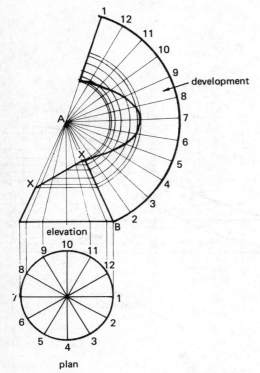

Figure 351   *Development of the frustum of a cone*

hexagonal column which supports an inclined concrete ramp. The problem is to find the true shape of the hole required in the formwork for the soffit of the ramp. This problem is solved using a method similar to that used when drawing the true section of the frustum of a prism.

Figure 353 shows a plan and elevation of two walls A and B which are joined by a skew arch. The problem is to find the true shape of the soffit or lagging required for the arch centre. The method used is as follows:

Divide the semicircle into six parts. This gives points 1–7.

Project points 1–7 down vertically onto the plan to give points $1^1 – 7^1$.

Where vertical lines touch either side of the arch, project lines across horizontally.

Take distances 1–2, 2–3, 3–4, etc. from elevation and mark points $1^{11} – 7^{11}$.

Project points $1^{11} – 7^{11}$ down vertically where the same numbered lines intersect and draw the development of the soffit.

Figure 354 shows a sketch of a house with a dormer window in a pitched roof. The problem is

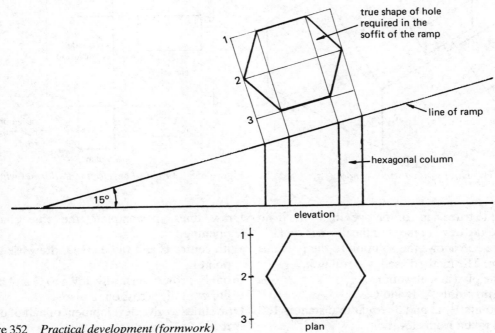

Figure 352   *Practical development (formwork)*

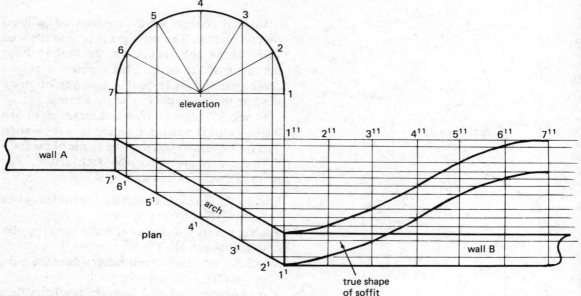

Figure 353 *Practical development (arch centre)*

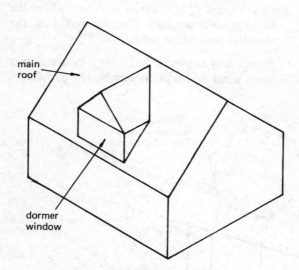

Figure 354 *House with dormer window*

Figure 355 *Practical development (dormer window)*

to find the true shape of the opening in the main roof and the development of the dormer roof.

Figure 355 shows the solution to the previous problem. The method used is as follows:

Draw the plan and elevations.

Project up points A, B and C.

Mark points 1^1, 2^1 and 3^1 equal to distances 1, 2 and 3 taken from elevation.

Draw lines to complete the true shape of opening.

With centre E and radius E D, draw arc to give point F.

From F, project vertically down to G and from G horizontally across on to plan.

Draw lines to give development of half of dormer roof.

Centres for arches

In order to construct a centre for an arch, the carpenter must first set out the outline of the required arch. The setting out of segmental and semicircular arches is covered in *Carpentry and Joinery for Building Craft Students 1*. The setting out for a number of other arch shapes is given in the following figures.

Figure 356 shows the outline of an equilateral Gothic arch. The method used to set out this arch is as follows:

Draw line AB equal to span.
With centres A and B and radius AB, draw arcs to intersect at C.

Note: Triangle ACB is an equilateral triangle.

Figure 357 shows the outline of a drop gothic arch. The method used to set out this arch is as follows:

Draw lines AB and CD equal to the required span and rise.

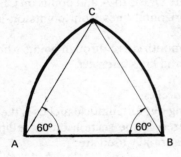

Figure 356   *Equilateral Gothic arch*

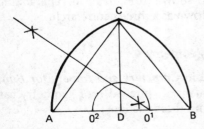

Figure 357   *Drop Gothic arch*

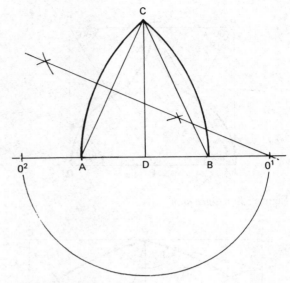

Figure 358   *Lancet arch*

Bisect line AC to give point O^1.
With centre D and radius DO^1, draw arc to give point O^2
With centres O^1 and O^2 and radius O^1A, draw arcs to intersect at C.

Figure 358 shows the outline of a lancet arch. The method used to set out this arch is as follows:

Draw lines AB and CD equal to the required span and rise.
Bisect line AC to give point O^1.
With centre D and radius DO^1, draw arc to give point O^2.
With centres O^1 and O^2 and radius O^1A, draw arcs to intersect at C.

Figure 359 shows the outline of an ogee arch. The method used to set out this arch is as follows:
Draw equilateral triangle AED with base equal to the required span.
Complete rectangle ABCD.
Draw lines from B and C at 60 degrees to give point F.
With centres F,B and C, draw arcs.

Figure 360 shows the outline of a Tudor arch which is also known as a four-centred arch. The method used to set it out is as follows:

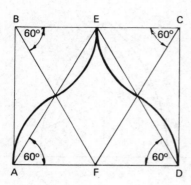

Figure 359   *Ogee arch*

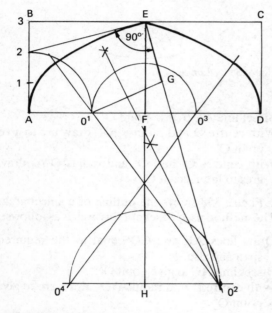

Figure 360   *Tudor arch*

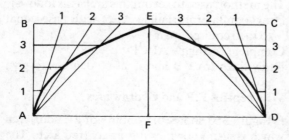

Figure 361   *Parabolic arch*

Draw rectangle ABCD equal to the required span and rise.

Draw vertical line FE from the centre of AD.

Divide AB into three equal parts. Join point 2 to E.

Draw line E O^2 at right angles to line 2E.

Make EG equal to A2.

With centre A and radius A2, draw arch to give O^1.

Draw line O^1G and bisect to give point O^2.

With centre F and radius FO^1, draw arc to give point O^3.

With centre H and radius HO^2, draw arc to give point O4.

With centres O^1, O^2, O^3 and O^4, draw arcs.

Figure 361 shows the outline of a pointed parabolic arch. The method used to set out this arch is as follows:

Draw rectangle ABCD equal to the required span and rise.

Draw vertical line FE from the centre of AD.

Divide lines AB, BE, CE and DC into the same number of equal parts.

Join points on BE to A and points on CE to D.

Draw horizontal lines from points on lines AB and DC.

Draw a smooth curve through points where same numbered lines intersect.

Elliptical arches

The setting out for elliptical arches is the same as that covered in the section on the ellipse. The methods normally used are:

For a true elliptical arch, the trammel method shown in Figure 331;

For an approximate or mock elliptical arch, the method shown in Figure 336. This method is also known as a three centre arch.

Roofing geometry

As stated in *Carpentry and Joinery for Building Craft Students 1*, pitched roof geometry can be divided into three sections:

the development of roof surfaces;
finding the true lengths of rafters, etc.;

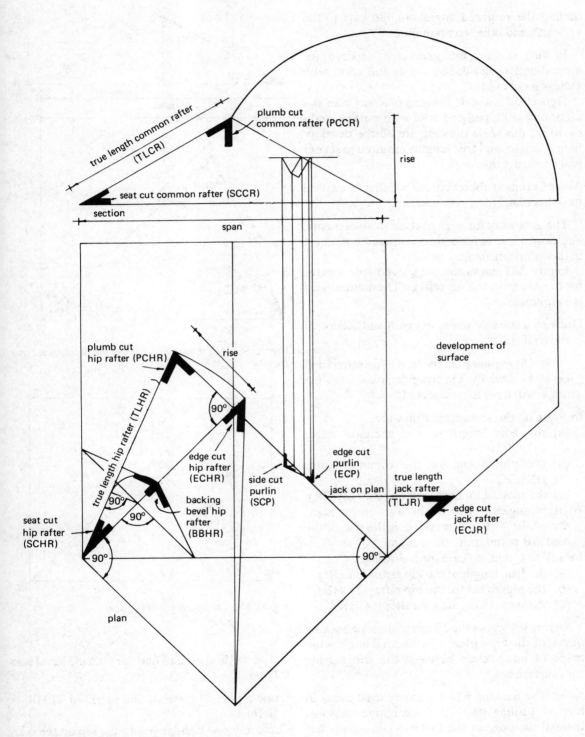

Figure 362 *Roofing angles and true lengths*

finding the required angles for the cuts to the rafters and other components.

In this section the geometry required for hipped-end roofs, double roofs and roofs with valleys is covered.

Figure 362 is a scale drawing of a part plan and section of a hipped-end roof with purlins. Indicated on this scale drawing are all the developments, angles and true lengths required to set out and construct the roof.

Note: Common abbreviations which may be used have been included in brackets.

The geometry for each of these developments, angles and true lengths are considered separately in the following figures.

Figure 363 shows the angles and true lengths for the common and hip rafters. The method used is as follows:

Draw to a suitable scale, the plan and section of the roof.

Note: On regular plan roofs, the hip rafters will be at 45 degrees. On irregular plan roofs the angle will have to be bisected.

Indicate on the section the following:
- (a) the true length of the common rafter (TLCR)
- (b) the plumb cut for the common rafter (PCCR)
- (c) the seat cut for the common rafter (SCCR)

At right angles to one of the hips on the plan, draw line A^1B^1 and mark on it the rise of the roof AB taken from the section.

Join B^1 to C and indicate the following:
- (a) the true length of the hip rafter (TLHR)
- (b) the plumb cut for the hip rafter (PCHR)
- (c) the seat cut for the hip rafter (SCHR)

Figure 364 shows the dihedral angle or backing bevel for the hip rafter. The dihedral angle is the angle of intersection between the two sloping roof surfaces.

Note: The backing bevel is rarely used today in hipped roofing work for economic reasons. Instead the edge of the hip rafter is usually left square.

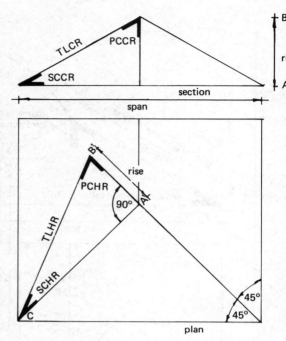

Figure 363   *Common and hip rafters, angles and true lengths*

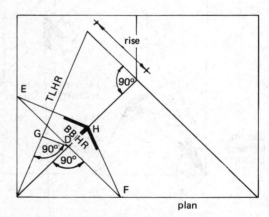

Figure 364   *Hip rafter backing bevel*

The method used to find the backing bevel is as follows:

Draw a plan of the roof and mark on TLHR as before.

Draw a line at right angles to the hip on the plan at D to touch wall plates at E and F.

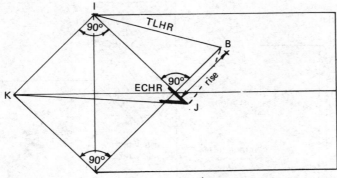

Figure 365 *Hip rafter edge cut*

Draw a line at right angles to TLHR at G to touch point D.

With centre D and radius DG, draw an arc to touch the hip on the plan at H.

Join point E to H and H to F. This gives the required backing bevel (BBHR).

Figure 365 shows the edge cut to the hip rafter. This is applied to both sides to allow it to fit up to the ridge board between the crown and common rafters. The method used to find the edge cut is as follows:

Draw a plan of the roof and mark on TLHR as before.

With centre I and radius IB, swing TLHR down to J. (This makes IJ, TLHR.)

Draw lines at right angles from the ends of the hips and extend the ridge line. All three lines will intersect at K.

Join K to J. Angle IJK is the required edge cut (ECHR).

Figure 366 shows the development of two of the roof surfaces along with the true length of the jack rafters (TLJR) and the edge cut for the jack rafters (ECJR). The edge cut allows the jack rafters to sit up against the hip.

Note: The plumb and seat cuts for the jack rafters are the same as those for the comon rafters. The method used to find the true lengths and edge cut is as follows:

Draw the plan and section of roof. Mark on the plan the jack rafters.

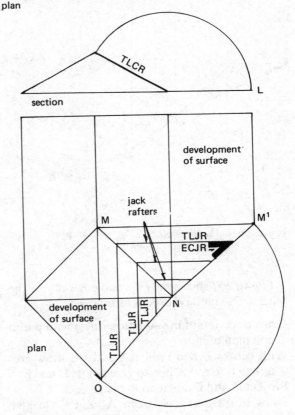

Figure 366 *Roof development*

Develop roof surfaces by swinging TLCR down to L and project down to M¹.

With centre N and radius NM¹, draw arc M¹O. Join points M¹ and O to ends of hips as shown.

Continue jack rafters on to development.

Mark the true length of jack rafter (TLJR) and edge cut for jack rafter (ECJR).

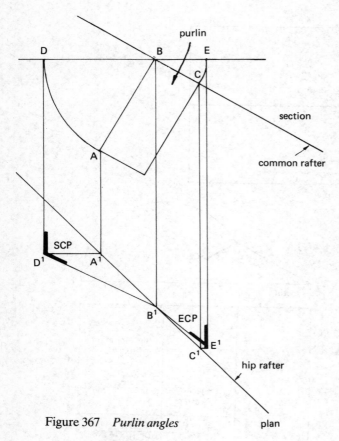

Figure 367   *Purlin angles*

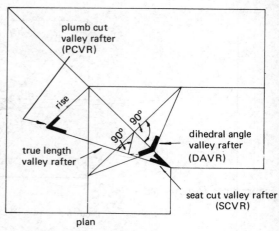

Figure 368   *Valley rafter, true length and angles*

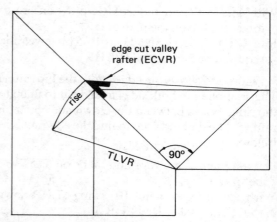

Figure 369   *Valley rafter edge cut*

Figure 367 shows the side and edge cut for the purlin. The method used is as follows:

Draw a section of the common rafter with purlin and plan of hip.

With centre B and radii BA and BC draw arcs onto a horizontal line to give points D and E.

Project D and E down on to plan.

Draw horizontal lines from A^1 and C^1 to give points D^1 and E^1.

Angle DD^1B^1 is the side cut purlin (SCP) and angle B^1E^1E is the edge cut purlin (ECP).

Roofs with valleys

Where two sloping roof surfaces meet at an internal angle, a valley is formed. Figures 368, 369 and 370 show the following:

True length of valley rafter (TLVR)

Plumb and seat cuts for valley rafter (PCVR and SCVR)

Dihedral angle for valley rafter (DAVR)

Edge cut for valley rafter (ECVR)

Part development of one roof surface

True length and edge cut for cripple rafters (TLCrR and ECCrR)

These true lengths and angles can be found by using similar methods as those used for the hip and jack rafters.

Pitch line

The single line used in roof geometry represents

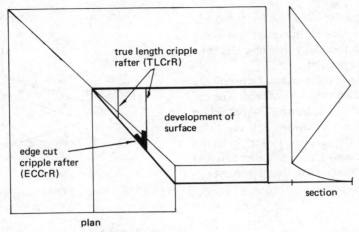

Figure 370 *Cripple rafter, true lengths and edge cut*

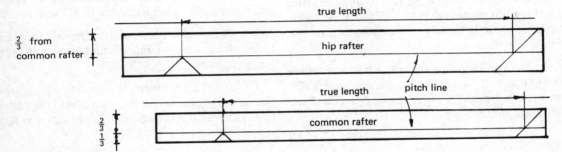

Figure 371 *Setting out rafters*

the pitch line, which is a line marked up from the underside of the common rafter, ⅓ of its depth.

As the hip and valley rafters are usually of deeper section, the pitch line on these is marked down form the top edge at a distance equal to ²/₃ the depth of the common rafter. This is shown in Figure 371.

The true length of the common and hip rafters is measured on the pitch line from the centre line of the ridge to the outside edge of the wall plate. For jack rafters, it is from the centre line of the hip to the outside edge of the wall plate; and for the cripple rafter it is from the centre line of the ridge to the centre line of the valley. Therefore when marking out the true lengths of the roofing components from the single line drawing, an allowance in measurement must be made. This allowance should be an addition for the eaves

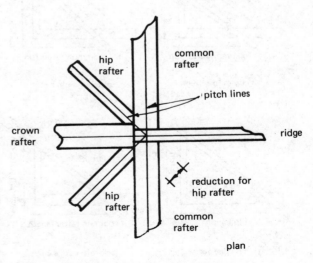

Figure 372 *Reduction for thickness of materials*

overhang and a reduction to allow for the thickness of the components. If this reduction is not apparent, it may be found by drawing the relevant intersecting components.

Figure 372 shows the intersection between the ridge, common, crown and hip rafters. The reduction of the hip rafters is shown. The reduction for the common rafters is always half the ridge thickness and for the crown rafter half the common rafter thickness. These reductions should be marked out at right angles to the plumb cut.

Roofing square

After having covered geometrically the lengths and angles required for hipped, double and valley roofs, the use of the steel square to find the same lengths and angles should be fairly straightforward, as it is merely the application of the geometric principles.

Note: Most roofing squares contain sets of tables on them which give rafter lengths per metre run for standard pitches, although in practice these tables are rarely used.

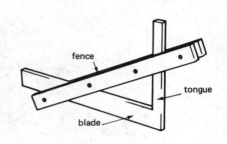

Figure 373   *Roofing square and fence*

Figure 373 shows an outline of the roofing square and its fence. The wide part is the blade and the narrow part the tongue. Both the blade and the tongue are marked out in millimetres.

Note: Most carpenters will make a fence for themselves using two battens and four small bolts and wing nuts.

To set out a roof using the roofing square, the rise of the roof is set on the tongue and the run of the rafter is set on the blade (run of rafter = half

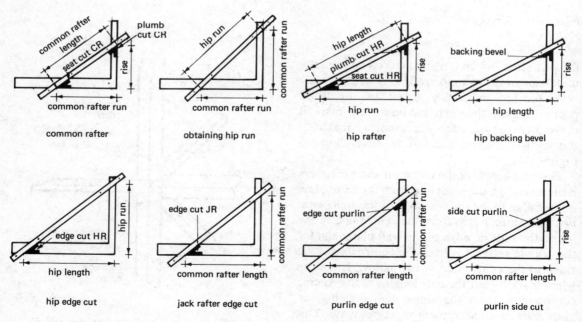

Figure 374   *Setting up a roofing square to obtain various scale lengths and angles*

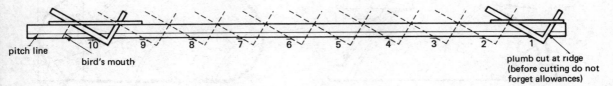

Figure 375 *Using a roofing square*

of the span). But in order to set the rise and run on the roofing square, these measurements must be scaled down and it is usual to divide them by ten.

For example: For a roof with a rise of 2.5 m and a rafter run of 3.5 m, the scale lengths to set on the roofing square would be:

rise 2.5 m ÷ 10 = 250 mm
run 3.5 m ÷ 10 = 350 mm

The illustrations given in Figure 374 show how to set up the roofing square and fence to obtain the required lengths and angles. The lengths will, however, be scale lengths.

Figure 375 shows how the roofing square may be stepped down the rafter ten times to obtain its actual length. Alternatively, the scale length can be measured off the roofing square and multiplied by ten to give its actual length.

Allowances

The roofing square like the geometrical method gives the true lengths of members on the pitch line. Therefore the same allowances in measurement as stated before must be made. The length for the shortest jack rafter can be found by dividing the length of the common rafter by one more than the number of jack rafters on each side of the hip. This measurement is then added to each successive jack rafter to obtain its length. For example, for the roof shown in Figure 376 with three jack rafters on each side of the hip and a common rafter length of say 2.1 m:

Length of short jack (1) = 2.1 m ÷ 4
                          = 525 mm
Length of middle jack (2) = 525 mm + 525 mm
                          = 1.05 m

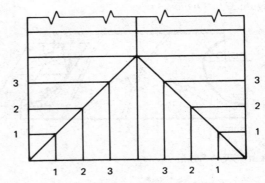

Figure 376 *Calculating jack rafter lengths*

Length of long jack (3) = 1.05 m + 525 mm
                         = 1.575 m

Note: The true lengths and angles for valley and cripple rafters can be found by using the same methods as used for the hip and jack rafters.

Mouldings

Mouldings can be either one of two types. These are:

Roman moulding, which is formed from arcs of circles;
Grecian moulding, which is formed from elliptical, parabolic or hyperbolic curves.

The following figures show various common mouldings on pieces of timber with Roman on the left and Grecian on the right. The setting out should be self-explanatory from the drawings. The Grecian mouldings are normally thought to be more aesthetically pleasing than the Roman mouldings. The proportions of the moulding and type of curve is usually left to the designer.

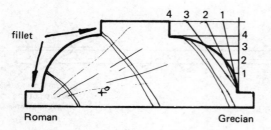

Figure 377   *Ovolo*

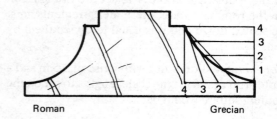

Figure 379   *Torus*

Figure 378   *Scotia*

Figure 380   *Cavetto*

Figure 377 is an ovolo moulding, which is a quarter of a circle and is the reverse shape of the cavetto. Where fillets are not used the moulding is normally called a quadrant.

Figure 378 is a scotia moulding which is formed by two quadrants of different radii giving a concave curve.

Figure 379 is a torus moulding. It is sometimes called a bull-nose or half-round moulding.

Figure 380 is a cavetto moulding which is the reverse shape of the ovolo.

Figure 381 is a cyma-recta moulding on a cornice. This moulding is often called an ogee moulding.

Figure 382 is a cyma-reversa moulding on a cornice. This moulding is also known as a reverse ogee mould.

Figure 383 is an astragal or bead moulding.

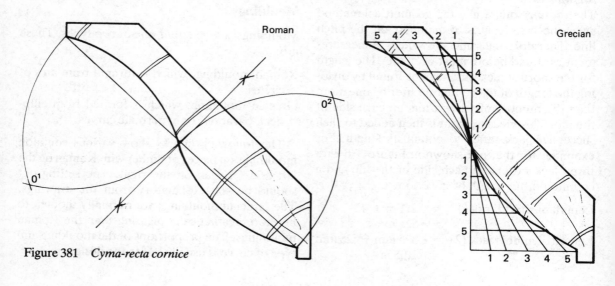

Figure 381   *Cyma-recta cornice*

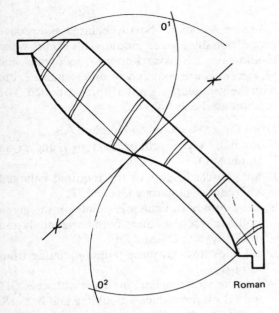

Roman

Figure 382 *Cyma-reversa cornice*

Grecian

Figure 383 *Astragal or bead*

Intersection of moulding

Where two mouldings intersect, the intersection is known as a mitre. When both of the mouldings are the same size, the mitre will be a bisection (half) of the angle of intersection. Two examples of this are shown in Figure 384. The 90 degree angle has 45 degree mitres and the 120 degree angle has 60 degree mitres.

Enlargement and reduction of mouldings

Figure 385 shows how to enlarge or reduce a given moulding in width only, e.g. for use where the architrave over the head of a door is required to be larger or smaller than the jambs. The method used is as follows:

Draw the given mould and the outline of the required mould. Project line to determine the mitre line.

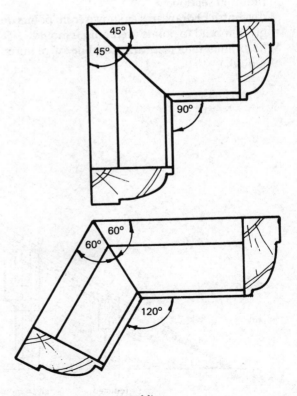

Figure 384 *Mitring mouldings*

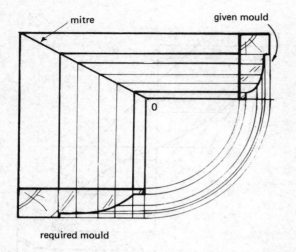

Figure 385   *Enlargement or reduction of a given mould*

Select a number of suitable points on the given mould and project these onto the mitre line.

Draw vertical lines down from mitre onto the required section.

With centre O draw arcs as shown from points on given mould to points on required mould.

Where lines intersect, draw outline of required mould.

Figure 386 shows how to enlarge and reduce proportionally a given mould. This occurs when mouldings such as architraves, dado rails and picture rails are required in different sizes, but with their mouldings similarly proportioned. The method used is as follows:

Draw the given mould on base line AB.

Draw line AA^1 touching the top of the given mould at D.

Draw vertical heights of the required enlarged and reduced moulding GH and JK.

Select a number of suitable points on the given mould and project these both horizontally and vertically onto DC and DF.

Draw lines through these points radiating from point A.

Where the radiating lines intersect with lines GH and GI on the reduced moulding and lines JK and JL on the enlarged moulding, draw lines horizontally and vertically. This then gives the points from which the outlines can be drawn.

Figure 387 shows that when curved and straight mouldings of the same section intersect, there will be a curved mitre. To determine the mitre the following method is used:

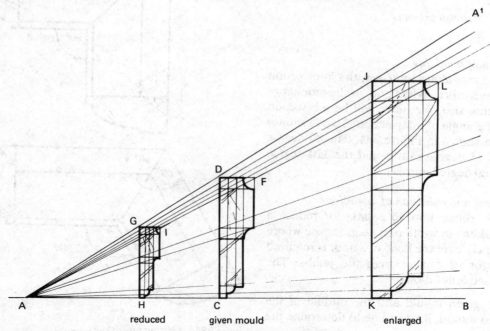

Figure 386   *Proportional enlargement and reduction of a given mould*

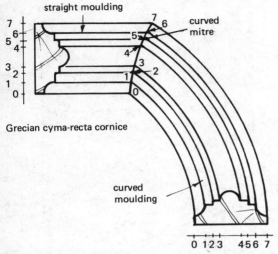

Figure 387 *Intersection of a curved and straight moulding*

Draw the section of the straight moulding and select on it a number of suitable points: 0, 1, 2, 3, 4, 5, 6 and 7.

Draw the section of the curved moulding and mark on it the same points 0, 1, 2, 3, 4, 5, 6 and 7.

From these points, draw lines parallel to the direction of each moulding.

Where the lines intersect draw a smooth curve to give the mitre.

Raking mouldings

When a raking mould and a level mould intersect at a mitre, the sections of the moulds will be different. Figure 388 shows the plan and elevation of a brick pier around which a dado height moulding is to be fixed. The moulding on the face is inclined or raking at 30 degrees. The two return moulds are level. Given the section of the raking mould, the method used to determine the sections of the two level moulds is as follows:

Draw the plan and elevation of the raking mould.

Mark the given raking mould section on the elevation.

Select suitable points on the given mould 1, 2, 3 and 4. Transfer these on to the required moulds as shown.

Where lines intersect, draw the required sections for the top and bottom moulds.

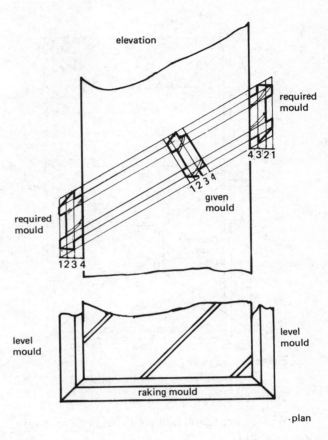

Figure 388 *Raking mouldings*

Splayed work

Hoppers

The following figures illustrate the methods used to find the angles and true shapes required to construct two types of timber hoppers.

Figure 389 shows a plan and section of a square hopper. The method used to find the required information is as follows:

Draw plan and section.

With centre B and radius BA, draw an arc and project down to give A^{11} on the line drawn horizontally from A^1.

Join A^{11} to O, repeat on lower corner and draw the development or true shape of the side.

Angle $A^{IV}A^{11}O$ is the required side bevel.

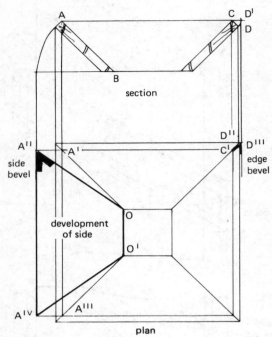

Figure 389   *Square hopper*

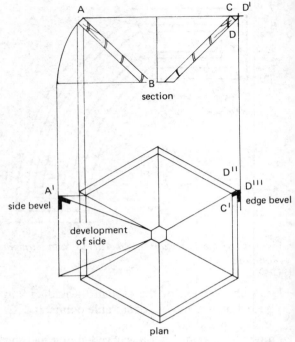

Figure 390   *Hexagonal hopper*

To find the edge bevel or mitre:

With centre C and radius CD, draw an arc to give point D^1.

Project down D^1 to give D^{111} on the line drawn horizontally from D^{11}.

Join C^1 to D^{111} to give the required edge bevel.

Figure 390 shows the plan and section of a hexagonal hopper. The methods used to find the required angle and true shapes are the same as those used for the square hopper.

Splayed linings

Figure 391 shows a part plan, elevation and section of a splayed timber reveal lining to a door or window opening. In order to construct the lining two angles are required.

The side or face bevel This is obtained by developing the inside face of the linings. The method to use is the same as that used when developing the side of the square hopper.

The edge bevel or mitre This is, in fact, half the dihedral angle and is found using a similar method to that used when finding the dihedral angle for a hipped rafter.

Bevel for struts

The following figures are of different arrangements of an inclined strut and a vertical post.

Figure 392 shows the plan and elevation of a post and strut. This is the most common arrangement where both the foot bevel and the top edge are apparent.

Figure 393 shows the plan and elevation of a post and strut. The edges of the strut in this arrangement need developing in order to determine the bevels. The method to use is as follows:

Draw the plan and elevation.

Draw the section of the strut, 1, 2, 3, 4.

With centre 4 and radius 4–1 and 4–3, draw arcs to give points A and B.

Project lines parallel to the edges of the strut, to give points C^1, D^1, E^1 and F^1 on lines drawn at right angles from C, D, E and F.

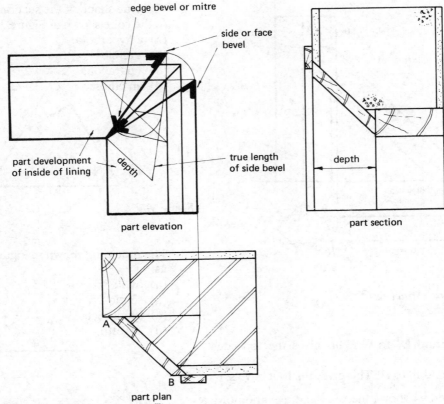

edge bevel or mitre

side or face bevel

part development of inside of lining

depth

true length of side bevel

part elevation

depth

part section

A

B

part plan

Figure 391   *Bevels for splayed linings*

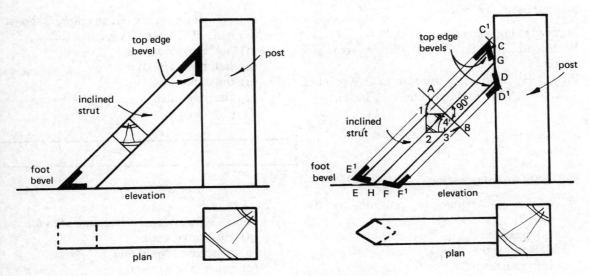

top edge bevel

post

inclined strut

foot bevel

elevation

plan

Figure 392   *Strut bevels*

top edge bevels

post

inclined strut

foot bevel

C^1
C
G
D
D^1
A
1
4
90°
2   3
B

E^1
E H F F^1

elevation

plan

Figure 393   *Strut bevels*

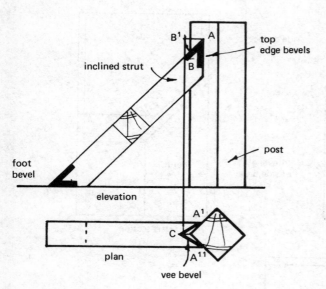

Figure 394   *Strut bevels*

Join C^1 and D^1 to G. This gives the top edge bevels.

Join E^1 and F^1 to H. This gives the foot bevels.

Figure 394 shows the plan and elevation of a post and strut where the strut is cut around the corner of the post. The top edge bevel is apparent but the vee bevel must be determined. The method used is as follows:

Draw plan and elevation.

With centre A and radius AB, draw an arc to give point B^1.

Project B^1 down on to the plan to give point C. Angle A^1CA^{11} to the required vee bevel.

Self-assessment questions

1 Which of the following polygons has five sides?
   (a) hexagon
   (b) pentagon
   (c) octagon
   (d) heptagon

2 The true shape of the section of the frustum of the cone shown in Figure 395 will be:
   (a) a hyperbola
   (b) a circle
   (c) a parabola
   (d) an ellipse

Figure 395

3 The moulding shown in Figure 396 is known as:
   (a) ovolo
   (b) scotia
   (c) cyma-recta
   (d) cavetto

Figure 396

4 A trammel for setting out an ellipse is shown in Figure 397. Length A is equal to:
   (a) half the minor axis
   (b) half the major axis
   (c) the minor axis
   (d) the major axis

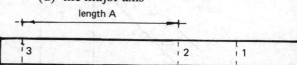

Figure 397

5 Figure 398 shows the development of the:
   (a) frustum of a cone
   (b) frustum of a pyramid
   (c) frustum of a prism
   (d) frustum of a cylinder

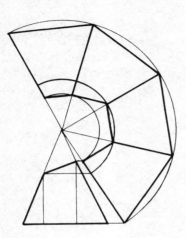

Figure 398

6 Figure 399 shows the plan and section of a roof. Which angle could be used for the jack rafter plumb cut?
(a) 1
(b) 2
(c) 3
(d) 4

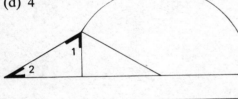

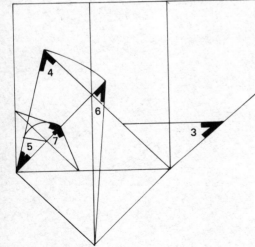

Figure 399

7 The edge cut to the hip rafter for the roof shown in Figure 399 will be:
(a) 4
(b) 5
(c) 6
(d) 7

8 The object shown in Figure 400 is of:
(a) a right square pyramid
(b) an oblique square prism
(c) an oblique square pyramid
(d) a right square prism

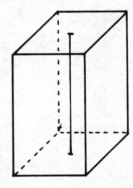

Figure 400

9 At the intersection between the head and jamb of splayed linings to a window or door opening, the edge bevel or mitre is equal to:
(a) the face bevel
(b) the dihedral angle
(c) half the face bevel
(d) half the dihedral angle

10 The centres used to draw the drop Gothic arch shown in Figure 401 were:
(a) 1
(b) 2, 3
(c) 4, 5
(d) 6, 7

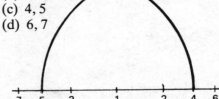

Figure 401

Answers to self-assessment questions

Chapter 1   Woodworking machines and powered hand tools

1	(c)	6	(b)
2	(d)	7	(b)
3	(a)	8	(d)
4	(c)	9	(c)
5	(a)	10	(d)

Chapter 2   Materials

1	(c)	6	(c)
2	(a)	7	(c)
3	(c)	8	(a)
4	(b)	9	(d)
5	(d)	10	(a)

Chapter 3   Scaffolding

1	(c)	6	(c)
2	(b)	7	(d)
3	(c)	8	(a)
4	(d)	9	(b)
5	(a)	10	(a)

Chapter 4   Site setting out and levelling

1	(d)	6	(c)
2	(c)	7	(c)
3	(a)	8	(c)
4	(b)	9	(b)
5	(b)	10	(a)

Chapter 5   Joinery

1	(d)	6	(d)
2	(c)	7	(c)
3	(a)	8	(a)
4	(b)	9	(c)
5	(b)	10	(b)

Chapter 6   Construction work

1	(c)	6	(a)
2	(b)	7	(a)
3	(a)	8	(d)
4	(c)	9	(c)
5	(c)	10	(d)

Chapter 7   Temporary construction and site works

1	(c)	6	(d)
2	(d)	7	(a)
3	(b)	8	(c)
4	(a)	9	(b)
5	(b)	10	(b)

Chapter 8   Drawing practice and geometry

1	(b)	6	(a)
2	(d)	7	(c)
3	(a)	8	(d)
4	(a)	9	(d)
5	(b)	10	(c)

Index